# THE COLLAR AND THE CAB

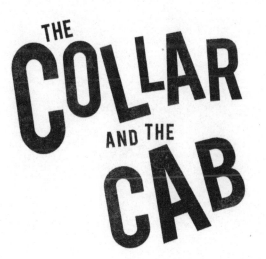

# THE COLLAR AND THE CAB

## PAUL RICHARDS

Matador
9 Priory Business Park,
Wistow Road, Kibworth Beauchamp,
Leicestershire. LE8 0RX
Tel: 0116 279 2299
Email: books@troubador.co.uk
Web: www.troubador.co.uk/matador
Twitter: @matadorbooks


ISBN 978 1785891 731

British Library Cataloguing in Publication Data.
A catalogue record for this book is available from the British Library.

Printed and bound in the UK by TJ International, Padstow, Cornwall
Typeset in 11pt Minion Pro by Troubador Publishing Ltd, Leicester, UK

Matador is an imprint of Troubador Publishing Ltd

*With thanks to John*
*for the introduction to the world of minicab driving*
*and to my obscenely gifted daughter Beckie*
*for the front cover picture.*

*This book is dedicated to my wonderful wife Lynn*
*without whose constant support I would never have survived,*
*and to my fantastic children, children-in-law and*
*grandchildren who enrich my life beyond imagination and*
*constantly make me proud.*

# 1

## WOODHOUSE - STRANGE NEW WORLD

It was two o'clock on a frosty January morning, and I found myself in the still well-populated main entrance of Leeds General Infirmary. Work was plentiful and my warm minicab was waiting just outside, but whether it was my semi-dormant pastoral instinct or simply a sense of common humanity I was unable to leave the side of the rather frail, elderly woman I had just transported from her home some twenty miles away, even though the ward staff had assured me that someone was "on their way down"; I had been around enough hospitals in enough cities in my previous professional capacity to understand what "just coming" was likely to mean in relation to the imminent arrival of the grossly overworked and underpaid members of the nursing profession.

A fare from Halifax to Leeds in the early hours of the morning paid for by the NHS was something to put a spring in the step of any taxi driver, but on this occasion the elation generated by the job was at least tempered by the knowledge that the lady I would be transporting had been summoned by the staff caring for her husband because he was nearing the end of his life.

Seamlessly and entirely subconsciously I found I had switched vocations when the customer emerged from her house, and functioned as a member of the clergy on the 30-minute journey to the centre of Leeds without ever mentioning the profession I had spent most of my adult life pursuing; I was somewhat relieved to discover that pastoral care of people in extremis still seemed to come quite naturally to me. Having announced our arrival at the reception desk I felt responsible for her until a designated member of staff had come to relieve me. This gave me an opportunity to look around and observe those who had little better to do than observe me. Until a little over a year previously in exactly the same place at exactly the same time of night, in many respects fulfilling the same function, I would have been dressed in a clerical collar, and that alone would have commanded a level of respect, possibly deference, even from members of the higher echelons of the medical profession. Now dressed in my company sweat shirt with a plastic badge announcing my credentials hung around my neck I would have looked like any other middle-aged private hire cab driver.

The delay gave me the opportunity to try to work out what others seemed to make of me. Making an allowance for a certain level of innate paranoia what I picked up was not pleasant; a combination of suspicion, mistrust and even latent hostility seemed to float in a vaguely malevolent fashion from the facial expressions and body language of medical, clerical and auxiliary staff, and even from the recalcitrant individuals who were compelled by recent legislation to leave the building in order to feed their nicotine craving.

None of this came as a great surprise. I was aware by this point of just how many people had had unpleasant encounters with members of the taxi-driving profession by being "cut up" in a line of traffic, "ripped off" by excessive fares or otherwise brutalised with some metaphorical sharp object. More particularly I was not surprised because I was reminded of my own views of only a few years previously.

Faces – always it was the faces, hazy and distorted through tinted lamination, like corpses beneath a sheet of ice. I would read expressions which intimated a way of life which, if not flagrantly in defiance of the laws most people are content to live by, certainly finds a home in the shadowlands of its border country. This perception, plentifully fuelled by a prejudice so entrenched as to be almost written into my genetic code, was given birth after a gestation period reckoned in decades, and was nurtured by a paranoid distrust of anything not readily understood. The latter condition, I would later realise, was a complex survival mechanism designed and constructed by the need to protect my religious bubble. It was the cerebral equivalent of the Maginot Line, assembled almost completely subconsciously, and offering a similar level of illusory protection. It was to take well over a year of being a cabbie before that particular defensive redoubt was permanently breached.

As with most assessments of personality, it was probably the eyes, the "windows on the soul" that seemed to give the game away. On the odd occasions I took the trouble to look at one of the members of this "great unwashed" fraternity I always felt as if the face had been sculpted by one of those caricaturists encountered on seaside promenades who will do a representation of you looking ridiculous for a modest fee. The eyes always seemed slightly too large, and the engorgement seemed to suggest a personality driven by sullen acquisitiveness. The immediate setting of the image didn't help either, generally occupying the space between a strip of gaudy plastic bearing a legend such as "A1 cars" and the top of a steering wheel polished and eroded by a million inconsiderate manoeuvres; were this a sculpture in the abstract section of an art gallery I would have entitled it "Malevolent Void".

A thousand times I must have glanced imperiously at the seemingly ubiquitous fleets of private hire vehicles plying their trade around the centres of commerce and leisure in the burgeoning metropolises of West Yorkshire; never once had I seriously questioned how so many taxis could possibly be occupied in gainful employment all day long, and until recently

I had assumed that anyone who sought a living from driving one probably emerged each morning from some Hades-like netherworld where nice respectable folk only go when dragged kicking and screaming by some demonic figure straight out of Paradise Lost. The negative images so firmly fixed in my cerebrum were the product of such premeditated ignorance, and were expressed through the kind of look a Hasidic priest might reserve for a pig farmer. In truth, of course, this was rather uncomfortably near to the actual truth. An entire adult life spent in the neo-puritanical cloisters of conservative Protestantism also brought an innate defensiveness to bear on what was one of a thousand things deemed unworthy of my serious interest. Disdain is a much more economical response than interest or respect for those things the very existence of which threaten our value system. In that sense I guess I was in religious terms a member of the Flat Earth Society, and carried my card conspicuously.

But now the face exposed to critical scrutiny was my own, and the negative opinions were irrational prejudices directed against a sub-caste. We were not quite untouchables, but were scarcely a level up from Dalit status, and most definitely unlikely to contain members of the human species a young lady would be happy to take home to meet her parents. I was to discover that, whilst mild to moderate paranoia is almost a precondition for a career in any form of taxi driving, such sentiments are not wholly without foundation.

A member of the nursing staff arrived to collect my customer, exuding the sort of warmth and compassion towards her for which the vast majority are rightly held in very high regard, and offered me only a passing glance as her attention fixed itself on the soon-to-be widow. This momentary perusal to which I was subjected appeared to leave in its wake an atmosphere of incomprehension and suspicion at my presence, so as they turned to go I tried to explain that I had just waited with her as I had brought her to the hospital and it seemed wrong to leave her until she was collected. The precise brusque professional words of peremptory dismissal cast over the left shoulder I cannot recall, but the sense of unwarranted hostility that her voice contained left me puzzled. As I was passing through the door the penny dropped; she thought that what I was really hoping for was a sizeable tip to reward me for a job well done – and how could I treat an elderly lady on the point of becoming a widow in such a fashion? I wanted to run after them as they disappeared into the labyrinthine corridors that are characteristic of most large hospitals that began life as Victorian infirmaries and had had extra bits welded on until they looked like some grotesque brickwork gorgon from an underground horror film. I wanted to try and explain myself, tell them I used to be a vicar and still did a bit on the side, but instinctively knew it would be a pointless and futile exercise. I opted to extract myself from the scrutiny of those who had little else to amuse themselves with at this time of night, and do another couple of hours' worth of work before heading for home.

The sojourn I had embarked on in this strange new world was to last for a total of two years, though the tariff allocated by the court of caprice was undeclared at the outset. The course of events that brought me to this experience is not as uncommon as many might imagine. Having completed my half century to respectable, if muted applause, and some twenty years in the supposedly selfless world of clerical ministry, I had been tossed onto the ecclesiastical scrap heap by a body of people purporting to be a Christian community in the northern suburbs of the city where my family and I had made our home.

I had become another victim of the popular British leisure pursuits of character assassination and power politics, a game played not merely in the corridors of power at Westminster, the boardrooms of the City and professional football clubs, but with unselfconscious gusto in almost every social and religious organisation you care to name. For those mercifully unacquainted with the version favoured in various putatively Christian institutions the rules and modus operandi are similar to their counterparts in politics, business and professional football management but these latter coliseums tend to be tame and genteel by comparison. Success is measured by an increased number of bums on seats, a growing membership list, a healthy bank balance and the somewhat more nebulous and subjective "feel good factor." Losing members is much like losing seats, market share or matches. Fewer worshippers on a Sunday is akin to smaller crowds or a dip in the opinion polls, and failure to pander to the sensibilities of all church members can result in the equivalent of a back-bench or boardroom rebellion or an unhappy dressing room. If one or more of these indicators slips seriously into red figures, the likelihood is that a group of disaffected church members will gradually introduce a whispering campaign which may eventually gain sufficient momentum to lever the incumbent out of office. Of course not all churches are like this, but where it happens the similarities with the world of professional sport, business and politics are remarkable. Apart from the viciousness of the religious version the subtle differences are threefold. Firstly it tends to be set in a framework of prayer and much quoting of religious texts. Secondly, since the pursuit of power and the removal of those who are in the way are technically outlawed by the rules of the religion, much pious language is deployed to make it look as if such actions are the product of a desire for what is best for all concerned and especially for the glory of the same God whose rule book seems specifically to condemn such behaviour. The third area of dissonance concerns the sums of money that change hands, where false piety is compelled to disrobe and succumb to the ravages of the kind of frugal pragmatism most churches are rightly forced to live by.

Having thus been the recipient of this brand of loving

concern from some of my erstwhile flock, and not benefitting from a seven-figure settlement, I now faced the challenge of finding a way of making a living for my wife, our four children and myself. Like most manse or vicarage families we had long since learned to manage with a relatively small income, but we did have to eat, clothe ourselves and keep a roof over our heads. The options were limited and generally unattractive. I had entered ministry as a life-long vocation in my mid-twenties and learned no other trade that would offer me a viable living. A job in the charity sector was always a possibility, but this would almost certainly entail moving to a different area. My children were at a critical juncture in their education, and there was no reason to intensify the relatively superficial damage inflicted by their vicarious participation in my mauling by pulling up our roots, especially after the traumatic events of the previous few weeks that culminated in my eviction. So it had to be something that would offer a decent salary and enable us to stay put in the area. There were a few ministers' posts going nearby, but returning to my calling so soon had about as much appeal as arm-wrestling a steam hammer and I was singularly unqualified for most other professions. Apart from these challenges I had also become psychologically incapacitated by my recent experience, which made any kind of work in a church environment unconscionable. The systematic dismantling of my self-esteem over six years that had been the onerous but diligently-observed duty of a number of earnest church members had left me in no fit state to care for my daughter's geriatric goldfish, let alone a religious organisation.

Thus it was that my personal road to recovery of self-confidence and the restoration of something approaching faith in the human race was to lie along the pot-holed thoroughfares scourging the flesh of the less presentable parts of West Yorkshire. The monotonous rattle of a diesel engine hammered into submission by a ruthless disregard for the red line of the tachometer and the crunching of a gearbox rendered arthritic from a million angry gear changes by disillusioned cabbies were to be my constant companions. Surprisingly, however, this symphony of mechanical dissonance was to become, over time, more like the gentle throb of a cruise ship's engines, lulling my exhausted emotions to sleep in order that the restoration of my personality and self-esteem could at last begin.

# 2

## ARMLEY – GIVE US A JOB

4.15 a.m. The last time my alarm had emitted its obscene cackle at that time was when a former friend enjoyed a practical joke at my expense. It was all I could do to resist burying him alive by way of reciprocation. All-night sittings at deathbeds were not unfamiliar territory, ironically one of the most rewarding features of being a vicar – finally being allowed to do something for a patient once the medical profession has exhausted its options and sympathetically shrugged its clinical shoulders. But this was no sort of time to be waking up for anything less than a life and death struggle or a day's golf. It was to be the hour at which, for much of the next year or so, I would be getting up for work.

Some months previously, when the self-righteous assassins of 21$^{st}$ century Puritanism had first etched "Mene mene tekel parsin" on the wall of my public ministry, I had begun to prepare for this eventuality "just in case." I had become good friends with a former industrial executive with a degree in chemical engineering, now compelled by the collapse of much of the region's manufacturing and the absence of transferable skills to seek a living in a different environment. He had found his way into private hire cab driving through a company that had learned to exploit a loophole in the law that allowed unlicensed ("unbadged") drivers to try it out to see if they could make a living before they committed themselves to the trouble and expense of registering with the local authority. Naturally phlegmatic and down to earth, he seemed to have adapted well to his new environment and was already briefed that I might value an introduction to the company he worked for.

So it was that my initial encounter with the world of minicab driving had taken place the day before the assault of the alarm clock courtesy of an introduction from this friend who appeared to make a decent living from it. Lulled into an expectation of relative refinement by his congenial demeanour I could scarcely have anticipated the seismic cultural shift I was about to experience, and whether motivated by a sense of fun or a desire not to frighten me off he had deemed it sensible to allow me to discover first-hand what I was letting myself into without prior warning.

It was perhaps as well that the intellectual and educational requirements for entry into my new vocation were undemanding, since my journey from leafy suburb to the sort of area in which private hire companies often thrive had taken me to another world, a hostile and threatening planet virtually devoid of the genteel humour and banal pleasantries that had been my stock-in-trade as a respectable cleric.

It is difficult to describe adequately the sense of rising panic I experienced in the next few minutes. To reach the office complex I had to navigate the treacherous swamps of this alien planet. A number of natives soon crossed my path; a mechanic wielding a wrench much like a terrorist brandishing an AK47; a handful of drivers rendering the verbal atmosphere a colourful shade of azure as they recounted tales of their most recent experiences of exploitation and victimisation; a couple of operators – the people who answer the 'phone – unable to last another minute without an infusion of nicotine, having spent all morning taking calls from people who were in one place and desired to be in another five minutes previously. Nearly all of these people I would come to appreciate, and some I would be privileged one day to count as friends, but on that particular day I felt as if I had entered another world, a planet with a jungle full of wild, dangerous animals; big cats running loose, the primate cage door left ajar, and someone had forgotten to replace the lid on the snake pit. Not that there was anything necessarily intimidating about the appearance or demeanour of the human specimens dotted around the place – even the bloke with the large spanner wouldn't have been physically intimidating in a different context. It was simply the case that I had left behind anything vaguely resembling a comfort zone what felt like half a galaxy away. It was, perhaps, like being dropped in the Amazon rain forest thousands of miles from civilisation with a beach towel and a tube of sun cream and expected to make the best of it. Like all manifestations of paranoia it was, of course, mostly in the mind, but however hard I tried I couldn't get my subconscious to listen to the voice of reason. The absence of friendly smiles from those who had nothing better to do than stand and stare didn't help; I guess I probably looked as much out of place to them as I felt, and those who gave me more than a casual glance almost certainly saw nothing more than a lump of fresh meat ready to be mercilessly processed by the relentless grinder in which they were merely insignificant and passive components.

Standing in the "Yard" – the place where drivers, mechanics and telephone operators gathered when not working – waiting for the arrival of the person I anticipated might be a suitably qualified director of human resources I had ample, if unwelcome, opportunity to take in the conversations going on around me. The shock to the system was, perhaps, something like the reports I had read in history books of the outrage felt by the first Victorian missionaries who, having penetrated the jungle of darkest Africa, beheld savages who were not merely naked but adorned their portable furniture with the shrunken heads of defeated enemies. In this instance, nakedness was perhaps represented by language seldom encountered by genteel clerics with obscenities replacing punctuation marks and generally featuring the copious use of the present participle of an Anglo-Saxon term for copulation; anecdotes of recent catastrophes that had befallen the veritable multitudes for whom Schadenfreude was an appropriate sentiment were the shrunken heads of the tribe.

It wasn't that I was shocked or outraged by bad language as such. I had spent a lot of my younger life on the terraces of football grounds in the good old days when you were allowed to stand whilst chanting profanities at the opposing players, supporters and the "Bastard in Black" whilst anticipating the punch-up that was de rigeur following the final whistle. I knew what the words meant, but it was the all-pervasive and unremitting nature of the conversations I witnessed that created my unease. Not that I was included in any conversation – it would be months before I earned that right – or even, as far as I could make out, regarded as anything other than a redundant piece of jetsam washed up on the tide.

I was later to understand why potential new drivers were about as welcome as a dog turd on the sole of your best pair of brogues, but the failure of anyone even to acknowledge my presence coupled with the alien atmosphere made me feel like beating a hasty retreat before I made a complete arse of myself. There was surely no way in which I could find a home working in this environment.

Just as the flight response was delivering the coup de grace to its more aggressive counterpart and I was debating how to exit rapidly but with a modicum of dignity intact the member of the management team who dealt with drivers showed up and almost politely directed me to a rather pleasant glass office at the top of the stairs – things were looking up perhaps. Or perhaps not.

My job interview consisted of being subject to a cursory visual examination, presumably to confirm that not only did I have the requisite number of limbs but failed to carry a white stick and was not accompanied by a Labrador. Professional training consisted of five minutes in a company vehicle being offered a succinct explanation of the limited range of buttons sported by the on-board computer terminal otherwise known as a datahead.

A sure sign of things to come was the method of ensuring that a company vehicle in my charge would have a better than even chance of making it back at the end of a shift in no more pieces than it had been dispatched with at the start, and that there would be reasonable odds on the company's reputation not being damaged by an aspiring stock-car driver. I was invited to go for a rather undemanding ten-minute driving test in the company of a subcontracted driving instructor (who also seemed completely out of place in this environment) to ensure that I would not "fuckin' frighten the fuckin' old ladies" following which I was relieved of £10 to pay the driving instructor who was able to reassure the management that my driving style was not especially suited to the world of the Destruction Derby; finally there were endless forms to complete whose purpose seemed to be that of making sure that I would be held personally responsible, both fiscally and legally, were any one of about 50,000 things to go wrong.

The warm handshake of congratulations upon my appointment was taken as read, the interview with the human resources department to ensure I was properly briefed for my new career failed to take place, and I was left in complete ignorance about any benefits to which my position entitled me. Conversely I was left in no doubt about my potential liabilities and their cost in cash terms should I step or fall out of line in any way. Essentially I was self-employed, I was to pay the company for the use of the vehicle, make sure it had enough fuel, and everything else was down to me.

I was sufficiently competent at reading body language and changes of intonation to recognise that the person across the table had evaluated the chances of me making a success of the job, and reckoned my life expectancy at something slightly less than that of a soldier on the front line at the Battle of the Somme. I was grudgingly told I could give it a go – if I wanted to – but the sub text read "I wonder if we can make a few hundred quid from you before you go back to the soft furnishings of white collar land." He was, of course, something of an expert at rating the chances of new drivers, and hard-nosed enough to recognise that the attrition rate in this work was likely to take care of me pretty quickly. My subconscious instinct was undoubtedly to concur with his evaluation, and it was probably more of a tribute to my innate bloody-mindedness rather than to any congenital resilience that I was determined to prove both of us wrong. My current account of personal resources had long since slipped into the red, and a sparkling, lucrative career in this business seemed about as probable as a lottery jackpot. As I was later to discover, the likelihood of being turned away as a potential driver by this, or any other private hire company, was much the same as succeeding in persuading a traffic warden to tear up a parking ticket, but at this point I was perhaps just slightly encouraged that I was not dismissed without a second thought. At the very least here was someone who was willing to give me a chance.

# 3

## WORTLEY – FIRST DAY

Being advised to pick up my car for the next day's shift any time from 5.00 a.m. onwards, and wanting to give this job a decent chance of success, I felt compelled to introduce the alarm clock to the aforementioned unfamiliar arrangement of its digits. I decided that I would arrive early, though probably not bright, for my first shift. Starting work a full four hours before I was used to doing anything more than emerging from a stupor and imbibing coffee was, to put it politely, a novel concept, but I was off to bed at 10.00 p.m. – the time I was normally settling down for a few hours of decent telly – with the alarm locked and loaded and anticipating a good six hours of dreamless repose before rising refreshed and prepared for a new challenge.

I should have known by then that life is never that simple. Perhaps it was that bed was unfamiliar territory at that time of night, and however many yawns I forced out I was simply wide awake. Then there was the constant thought that I had better get to sleep quickly otherwise I would be too tired to start work, accompanied by an ominously undefined and unspecified dread about what tomorrow would really be like; whatever the case the next six hours and fifteen minutes were spent counting enough sheep to fill a Yorkshire Dale and changing positions more times than a politician caught fiddling his expenses.

I believe that my sleep tally that night was exactly zero; thankfully this would never be repeated until long after I ceased driving for a living. But the night dragged on and on, feelings fluctuating between wanting the time to go so I could get up and wanting it to drag every time I felt as if at long last I might actually be dropping off. I watched digits change sometimes at a snail's pace and sometimes unrelentingly as frustration competed with anxiety and futility on the podium of top emotions and I recalled Christmas Eves of childhood. Then I would be torn between a desperation for the excitement to subside so that Santa wouldn't arrive to find me awake and leave me without any presents on Christmas Day, and a longing for the morning to arrive because how on earth could I be expected to sleep at a time like this? This time, of course, there was precious little excitement, but plenty of anxiety and apprehension, both of which increased as sleeping time ebbed away and this vicious circle cruelly made it less and less likely that I would be visiting the land of nod this night.

The long dark night of the soul finally drew to its premature end, and I slipped out of a bed which had vindictively increased in comfort and cosiness in the previous quarter of an hour and with almost resentful feelings towards my motionless long-suffering wife who was totally dead to the world and had been almost since she joined me some five and a half hours earlier. Along with the appointed hour there arrived fresh anxieties about completing a long shift in a new job without the benefit of sleep to augment the more general worries about the wisdom and viability of the project on which I was embarking. But having rarely been one to bottle out of a challenge, however desperate the odds stacked against me, there was nothing for it but to drag myself out of bed into the darkness of an early autumnal Yorkshire morning.

Envy of the recumbent state of my wife competed with feelings of anxiety about falling asleep at the wheel and a sense almost of panic about what I had let myself in for as I moved from bedroom to bathroom and back again before making myself a coffee nearly strong enough to slice as a filling for my lunchtime sandwich. Then it was time to find my way back to the place that barely 12 hours earlier had made me feel as much at home as a nun in a brothel.

Over time I was to elevate the process of transporting my body from bed to work in 35 minutes to an art form of the subconscious; my mind, not constrained by the same physical limitations, would follow about an hour later. After a few months I would find myself picking up my car with no conscious recollection of the process by which it had happened, my body repeating actions that had long since eroded a channel in my survival reflexes.

But this was 16th September 2005, and an entire continent of new experiences awaited me. Unlike our plucky colonial ancestors, cutting swathes through virgin territory to plant their flag and impose their way of life upon reluctant beneficiaries, I was scarcely able to force myself through the practical processes by which I began work. Apprehension and determination fought for control of muscles still atrophied by the absence of sleep I had endured in the course of a night when the clamorous voices of certain failure announced their verdict on my latest stupid idea.

Fuelled partly by caffeine and partly by a dogged commitment to what seemed an increasingly bizarre exercise I arrived at "Base", the name given to the complex of buildings and their associated activities from which private hire vehicles were collected for the day's work. After a while I discovered this epithet functioned equally well as a moral metaphor as for a quasi-military one, but today I was the new boy in class and hoping that the teacher was nice, that the school bully wouldn't notice me and that I wouldn't have to undress for P.E.

Although the business of running a private hire operation is a round-the-clock affair there are some times that are quieter than others, and 5 a.m. is one of them. It marks the final hour for night shift drivers who were late starting and an early one for their diurnal counterparts; work is pretty scarce, but there are relatively few drivers operating, so what work there is can be quite lucrative on quiet roads. There are still some remnants of contract work from city centre establishments like casinos and as the buses are not really up and running at that time there are people without independent transport on early shifts for whom a taxi is the only option. Not that I had the first clue about any of this when I turned up holding my bag of essentials that first morning.

I had hoped to meet a mild-mannered avuncular figure anxious to calm the nerves of a new boy who would dispense the keys to one of the myriad Skoda Octavias sitting in the convalescent unit called "The Yard" with genteel good-humour. Instead I encountered Dave – at this stage the visual epitome of all that I dreaded in this strange new world, though later someone I recognised as one of the most genuine people I was privileged to meet on my new planet.

Dave's job was to arrive at the office in the middle of the night and issue car keys to drivers working the "day shift", a technical term for any stretch of eight hours or more from 3 a.m. to 6 p.m. the same day. This function he carried out with a unique and at times beguiling mixture of belligerence and affection. Dave's physical appearance could best be described as intimidating, the sort of man who would be picked out by a witness at a police line-up almost on principle. From the waist upwards he was more or less cuboid in form, his torso sporting accessories consisting of a prop forward's neck, a closely shaven head and arms whose girth provided ample space for tattoos recalling past love affairs. Funnily enough I still cannot for the life of me recollect what his legs looked like – though I'm pretty sure I saw him walking on more than one occasion.

The paradox of Dave's personality consisted in the relative disdain with which he addressed drivers, each sub-clause decorated with a profanity or expletive, and his penchant for inappropriate terms of endearment. "Aven't got any fuckin' decent cars in the fuckin' yard yet, but you can have this pile of crap if you like, love." "Love??" Who was he calling "love?" Must be me – so I took a cautious step backwards now feeling threatened by a questionable sexual appetite as well as a gargantuan physical presence. But his manner and tone were good-humoured, and he made no attempt to vault the piece of furniture between us to land either fist or lips on my face. The feeling of imminent danger gradually subsided and adrenalin levels returned to merely critical level, so I took another look at Dave. There was something both confusing and disarming about this colossus calling middle-aged men "love"; the decorative earrings he wore fuelled the unspoken suspicion about his sexual inclinations, but the romantic legends inscribed on his arms witnessed only a heterosexual past. Which one of us was confused? Well, I still don't know, but over time simply came to accept Dave for what he was, and regarded him as a welcome friendly face with a reassuring voice, and the brief exchanges we shared at 5 a.m. as a comforting slice of social intercourse with which to start the day.

Clutching the key to the "pile of crap" between anxious fingers I located the four-year-old yet geriatric vehicle allocated to me, tried with limited success – and enough creaking and groaning to wake the neighbours from their beds – to adjust the driver's seat and experienced mild surprise when the engine spluttered into life with the kind of sound you would expect from a dozen chain smokers all coughing at the same time. Dave checked the vehicle over, a vital task since he knew every dent and every scratch on every car – material enough to fill half a volume of an Encyclopaedia Britannica – and so could verify whether any further damage was caused by the driver taking the car out or had been inflicted by its previous incumbent. He listed the not insignificant damage to the bodywork he already knew about, and with an imaginary V-sign to lung cancer disappeared behind the smoke from what I once calculated could have been his 25<sup>th</sup> cigarette of the day.

Procrastination has always been the enemy of, as well as the antidote to, human enterprise, and I had certainly been dilatory in the preliminaries. The various pieces of equipment required for a day's work had been laid out with the level of care usually demonstrated by a Masonic grandmaster preparing his regalia for the annual general meeting of the lodge. This prevarication was not to impress anyone, but to delay the arrival of the moment of truth. The car had been fuelled, and seemed to be asking what I was waiting for in the same way a battered spouse greets the return of a drunken partner. The dreaded moment had arrived. It was time to press the relevant buttons and wait for work to arrive through the screen that seemed silently to mock my reluctance and challenge me to give up now before I made an even bigger prat of myself. The investment of nearly £50 in costs and the thought of facing my family with the ignominy of such abject surrender – not to mention that it was still only quarter past five in the morning – were probably the only thoughts that stood up to be counted.

Having "signed on" I awaited my first job much as a condemned man anticipates his final breakfast – the vizier of certain and terminal failure. Later on I would come to loathe gaps in time between jobs, but this day gastric turmoil and cold sweat betrayed a slender and irrational hope that unexpected deliverance might arrive from heaven or, more probably, from the technology that drove the business. Ever since my days in Sunday School I had been familiar with the dramatic tale of Abraham preparing to sacrifice his only son at God's seemingly irrational whim, only to be rescued from the ordeal at the last moment. Strangely enough it had always seemed quite a reasonable thing for God to do, but I had often wondered as a child how Isaac felt lying on the pile of wood waiting for his father to plunge the knife between his ribs. Now I had some notion – he was petrified, and would have been casting frantically around for some last-minute means of reprieve, promising to keep his bedroom tidy and from now on always to eat his greens. My last hopes of a reprieve lay with a mechanical failure of the car, the central computer ignoring my existence or a natural disaster – where was God with a decent earthquake or flood when I most needed it? Perhaps I would at least be granted a stay of execution long enough to allow time to brace myself for the ordeal.

The famous British hangman, Albert Pierrepoint, allegedly claimed that at the height of his powers he had been capable of taking a prisoner from the condemned cell to the gallows, and snuffing out his life at the end of a long drop before the clock finished chiming the hour of execution. This process involved securing ankles and wrists, covering the unfortunate victim's head in a hood, applying and adjusting the noose before pulling the trapdoor lever. Presumably he preferred late morning rather than dawn executions when the clock would be at its most generous! I had wondered whether the condemned prisoners were grateful or not. Whilst my ordeal was far removed from death row (though the backdrop of Armley prison did lend itself to the atmosphere) I was perhaps able to share something of the ambiguity of emotions inevitably generated by this experience; a combination of the natural fear of imminent demise with a shrinking curiosity of what would follow – if anything. Perhaps it was a mercy that my anxiety-filled indolence was not to last very long, and the transition to the next life was to be swift, if not pain-free.

# 4

## GILDERSOME – WHERE THE **** IS THAT?

At the midway point between an old-fashioned alarm clock of the sort with a little hammer and bells on top and a dustbin rolling down a cobbled street. That's about the nearest I can come to describing the sonic emission that assaulted my aural sensibilities when the computer screen sprang into life at 5.16 a.m. that first day. Like Orwell's telescreens in "1984" the sound both demanded attention and offered unspoken malevolence to those who refused to comply with its commands. My first job had arrived.

Private hire companies in West Yorkshire are a bit like molehills; you just never know when and where another one is likely to pop up. Rarely did a month pass by that was not marked by the apparent parthenogenesis of a fresh face in the minicab world. Such companies would frequently opt for names that exploited the negative past experiences of potential customers, for instance "New Deal", "Neighbourhood Cars" – or anything that could offer a hint of a more positive experience than what went before. The molehills can proliferate because the only functional pest control is carried out by the harsh reality of economic viability, since each operator has to attract enough customers to supply its drivers with work, and enough drivers to make a profit from "rents" – the fees paid by drivers to the companies they work for. Most of the public labours under the apprehension that minicab drivers work for the companies whose legends adorn the vehicles they operate, a myth perpetuated by the companies concerned both within and without the business. The reality is, in fact, almost exactly the opposite, the relationship being in practice that drivers are effectively the customers. Private hire operators make the majority of their living by attracting self-employed drivers who pay for the privilege of access to the workload of their company. Seasoned campaigners will run their own vehicle with the logo of the operator sported on each side of their car along with a licence plate; they merely rent the radio and datahead. Many of the larger firms provide a fleet of cars, which are then hired out by individual drivers who have reservations about sending their cherished four-wheeled friends to an early grave. Needless to say that generally speaking these courtesies are not extended to the company vehicles they savage in the course of an average shift.

That I was working for the biggest mole in the park was more accident than design, but it did offer a number of important advantages – particularly when the legend on the screen detailing the next pick-up point might just as well have been written in Egyptian hieroglyphics.

Optimistic self-delusion had supported the myth that having lived in a city for six years I "knew my way around." An hour gazing in bewilderment and incomprehension at a string of addresses shattered it. The meagre grasp of local geography I possessed related to the kind of area where respectable churchgoers made their home; I would be working mostly in areas unlikely to be frequented by genteel men of the cloth trading pastoral care for a warm beverage in a china cup.

In London it is said that the Thames creates a psychological barrier that separates the rival domains of north and south of "the river", and longstanding residents identify themselves according to which side of this psychologically impenetrable barrier they call home. In Leeds that responsibility lies with the

Kirkstall Road, running more or less parallel with the River Aire and the Leeds to Liverpool canal. With just two crossing points between the centre and the edge of the city most inhabitants choose the north or south side, and many will rarely cross into foreign territory. The sketchy geographical knowledge I possessed was exclusively contained within the "north" section, and Armley, dominated by Her Majesty's prison and a plethora of taxi companies, was in the south.

I gazed at the legend on the datahead, fighting the rising panic. The realisation I had suppressed for the last day or two – that the city I had come to call home was as familiar as the back streets of Calcutta – crashed through the flimsy screen of optimism as a high velocity bullet through a water melon. Six months later I would have a Sat-nav to do the job for me. At this stage the frugality that was an essential tool for survival for a cleric bringing up a family of four children militated against that kind of profligacy, certainly until I had established whether I could make a living out of the job. I consulted my five-year old yet pristine A-Z, and with a huge sense of relief located my initial destination.

Private addresses were a lesser problem that first day. One of nature's quirks was to equip me with an ability to visualise map pages and retain simple instructions like "third right, second right and fourth left". The first panic was over as with a sense of triumph and a newfound optimism I arrived at the address and awaited my first customer; I pulled myself upright in my seat and tried to exude the pheromones appropriate to a seasoned professional taxi driver. I tried to glance nonchalantly at the young woman towing her semi-comatose toddler down the path to the car whilst holding on with the other arm to a new-born infant who must have only recently shuffled onto the mortal coil. In a month or two I wouldn't regard the sight of a young mother with two small children calling a taxi at this hour anything other than normal, but this was one of many sights and sounds that caused my jaw to drop alarmingly during my first week. Having taken a second or two to regain an air of competence I decided I could afford a fleeting smile and even condescended to collect the folded buggy from the front doorstep where the disability of only having two arms had necessitated it's abandonment. I have always wondered why God didn't equip those women who he knew would become mothers with an extra arm and had come to regard it as a design fault along with the appendix and nasal hair. Of course what I should have been doing all this time was scrolling down through the writing on my screen to see where the customer was going and try to work out where it might be. I soon paid for my mistake as I suddenly realised that I had not been summoned because she fancied a cosy chat in the company of perhaps the only taxi driver in the county with a degree in theology. The euphoria was short-lived, and even the earlier panic was made to look insignificant by that occasioned once I remembered that we were supposed to be going somewhere.

Tracy (there seemed an oddly disproportionate quantity of customers called "Tracy", followed quite closely by those who revelled in the appellation of "Stacey") would expect to find a taxi driver occupying the vehicle. I was a taxi driver in the same sense that an eight year old boy is a gunfighter because his parents have bought him a cowboy outfit for Christmas, though perhaps I enjoyed fewer natural resources than the said juvenile.

I don't recall the destination of this particular Tracy, but future Tracyesque interchanges those first few days followed a familiar pattern and developed about the same level of unpredictability as a set of rail tracks: –

TRACY: –  I want to go to Priory Medical Centre please love
ME: –     Gulp
TRACY: –  You know – just off Green Lane
ME: –     Errrrr… Is that in Armley?
TRACY: –  O no, not another fuckin' new driver without a bleedin' clue.

Without exception this awkward exchange was followed by the humiliation of taking detailed directions from a customer who was expected to cough up a not inconsiderable fare after doing half the work for me. To my surprise and relief they always seemed to regard this arrangement as normal, or possibly they enjoyed the bizarre comfort afforded by the feeding of an indigenous paranoia ("They always send me the fuckin' new ones.")

The prevalence of "Tracys" in my new world was something of a surprise, because I didn't see them as likely users of taxis from a socio-economic perspective. I was able to number the times I had called for a cab on the fingers of one hand and still make a vulgar gesture, generally preferring to wait an hour in the pouring rain at a bus stop rather than spend several pounds on the luxury of a car with someone else doing the driving. Since I couldn't afford taxis, I embraced the illusion that the average customer would be a businessman or other white collar professional who for whatever reason was not able to take his car where he was going; likewise I imagined that the common destinations would be business parks and transit centres like airports and railway stations, and few journeys would be of less than five miles. In fact most journeys were less than two miles and ten minutes in length, and serviced people who couldn't afford to run a car but who, for a wide variety of reasons, were not patronising the bus service.

The reputation of buses in Leeds and West Yorkshire was not great at this time. Certainly the unpredictability of most services was a major incentive for, and a significant contributory factor in, the prodigious growth of the private hire trade. There were other reasons that caused more sombre reflection; some elderly people would not use buses because the drivers would not wait for them to sit down before pulling away, causing in some cases quite serious injury. Others used taxis because they were fearful for their safety in the neighbourhood they inhabited if they chose to walk to the bus stop. Sadly for many of these customers a return taxi to the shops or the health centre resulted in cutbacks on more essential commodities like food and heating. It was not uncommon for me to feel more than a pang of discomfort, or even guilt, when a pensioner was fishing around in a small battered purse for the pound coins she knew were in there somewhere as I was torn between the need to earn a living and the relics of a vocational philanthropy. I have to confess that mammon usually won the day, but occasionally sub-dermatological altruism resulted in reduced fares. Embarrassingly it was often the elderly poor who were the most insistent in offering a tip. There was something endearingly innocent about the insistence with which 20p coins were pressed into the hand in appreciation. The sincerity of the gesture signalled in no uncertain terms that to decline would have caused both offence and embarrassment. After all, 20p used to be four shillings, more than enough for a cinema ticket, fish and chips, a bottle of pop and a bus home, and still a few coppers for the piggy bank.

The problems of finding a domestic address for such a job paled into insignificance compared to performing the operation in reverse, when the A-Z might as well have been a copy of the Kama Sutra in the hands of a eunuch. Those jobs where the pick-up was from commercial premises or local amenities and services were to involve all the humiliation of the "Tracy" exchange plus the trauma of a radio conversation with an operator.

"Don't worry if you need help finding somewhere," had quoth my taxicab guru and mentor during my brief initiation the previous day. "The operators will help – it's what they're paid for." What he didn't tell me were the three principal obstacles involved in securing assistance: –

1) Would there be someone willing to respond on the radio for help? Eventually perhaps

2) Would they have any idea where I was supposed to be going? Have your lottery numbers ever come up?

3) Would I be able to understand what they were saying? This depended on the level of radio distortion and the strength of the operator's accent or, to put it another way, "are you feeling lucky?"

Having initiated a conversation with these founts of cartographic knowledge there was then the problem of understanding them. 'It's by the Butcher's Arms off Lidgett Hill' made perfect sense to someone looking at a giant map in an open plan office. My attitude to pubs resembled that of a slug in the presence of a tub of salt, unless they were of the very genteel sort with a cheap carvery.

All this gave rise to a further frustrating exchange: –

| | |
|---|---|
| ME: – | Did you say "Widget Hill?" |
| OPERATOR: – | Lidgett Hill |
| ME: – | Can you spell that? |
| OPERATOR: – | Crackle …tt Crackle …ll |
| ME: – | Sorry, didn't catch that |
| OPERATOR: – | Snap.. your …Pop ..A-Z |
| ME: – | Can you stop eating your breakfast and spell the name of the road? |

By the time I had understood the directions, located the place on the map and driven there the customer had frequently decided it would be quicker to travel by pogo stick. It was only those who were too sick, too drunk or had just had their hair done that would be likely still to be waiting when, with a sigh of relief, I finally arrived.

The relief was short-lived, of course, because as well as the ire of a frustrated customer now late to pick the kids up from school I had all the humiliation of another "Tracy" exchange to look forward to as they guided me to their destination street by street. 'Turn right here, love. No, not there, I mean the next fuckin' street; God, why can't I have a driver who knows where he's fuckin' going?' Asking for the fare gave me an understanding of what it must be like to work in one of those cafes you can still find at remote railway stations where stale sandwiches and anaemic tea are dispensed at a cost only made possible by the operation of a monopoly. Sometimes I was quite amazed when they actually agreed to pay up, expecting to have to barter as customers negotiated a discount based on the amount of my work they had been compelled to perform. Needless to say tips were in short supply in those first few days.

# 5

## Drighlington – Survival Day

The journey from the first shift to becoming an established driver is straightforward in the same sense that a solitary egg in a lump of frogspawn is guaranteed a transition to royalty courtesy of a kiss from a princess. A minority would reach tadpole status, but the odds against making a good living over the longer term are heavily stacked against anyone entering the minicab world. Because attrition rates are so high most companies adopt a policy in keeping with the laws of natural selection – recruiting as many new drivers as possible, knowing that the majority will not last beyond a few weeks, many not beyond the first few days, and not grieving too much over the inconsequential loss to the collective gene pool of the taxi world. The level of mourning expressed over the premature demise of yet another would-be cabbie is generally on the level accorded by evolutionary biologists to the extinction of a primitive protozoon.

Each week new drivers would appear at Base clutching their bag of equipment like eleven-year-olds on their first day at senior school. In keeping with their juvenile equivalents the bag was as much a source of security as anything, containing a packed lunch with some comfort food, as well as a pristine street map, a pile of change and a money bag with a far more substantial appetite than was ever likely to be satisfied.

Survival for the first two weeks or so was the key for most, the feat of completing ten or twelve days work depending on a number of factors, only some of which were within the individual's control.

Recognising the importance of some of the tadpoles surviving to maturity most companies try to manipulate the process of natural selection somewhat by creating a favourable environment for the genes of the vulnerable new drivers. In my case this meant a reduced rent for the first week or so, and a certain level of preferential treatment in terms of jobs that were allocated to me. This practice provided substance to the perennial complaints of many experienced drivers who were convinced they were only being offered unrewarding work (I will return to the various manifestations of this paranoia in due course), but without some kind of differentiation it is difficult to see how any new drivers would ever survive. Even with this positive discrimination the great majority of those who arrived to pick up cars with bright hopes of a lucrative new career did not make it beyond the first few weeks. Perhaps the record for brevity of life is held by a driver I encountered returning his car to the yard at 6.30 one morning; he had realised this new world was not for him just after charging the fuel tank for his first day's work. He drove straight back, paid the rent on his car and left for home. Another crashed out in a more literal sense when his car collided with a bus within the first few minutes of work and decided to call it a day. Others managed a full shift but found the next morning that the only response to the insistent summons of the alarm clock they could muster was to reach for the snooze button. In fact my first day ended with some fairly deep anxiety – I had worked 13 hours, and was taking about £72 home – a figure that would reduce to something nearer £55 once I was paying full rent. The anxiety was short-lived – the second day I was taking home £90, and by the end of my 5-day low-rent period was making between £90 and £100 after costs.

Like soldiers arriving at the Western Front in 1914 full of romantic hopes of Christmas in Berlin after a couple of minor skirmishes there was little that could prepare most of us for the feral and, at times, psychologically brutal life of the average taxi driver. The apparently mundane reality of the mud of the Somme concealed seemingly limitless possibilities for demonstrating the vulnerability of the human body to shrapnel, machine gun bullets and barbed wire. Climbing into the driver's seat of a private hire car was unlikely to cost anyone their life, but would ruthlessly expose human frailty, psychological and physical, to a wide variety of unseen hazards.

Balancing the odds against premature extinction in my case were a number of genetic mutations that worked strongly in my favour. For one thing I enjoyed driving, and over the course of my life I had done more than my fair share. A teetotal lifestyle that was the consequence of a dislike of the taste of alcohol meant I never needed to fear being unfit to drive through intoxication. An ability to survive on five or six hours sleep a night, and an optimistic demeanour that had somehow survived recent experiences relatively unscathed also shortened the odds on my survival. Nevertheless each night I dropped into bed exhausted without being able to enjoy the funny story that was usually appended to the ten o'clock news in order, it seems, to throw into sharper relief the otherwise unrelenting litany of disaster and scandal that had preceded. I knew that when the alarm heralded a quarter revolution of the earth (at what must surely have been twice its usual velocity) I would face a strong urge to remain exactly where I was. I felt like a family pooch which, having been favoured by a comfortable home and regular meals, was now invited to share a new life with a pack of hyenas. Even at the best of times in those early weeks I knew that the abyss of meek surrender was perpetually lurking just one bad experience away.

It would stretch the bounds of credibility somewhat to describe 5.00 a.m. as a civilised hour; often I felt physically sick until well after normal breakfast time, probably the result of being in a vertical rather than a horizontal plane, but after two or three weeks I became quite used to it. Among other things it presented irresistible opportunities for one-upmanship in the Protestant work-ethic stakes, being able to describe the time my family ate breakfast as "almost lunchtime." Another advantage was that I would have two hours or so before traffic built up in which to earn some money and familiarise myself with the main routes around the city.

Those first weeks were precarious to say the least; it felt as if the juggernaut of my life had come to rest with almost half hanging over the edge of a cliff. It would not take a great deal of weight transfer to terminate my existence; one or two bad experiences and the elusive terra firma I still held would slide into the ocean of ignominious defeat after breaking my back on the malevolent rocks below. Whilst there was a part of me that sought the comfort of noble failure the constant, if largely mechanical, discipline of leaving home early and working long shifts boosted not only the family bank balance, but also, more importantly, my self-respect. I may have had to work mercilessly long hours to achieve the objective, but here I was doing something I had never tried before, and making a living out of it. I was becoming dependent only on myself and the natural resources with which I had been endowed. It was so much better than feeling held to ransom by the whims and prejudices of a religious institution obsessed only with its own preservation from the infections of a world it was finding ever more difficult to keep at bay.

On one particular day, and for no particular reason, I experienced a sensation familiar from what seemed a previous aeon. It was akin to rummaging through the boxes in the attic on a rainy Saturday afternoon, and encountering my county schools under-15 cross country trophy, and sensing the same feelings as on the day it was presented to me as a spotty youth. This strange feeling I was experiencing, rising through the swamp of years of morale-sapping criticism and a mire of self-doubt was pride;

not the nose-in-the-air self-promoting X-Factor sort of pride, but a tangible response to a tangible accomplishment. I seemed to have reached a point where at the very least I would not add taxi driving to the substantial catalogue of things I had tried and failed at in recent years that had so substantially filled my well-stocked store of personal disasters.

Once the feelings of panic I experienced every time I signed on for work subsided this time of day became one of my favourite periods for work – particularly on Saturday and Sunday mornings. Work was not plentiful, but neither were drivers for whom this was the cross-over point between day and night shifts, and there was always something interesting just round the corner. Whilst much of the day shift became fairly predictable, you just never knew who you were going to meet at that time in the morning. Apart from the regular runs – taking casino and night club staff home after their shift had ended, or airport runs for those off on holiday – it was generally the case that the people I picked up were, in one sense or another, not quite where they should have been, and engaged in activities that might attract the unwanted attention of a spouse, Her Majesty's Constabulary, or both.

# 6

## Holbeck – "Working Girl"

It was at this time of day one Sunday when the sterile sanctuary of the puritanical cell I had constructed for myself was violated for the first time. So long as I was able to consign anyone whose manner of life was out of sympathy with my sacred creed to a large box marked "Sinners" it was never necessary to see them as people. The lazy, undemanding and safe thing to do with anyone who made a living from the sex industry in any form was to consign them to the moral cesspool from which they had emerged and was, I had convinced myself, merely a staging post on the fast track to hell. It was that morning that I encountered Debbie, the first person to challenge my warped value system and compel me to take a long hard look at myself and my prejudices.

Months later I would have known that collecting a young woman from this particular area so early in the morning could mean only one thing, but I had not yet had sufficient experience of the reality of the seedier side of life in a large city to anticipate the existence of someone like Debbie. I understood that not all young women were tucked up in bed by protective parents with a nice cup of cocoa by ten o'clock in order to protect their virtue, but nothing could have prepared me for her, or saved me from the subsequent collapse of the prejudices I had heretofore seen as cardinal virtues.

Debbie was, I would judge, in her early 20's, but her youth

was marred by the scars of abuse – some self-inflicted. Dressed in denim jeans, cheap slip-on shoes with no socks she was struggling unsuccessfully to keep out the sub-zero temperatures by drawing round her neck a quilted top that reminded me of something left over at a church jumble sale that nobody could be persuaded to take. Her appearance aroused a curious combination of sympathy and curiosity – even a protective reflex, since she was about the same age as my daughter who was away at university at the time. Her mousy hair had clearly not seen the business end of a hairbrush all night, but the smile was disarming and warm, girlish yet engaging – what you might call "cute". Whilst this was probably in part a look that was cultivated to appeal to her customer base it seemed far from artificial. My turgid brain (well it was only 5.30 a.m.) and my imagination finally cooperated sufficiently to cause me to wonder if this was one of those scarlet women I had heard of and believed to be as good as doomed to hell, and if so should I make myself ritually unclean by transporting her anywhere, but I dismissed the thought as she was wearing neither a short skirt nor layers of cheap make-up, which were surely what all such people wore, didn't they? My natural defences receded and my previously inert better nature invented several naïve explanations to account for her walking the streets at this time of day. The self-imposed delusion didn't last long; five minutes into the journey and in the middle of an inane conversation about something as riveting as the Yorkshire weather she let slip casually that she was a "working girl" and had been out all night. By then it was too late; I had neither will nor desire to turf her out. I had realised she was friendly, interesting and – well, just plain nice. The barrier had been breached, and I was talking not to a prostitute, but to Debbie, who seemed normal and pleasant, and could have even been a member of my flock. Try as I might, I could no more see her as a member of a subclass of undesirables than as a Carmelite nun.

It was to take more than twelve months for the puritanical defensive wall to be permanently breached, when I worked the night shift and encountered more Debbies than I could have imagined existed in one city, but it was perhaps this encounter that dislodged the first brick.

Whether it was a vestige of my semi-dormant proselytising instinct or simply that I like to talk about myself I am not sure – but somehow conversations with society's supposed "undesirables" always seemed to visit the subject of what I did before I drove a cab. Whilst I had frequently asked God why the things that had happened to me had been allowed to take place I had never blamed him for them. I still thought of Jesus Christ as the answer to most of the problems human beings create for themselves and the Christian message the most philanthropic thing I had to offer. At the same time confessing that you had until recently been a man of the cloth was a bit like one of my childhood hobbies – dropping a lighted match into the petrol tank of a derelict car to see if there was any fuel left. The disclosure that I was an "ex-rev.", even when followed by an apologetic "but other than that I'm quite normal", could lead to the verbal equivalent of anything from singed eyebrows to third degree burns. It would usually take about ten minutes with an average customer before the nature of my previous calling would emerge into the conversation, but Debbie had given me the opportunity by her candid revelation, and I felt as if a reciprocal admission of belonging to a profession many regarded as undesirable was an appropriate quid pro quo. I braced myself for her reactions to this revelation, which I judged might vary from deference to diffidence on the north to south scale, and from scorn to respect on the east to west. I half expected her response to be one of panic – "let me out of this car now before he drives a bloody great stake through my heart" – then I remembered that she had probably encountered a fair number of my colleagues in her professional capacity, some with rather elevated ecclesiastical positions, and had learned not to bat an eyelid. But there was no mistaking the tone of shame and embarrassment that entered her voice and demeanour once she had comprehended that she was in the company of a Christian cleric who was not a potential customer. Ironically, though, the resulting conversation was one which left me with a great deal of soul-searching to do as my pious but wholly misguided judgments were shown to be the prejudices they were. The job of transporting Debbie was to be formative, perhaps not immediately but certainly once I had processed the emotional and spiritual turmoil she left in her wake.

We had about twenty minutes in each other's company since there were two destinations, the first of which was the home of her drug supplier. This was the first occasion on which I wondered if I was technically committing on offence by aiding and abetting someone buying illegal drugs, but I decided to sort out the finer points of the law at some indefinite point in the future. In any case I was less concerned about a technical illegality than the heart-breaking truth that a substantial proportion of her night's earnings were being spent on heroin. I paused to consider – in a not totally innocent manner – what acts Debbie had had to perform with men she hardly knew in dark cold alleyways in order to line the pockets of someone who probably made more money in a night than she did in a week by exploiting vulnerable people like her. The unbidden and somewhat unwholesome frisson that took place in my imagination was rapidly swamped by the sense of shame resulting from the process and this in turn by a feeling of impotence that a real-life tragedy such as this could be playing out under my nose while the only practical thing I could do to help was to make sure this vulnerable young woman reached home safely. To be fair she expected nothing more, but here was I – someone who had always considered himself the Indiana Jones of the Christian world – meekly sitting in my cab without the faintest clue as to how I might help this scrap of wasted humanity. The resulting silence – embarrassing only for me I suspect – as I sought in vain for something concise but incisive to say that would give God the upper hand, was mercifully interrupted by an instruction to pull up in a street adjacent to the one housing the purveyor of illegal narcotics; later I would learn that she could have chosen any one of half a dozen houses in this particular road. As Debbie made off with the nonchalance of one all too familiar with streets I would be reluctant to allow my wife to walk in broad daylight without a sizeable detachment from the SAS I tried to prepare for the second leg of the conversation by trawling through my database of ready-made conversation scenarios guaranteed to bring sinners to their knees in repentance, and succour to them once they displayed the appropriate contrition. It was like playing a game of chess where your opponent has just made an opening move you have never come across before and you try to work out what sort of defence, gambit or counter-attack might bring you the required result.

I had considered and discarded a dozen or more when Debbie returned with the same relaxed air that had characterised her departure and we headed off for what passed as home. My rising sense of frustration, even panic, at not being able to work out something worthwhile to say was almost palpable when, unexpectedly, Debbie herself broke the silence with a bombshell.

'I believe in God … I used to go to church when I was little.' I turned to glance at her, trying unsuccessfully I suspect to keep the astonishment I felt from displaying itself across my features. But Debbie's expression seemed to have altered. Quite suddenly years of wear and exploitation had fallen from her face and I was talking to a young girl who had once been a respectable churchgoer, Sunday School scholar, and the bearer of dreams of a normal, happy and fulfilled life.

I had no idea how to respond to this disarming revelation – indeed whether I should respond at all. How could it be that a young girl who was a regular worshipper at the hallowed premises of a Christian church could be selling her body to feed a heroin addiction? Should I tell her now that since she was doomed to the flames of perdition there was no real point in me risking some kind of moral infection by opening ears or mouth, or listen some more and allow the demolition ball of her engaging personality to smash another hole in the fragile wall of my private piety?

While I was deciding Debbie just carried on, telling her life story with honesty and a near-absence of self-pity to someone she had only just met, but seemed to see as some kind of Father Confessor. Whilst there was an element of shame in her manner – after all she was sharing a car with a reverend – and perhaps even a remote hope of absolution, she was probably unaware that the greater sense of shame by the end of the journey was my own.

It was to become a not unfamiliar story line over the coming months, generally related with nonchalance and simplicity, and certainly in Debbie's case an almost total lack of self-pity. As a minister I had been on the receiving end of more hard luck tales than you can shake a big stick at, all ending with an apparently reasonable explanation of why myself or my church should hand over a wad of cash as a loan to assist the unfortunate narrator, which of course would be "paid back by the end of the week". After a few years being in charge of a church I learned that the litmus test for sorting out the very occasional genuine case of hardship from the fairy tales was by the level of elaboration; the short, simple stories were the ones that were genuine, the convoluted ones the spurious. Debbie's story very much fitted the former category, not that she was asking for money – she paid her fare with no demur whatever. But as one who had become accustomed by painful experience to sifting invention from truth I had no doubts about the essentials of what she told me.

'My Dad walked out when I was about five; he found someone else, and my Mom drank herself senseless most days. I was usually left alone locked into the flat, and she kept bringing boyfriends home from the social club she worked at. They usually only stayed one night, but sometimes they moved in for a few days, or even a few weeks. Mostly they ignored me, until I got to about twelve or thirteen, when they started taking an interest once they had had enough of Mom. Usually it was just a bit of groping and dirty talk, but when I was about fifteen this one bloke actually moved in with us, and Mom was really sold on him. What she didn't know was that as soon as her back was turned he was trying to feel me up, or unbutton my blouse or put his hand up my skirt. Then one day when I was home from school and Mom was out working it went too far and he would have raped me. I scratched his face and ran out of the house and went to find Mom to tell her what had happened. The trouble was that he had already 'phoned her by then and told her I tried to get him into bed, and when he refused I had scratched his face. I don't know whether or not Mom really believed him, but the point was that she had to make a choice between him and me; guess who lost out? I was kicked out and had to find somewhere to live. I managed to stay at a few friends' houses for a bit, but eventually found myself out on the street. Well, I knew this bloke who did drugs and stuff, and he had already said he would take care of me if I needed somewhere to go, and I was desperate enough to take anything by this stage. He was very clever, but before long had me hooked on hard drugs and having finished with me himself was finding me customers to pay for the drugs I couldn't live without. Now here I am selling my body to buy heroin with a 2-year-old child to look after.'

The bare bones of this tale became like the relating of a recurrent nightmare over the next couple of years. A broken home, the arrival of a step-parent who was abusive – physically, sexually or both – eviction onto the street, usually at the behest of the natural parent, and the seemingly inevitable drift into prostitution and drug addiction became landmarks on an increasingly familiar landscape. Frequently the process was accelerated by drug dealers and pimps offering a mirage of affection and respectability while the girl became hooked on both narcotic and lifestyle. It took only a couple of weeks and a little artificial warmth to turn a young woman with hopes and dreams into a unit of production, fuelled by imaginary love and producing wealth for both pusher and pimp – roles sometimes combined in the same person. I could scarcely have imagined how common this scenario was for those who worked at the seediest end of the sex industry, or the matter-of-fact way in which their stories would be told.

We had arrived at what Debbie called home several minutes before the story ended, though so compelling was the narrative I scarcely noticed it until she left me. Little more than a hovel, her flat was in one of those post-war high rise blocks where clinical depression is contracted by the time the lift reaches the fifth floor – on the rare occasions it is not out of order due to vandalism. Nothing of value could be kept in this particular block since break-ins were so common the door frames were scarcely capable of holding the hinges, so many times had they been broken down. It was one of those addresses that were, to all intents and purposes, out of bounds to the police and on the rare occasions when crimes were reported there was about a snowball's chance in hell of anyone in uniform actually turning up to take a look. Here in these salubrious surroundings her two-year old daughter was asleep (hopefully) and unaware of how Mommy had been spending the night.

My difficulty was that it was not just Debbie and her appealing personality that was wreaking havoc in the china shop of my refined sensibilities; the part of my brain not engaged in the conversation was entertaining another rampaging bull; uncomfortable questions were charging round my cranium in search of honest answers – answers that were much easier to provide in my former profession when people like Debbie simply never featured on my radar other than as exemplars of how far society had fallen once Christian values had been abandoned – as if they were ever in fashion in the first place. These exemplars were always stylised caricatures that were so much easier to lampoon – and harpoon – than the real thing.

I found myself going back to basics – not the basics of the respectable ecclesiastical smoking room of my particular gentlemen's club, but those of the person who began the whole story some 2,000 years previously. The founder of my faith (interestingly the person of Jesus never seemed to be too far removed from my consciousness throughout my time as a cabbie, though I found it very easy to forget about the institution of the Church) was frequently lambasted for spending time with prostitutes, among other undesirables. Among his many ripostes was that a medic should be among the sick, not the healthy. So on this particular Sunday morning, when congregations were gathering in buildings of all shapes and sizes for a range of rituals, from bells and smells to swinging from the chandeliers, where would Jesus be more likely to be spending his time – in church with the faithful or with Debbie in her downtrodden flat trying to meet the twin challenges of a heroin addiction and a demanding toddler? The answer was palpably and painfully obvious almost before I asked the question, and very quickly I overtook Debbie in the shame stakes. How could I have lived as a Christian for all these years and never understood that Christ spent so much time with people like Debbie because they were the most likely to respond to his message of love and reconciliation and because theirs was the greatest need? I have never belonged to the class of cynic that regards all churchgoers as self-righteous hypocrites; most Sundays when I sat in church I began my liaison with God by clearing my considerable pile of moral debts so that I would feel less uncomfortable in his presence, and most of the people I had known in churches over the years would echo the sentiment; on that level church had been anything from a treatment centre for minor injuries to an intensive care unit for the critically ill. Nevertheless I had little doubt that were Jesus walking the streets of Leeds that morning he would be far more likely to climb the stairs to Debbie's flat and have a cup of tea with her and her child than he would be to grace the pews of even the most vibrant place of worship.

Just as worrying was the question of where her church was when she stopped attending and found herself pregnant and homeless? Just possibly they did everything they could to help but were thwarted by her self-destructive wilfulness. Somehow I doubted it.

Furthermore, why had none of the churches I had ever been involved with done anything for social outcasts like Debbie? Did we not want to dirty our hands and reputations? Were we simply unable to believe that there would be any kind of positive response to an expression of Christian outreach in such an unpromising field? Or were we afraid that there would be? Perhaps we had such a struggle holding on to faith ourselves that a few negative encounters or derisive rebuffs would have demolished what was left of it. Was it too late for Debbie? Was it too late for me?

I left her at the entrance to her high-rise block after promising that I would watch until she was safely inside, as she had before now been beaten up in the car park by mindless morons who considered her way of life ample justification for their prejudice. Generally speaking the mindless morons were not likely to emerge at this time of the morning, but there was always the possibility of encountering those for whom 6.00 a.m. was the end of their night out rather than the beginning of another day.

I drove away slowly, close to tears, with a head full of unresolved issues, and with enough food for thought to fill a long shelf at Sainsbury's, though I knew it would be some time before I had the appetite to digest it.

# 7

## Stanningley – Road Works

"Time is money." Thus Benjamin Franklin putatively advised a young businessman about to embark on the adventure of the American dream, presumably while the profits from the lightning conductor, his most recent brainchild, were rolling in with the vitality of waves at a Hawaiian surfer's paradise. This is one of those hackneyed and timeworn phrases like "you are what you eat" that are trotted out to general opprobrium and sage nods of grizzled heads by those who try to create the impression that their IQ has a digit in the hundreds column. Or else you encounter it in one of those motivational courses that will extract you from your self-limiting humdrum existence and propel you to galactic wealth and influence through the sheer force of your new-found confident personality and thank you very much that will be a hundred guineas please.

But we are not simply what we eat, and for most people time is not money. Incomes do not generally grow or shrink according to how we use the time for which we are employed, and whilst salary may reflect performance to some extent most of us know that it is the anal orifices of this world that often earn the most and enjoy a level of influence in direct inverse proportion to their work rate and efficiency.

Driving a private hire car, however, is one of the few professions for which the adage can be said to possess more than a modicum of truth. This is because in general terms fares for minicabs are calculated by the mile, or, more accurately, by the tenth of a mile. Real taxis, discernible by the word "TAXI" adorning some part of the vehicle and bearing a plate with the legend "Hackney Carriage", run on meters, which means that the driver is earning money even if he is sitting in traffic, held up at lights or caught up in road works – so long as he has a customer on board. The meter may advance a little slower than the usual rate, which is something like an Olympic 100 metre champion on steroids, but the smug expression on the face of the black cab driver betrays the comfort of knowing that whatever the traffic is doing the wolf is too far from the door to huff and puff anything substantial to matchwood. Private hire (minicabs) was the system I worked to during my time in the business. Latterly a number of minicab companies have experimented with meters to try to compensate drivers who work in the rush hours for the paucity of their takings in heavy traffic, and the use seems to be on the increase, particularly for companies that deploy a significant number of vehicles. This use of meters has not gone unchallenged; in that one of the basic conditions under which private hire cars are allowed to operate is that they are ordinary, unmodified vehicles, the innovation may have to be abandoned in response to the cacophony of howls of "foul" from black cab drivers. The company I worked for is currently using them to a somewhat mixed reception from customers and drivers alike. It says something for the triangular distrust between management, drivers and clients that most drivers are convinced they are making less money as a consequence of this innovation whilst many customers are equally certain that they are paying higher fares; this brand of reciprocal paranoia is one of the permanent and, at times, rather endearing features of the minicab world.

One of the ironies of driving a private hire car is that the time when there is a lot of work to be done is also the time when it is most difficult to make a reasonable living. Sitting in a traffic scrum next to a black cab and knowing that the meter in the other vehicle is regularly making satisfying clicks as another 20p is added to the fare is one of the private hire driver's recurring nightmares, and the cause of much angst; it has even caused some drivers to switch codes and join the black cab elite.

Any driver who has been in the game for more than a few months will have learned what tricks there are to avoid the worst of the traffic, much as a teenager learns the cheats and shortcuts to his favourite X-Box games. My personal favourite was a devious route known only to cab drivers and a few locals that involved passing through the grounds of Armley prison. Even so the frustration of sitting in heavy traffic was an unavoidable part of minicab life, and was augmented by the vexation of seeing a plethora of jobs waiting to be done on the datahead. Being unable to complete more than two or three jobs at most in an hour caused a fair number of drivers to risk the wrath of telephone operators and management alike by taking a break during morning rush hours, simply not starting work until 9 a.m., or finishing before the evening rush hour began. In the company I worked for this presented a potential catastrophe for the directors, because much of the work during this period involved fulfilling contracts with large organisations. For this work the driver was compelled to fill in a "docket", the value of which was set against his rent. The company charged corporate customers more than the dockets were worth to the drivers, thus supplementing the income received from rents. Having insufficient drivers available meant not only loss of revenue but the threat of a business or organisation taking its custom to a competitor.

Thus a cat and mouse, or perhaps more accurately a carrot and stick game ensued, in which the company would use a combination of threats and inducements in order to keep sufficient drivers working during the rush hours to complete all the contract work that was booked. This is perhaps what lies behind the innovation of metered fares, keeping disgruntled drivers working through the worst of the traffic by offering a modest inducement – that and keeping something of a rein on the drivers' propensity to be creative when determining fares; think of a number, double it, add ten per cent and hope for a tip.

Up to the point when I drove cars for a living, things like road works or new sets of traffic lights were a bit like in-laws; necessary up to a point, best avoided but endurable most of the time in moderate doses. Like most generally law-abiding citizens I had never seriously thought about what was going on when sections of road were coned off, temporary traffic lights were erected and miscellaneous items of machinery were scattered about the roadway with as much apparent forethought as driftwood at high tide. Call it naïve if you will, but the assumption many of us make is that essential maintenance, repair or renovation work is taking place and is being undertaken by hard-working contractors with a conscientious concern for the cumbersomeness to which the hapless motorist is being subjected. Work is therefore proceeding as quickly as possible in order to relieve the decent hard-working road user of any unnecessary delay or inconvenience. The absence of workmen at any given time may be attributed to shift patterns, unfavourable conditions due to climactic variables or an unfortunate delay caused by necessary supplies being unavailable at this particular time. The road remains coned off, we trustingly assume, because the workforce are taking a richly deserved tea break, and at any moment now a veritable army of road builders armed with tarmac, paint and pneumatic drills will return to continue the good work. Given that most commuters will only pass the road works on their way into and out of the city, before and after a day's work, the illusion that back-breaking labour is on display during office hours is somewhat easier to maintain. For me the frequent observation of the Stanningley Road / Armley Ridge Road renovation works was to evaporate that myth like so much salt water in a child's bucket, gradually perhaps, but relentlessly nevertheless, as the realisation grew that what one was encountering was not a strange combination of circumstances but more of an immutable law of nature.

My debut as a private hire driver had coincided with the commencement of these road works at a junction that had seen far too many collisions, some fatal. Quite reasonably, the Highways Agency had decided enough was enough and a new set of traffic lights to enable traffic and pedestrians to cross the main highway in safety was deemed necessary to prevent further loss of life and limb. Stanningley Road is to Leeds something akin to what the aorta is to the human body. Cut the flow of traffic and the city will very rapidly cease to function due to the massive internal haemorrhage of cars and commercial vehicles that will be compelled to find an alternative route through the capillaries of Armley and Wortley. Even if half of the road is out of service journey times are significantly lengthened, the road rage barometer rises alarmingly and there is a perceptible rise in the collective blood pressure level. Anger is tempered and hypertension moderated by the "common sense factor." Most of those who used the route regularly could see the thinking behind this decision to dig up a bit of the road. The advantage – or disadvantage if you will – of the taxi driver is that he is likely to pass such a point several times during a shift and observe what is really going on – or, more to the point, what is not going on.

It was in my former selfless mood of public-spirited altruism that I spent the first couple of weeks avoiding the jams or, when absolutely necessary, sitting in them willingly doing my bit for world peace by not ruing too much the cost in takings, calculated by the millisecond by the average minicab driver in such situations, particularly when in close proximity to a Hackney Cab with its meter running. On a good day I would even allow the odd driver to shoehorn his or her vehicle into the space in front when traffic merged into a single lane, though it depended on the classification into which the driver fitted – on which see later chapters.

But to return to the Stanningley Road junction renovation work this was to be the eye-opener to what actually happens when a reasonably chunky piece of road needs digging up, reshaping and adorning with that seemingly ubiquitous bane of taxi drivers' lives, yet another set of traffic lights.

During the course of an average day shift I must have passed these road works at least twenty times, and early on I tried to assess just how much work there was to be done and how long it was likely to take. A bit of central reservation had to be dug up, a short stretch of each carriageway resurfaced, road markings altered, cables laid and traffic lights installed and sequenced. I am no civil engineer or highway expert, but it was difficult to see how it could possibly take more than a month, and given a fair wind maybe the whole project could be completed in a couple of weeks. So when the crossing point of the road was put out of use, and blood supply through the artery was reduced by 50%, I anticipated a speedy return to traffic normality, when the whole situation would be greatly improved for everyone concerned.

The penny began to drop when, after passing the same spot for what must have been the 100th time in a week, I recalled that not on even a single occasion had I seen anyone actually working there. Roads were blocked off, and lanes were closed, but workmen were once again conspicuous only by their absence, and a similar state of affairs had persisted for the whole of the week. The weather was as benign as it was ever likely to be in a Yorkshire autumn. I could see the necessary equipment was available to do the work, much of it chained to lampposts blocking the pavement, as if some eccentric sculptor had hit upon the idea of a grotesque mechanical charm bracelet to exhibit to the commuting public. So why was nothing actually happening?

Some three months later I was inspecting an almost

identical landscape, a veritable Marie Celeste of the work site world, differing now only in the somewhat dilapidated state of the red and white cones adorning the central line of the carriageway and in the absence of a small stone wall that could comfortably have been tackled by a ten-year-old girl with a large hammer, and asking the same question. At a rough estimate seven out of every ten times I passed the spot there was no one there. On two of the other three occasions there were council employees or sub-contractors present but they were not actually doing anything, other than drinking warm beverages or casting "expert" eyes over the miniscule amount of work that had actually been completed whilst scratching heads and stroking beards. In an impressive display of multi-tasking these onerous tasks were often combined, the hot tea appearing to provide fuel for the high-powered internal engine of the cranial cavity and lubrication for the lower jaw. On one occasion out of ten there was activity – usually being conducted at the speed of a snail on Valium.

I was conscious of an evolution of emotional responses to this perennial inactivity. Acquiescence gave way to confusion and confusion to irritation, which in its turn gave way to anger, disillusionment and ultimately to cynicism – the last resort of the powerless commuter classes whose voyage to middle age has been through a mildly turbulent sea of disappointment with those who purport to make our lives safer and more satisfying. Contrary to Darwinian Theory this process of emotional evolution appeared to be heading in a direction that made survival increasingly unlikely, finally reaching a state of despair. The resignation that accompanied this nadir was at least comforting in that it came with some kind of assurance that I had reached the bottom of the emotional pit. Men who dig up roads have joined the illustrious ranks of politicians, financial advisers, self-assured preachers and estate agents in the premier league of those whose rhetoric fails to match the reality they embellish and whose true motives are far less fraternal and altruistic than their publicity suggests.

Just occasionally there would be a flurry of activity. After about four months of chronic inertia a crew of seemingly highly motivated and organised men arrived to install the new traffic lights. Holes were dug and filled after poles were interred at a slightly faster rate than that which would have been achieved by an arthritic hedgehog. The pavement was repaired, and soon there were traffic light fittings with dangling wires all ready to be connected up so the junction could be reopened. At last someone had inserted a stick of motivational dynamite in the relevant orifice of the council body that had permitted this dilatory state of affairs to be perpetuated. Hope surged in the breast of the cab drivers' fraternity as we anticipated being able to cross the junction in less time than it took to read War and Peace. The evolutionary process went into reverse gear till the pit of despair was little more than a dark blob. Then, inexplicably, the workforce seemed simply to disappear like so much dew at sunrise. The wires continued to dangle from the sterile fittings, waving at passing motorists in the breeze as if to offer a two-fingered salute and revel in the sadistic pleasure that comes from seeing the hopes of the powerless cruelly dashed.

And so it continued, day after day, week after week, month after month. Even after the work was actually completed, lights tested and central reservation embellished with sundry flora nothing happened. I wondered whether, after the best part of a year of creative idleness, those in charge felt it a shame to alter the congested landscape, or whether the re-opening was considered by now to constitute such a major achievement that an inaugural ceremony could only be performed by someone enjoying the status of a senior member of the royal family. 'I name this junction "What a sodding waste of taxpayers' money." May God bless this crossing point and all who traverse her.' Just possibly the whole tableau had been short-listed for the Turner

Prize and was awaiting the judges' pleasure.

Whatever those responsible were hoping for, the reality was that one day I simply drove past and noticed that traffic was moving freely through the former vehicular aneurysm. Amazingly the new traffic light system even seemed to work efficiently. The relief was short-lived – there were plenty of other routes waiting for the application of a tourniquet, but the contempt for those who commission and carry out road repairs had become permanent. Even as I write I know that the busy trunk road less than a mile from where I live has half of one of its southbound carriageways coned off just before and after a busy traffic island creating havoc at rush hours and more than one minor collision due to inadequate warning signs. This state of affairs has now persisted for about ten weeks. Other than arriving with a copious supply of traffic cones tossed into the vague vicinity of the white lines separating the two lanes of the carriageway no actual work has been completed and no workmen have appeared, and the only sign of activity has been the guest appearance of a man in a suit and a hard hat. His contribution consisted of casting an inept eye over the place where some work might one day take place should a family of pigs be passing overhead. Perhaps it was protection from bovine excreta that prompted the wearing of the hard hat, since there was nothing present that could have collided with his head, and certainly no holes in the ground into which he could have fallen. Or perhaps it was protection from irate locals hoping to beat some sense into the apparently dormant cranium of the council representative that encouraged such seemingly superfluous precautions.

Now I have acquired the paranoid habit of looking out for cone-layers I seem to see them every week. Usually operating when traffic is just building up to a nice crescendo there he is – the scruffy individual in T-shirt, denim jeans and hard hat tossing traffic cones into the middle of the carriageway as they are offloaded by a similarly-dressed individual from the back of an equally scruffy-looking vehicle. This second operative conducts his activity with all the generosity and enthusiasm of Santa Claus at a children's Christmas party. These wretched pieces of red and white plastic are then thrown onto the carriageways with the accuracy of a paraplegic caber-tosser after a few whiskies. And then they simply drive away – disappearing into some black hole specially commissioned by the local authority where plentiful supplies of tea and biscuits are maintained to provide practical refreshment for those who have just completed an exhausting half-hour's worth of manual labour. The enthusiasm and alacrity with which the carriageway is blocked seems to be in direct and inverse proportion to the level of activity that follows. I have even seen cones removed from the road weeks later when absolutely no work whatever has been completed. I have long since reached the point of knowing where I would like to insert the offending shapes. Whilst they would prove to be slightly too large for this venture to meet with unqualified success, I would gain a significant level of satisfaction from making the attempt.

Thus I learned to treat the laying of cones and the erection of temporary traffic lights not as the necessary precursor of imminent and essential repair work, but as a vague future promise of road surfaces slightly less destructive of car suspensions than the concrete model resembling a teenager with acute acne that currently pertained. The assurances of better things to come I have learned to place in the same box allocated to the verities claimed by aspiring politicians regarding the economy and my parents' assurances of phenomenal sporting prowess and physical strength if only I would eat my spinach like Popeye. The damage, I suspect, has been permanent.

# 8

## Rodley – Long Hours

My final words to my wife the evening before my very first shift were to the effect that I would start work at 5 a.m., and whilst I knew I could keep my car till 6 p.m. I would not, of course, work anything like that length of time. Thirteen hours wrestling with the capricious and, at times, barbaric traffic of West Yorkshire sounded like a descent into a netherworld reserved for the purification of perpetrators of genocide, ethnic cleansing or some other war crime. To my astonishment all thirteen of those hours pretty much flashed by punctuated by a series of astonished glances at the clock which, amazingly, still functioned in the eponymous pile of crap. Having worked almost every minute of those hours with only a couple of toilet stops I returned home feeling exhausted, but scarcely able to believe that more than half a day had passed since I had left home. I reassured my slightly anxious wife that I would be unlikely ever to repeat such a marathon, it was only that I needed to spend a day or two familiarising myself with the way the system worked. Perhaps if I had known that a pattern was set that would become permanent I would have quit at that point. I opened my bag of takings; even with my reduced rent I had barely earned the equivalent of the minimum wage. Depression and anxiety competed with sheer exhaustion to overcome me.

The rest of the week was pretty much a repeat of day one, the welcome difference being the steady increase in my takings.

Out of bed at 4.15 a.m. and into a heap of excrement by 5, and struggling to return the car to the yard after one last job through rush hour traffic just in time for the rear end of a night shift driver to land on the vacant seat.

The cars were thus run almost continually, perhaps having a slight respite somewhere around 4 a.m. when work really did become hard to find – though there were some day shift drivers who liked to start about then. As I learned more about how to go about making money in this new world, and the geography of West Yorkshire became less like a Greek labyrinth, my takings steadily increased, but my working hours remained more or less the same. The working week of an average taxi driver is something that places EEC directives relating to employee hours in the "Noddy Goes to Toytown" category. Most people who climb into the passenger seat of a private hire vehicle probably expect that there are restrictions in place to ensure that drivers do not work such long hours that they become a menace to those inside as well as outside the vehicle. I was surprised to learn that whilst such regulations are in place for almost every other job involving being in control of a vehicle the taxi and private hire driving profession is inexplicably excluded.

This absence of regulation, combined with the fiscal incentives generated by the way vehicles are rented out, result in many drivers working at least twelve hours a day, and some as many as eighteen; on one occasion I encountered a driver who claimed not to have slept for three nights because he had been working constantly. One twelve-hour shift is, of course, little more than tiring, but by the end of the sixth such consecutive day something of a catatonic narcolepsy descends, raising quite reasonable safety concerns.

It would be unfair to describe the private hire operating companies as universally irresponsible, but they are also fully aware that the way they run their businesses is likely to encourage drivers to keep working long after it is safe to do so.

Once the way the system operates is understood, long working hours and driving whilst struggling to keep eyelids open is almost inevitable.

This is how the system worked in my company, and in most others that hired out cars. I was a day shift driver, and in common with all other shift drivers almost all of my costs were incurred as soon as I picked the car up. I was charged a daily rent, and since the policy was for drivers to return vehicles with empty tanks another sum was spent putting fuel in for the duration of the shift. This resulted in spending about £50 before taking any money. The arithmetic then became simple. Once those costs had been covered, everything else was profit (I sometimes used to ring my wife – usually around 9 a.m. and announce proudly that I was now working for myself!), and the difference between going home with £75 and £100 was the difference between stopping work when I felt tired and pushing myself to the end of a thirteen hour day. Put another way a ten hour shift would generate an income only a little above the minimum wage, whereas a thirteen hour day could provide an additional 65% and furnish butter and jam for the bread I had won. A really good shift meant scones and clotted cream.

The same principle related to those who hired cars by the week; once costs were met everything else was profit, and the longer the working hours the greater the margin.

The system seems ill-advised, and even potentially dangerous to public safety, but it is the way most companies work, and in truth it is quite difficult to see a preferable alternative. There are a few private hire companies that operate a different system, settling for a percentage of the driver's gross takings, but this is rare. It would require honesty and a level of trust between operating company and driver that would have meant a wholesale abandonment of the qualities that characterised the typical bond. The relationship generally fluctuated between genial suspicion and psychotic paranoia depending on what sort of a week each party was having, and is seemingly almost embedded in minicab culture.

After some weeks the routine of early mornings, early bedtimes and precious little time to do anything other than work, eat and sleep was established. The psychologically soporific effect of this routine would, years previously, have been a cause for major resentment, but in my yet fragile state of mind it applied its own therapy rather effectively, as if aching emotional muscles were being gently manipulated by these demanding ergonomics to provide progressive relief and healing.

In any case time rarely dragged. I can imagine few, if any jobs I could do where a twelve-hour plus shift could pass without a dull moment or a wish for the time to go more quickly. The difficulty with the length of my working week was not so much the hours I needed to work, however, as the almost complete absence of opportunity to do anything else. Working six days a week, thirteen hours a day, and having to travel to and from a place of work on top of this meant one day a week to do everything else – see family, return 'phone calls, meet with friends, pay bills, visit the dentist and perform all the other duties that had been part of my role as husband and father ever since our first child was born. Golf was the most tragic casualty.

One of the perks of my existence as a clergyman had been admission to one of Yorkshire's best golf clubs as a clergy member – paying only a small percentage of the cost for ordinary members. Before my change of career I had recuperated from my regular verbal and psychological beatings by spending more and more time ruining a good walk by hitting and chasing a small white sphere. My handicap had assumed almost respectable proportions and I had at least some compensation for the failures, perceived, attributed and actual, in my professional life. Now I had barely enough time to put my golf shoes on, and certainly not enough to spend three hours or more on the links.

Autumn was beginning to yield in its unequal and futile

struggle with winter. For several weeks I had begun my working day before the increasingly pessimistic sounding birdsong had heralded dawn, and had dropped my car off well after the most resilient creature had given the day up as a bad job. But if the mood scales were weighted down on one side by the natural melancholia of shortened days, the balance was more than retained by ever-increasing quantities of available work and my rapidly improving knowledge of the business I had entered. In a formula of seemingly almost mathematical precision unpleasant weather equated to increased demand for taxis. A dark, cold, rainy early morning would witness hundreds of residents reaching for that little card they had put somewhere advertising the services of a local taxi company, rather than braving the walk to the nearest (probably vandalised) bus shelter to be at the mercy of both the elements and the largely fictional bus timetable.

By early December I began to feel that I had more than the vaguest of notions of how to navigate the byways – mental and geographical – of my new world, though this had been at the cost of something like half a small tree; my earlier, good-as-new street map, whose pristine state had remained unsullied for five years, had long since fallen into a dozen or more pieces and been consigned to the recycling box. Three unsuspecting successors had suffered similar fates, used and discarded at the rate of medieval royal concubines. In a vain bid to save the rain forest from further savagery I bought one of the more robust varieties featuring a wire-ringed spine whose reputation for longevity had clearly not been tested by anyone new to taxi driving. They were mauled to death by grubby, impatient fingers with the dexterity and elegance of a toddler attempting a Beethoven piano concerto. The arrival of a new job on the datahead seemed to reduce fine motor skills to infantile levels, hands driven to a frenzy by an irrational sense of anxiety previously experienced only once, when fell-walking through thick cloud and suddenly finding myself barely a metre from a sheer precipice. The memorising of the route from the A-Z preceded the somewhat simpler task of plotting a path through labyrinths of terraced houses to reach the promised job. All this had to be accomplished before the customer thought better of incurring the expense of a taxi and rang to cancel it or, more likely, simply left home and allowed the driver to waste both time and money. Having willingly yielded its information the cartographic fount of wisdom was mercilessly and ungratefully tossed aside while the race to reach a customer, and a few pounds towards the day's takings, became the sole foci of attention. Whilst work could take me to any point in West Yorkshire, as with most private hire firms the majority of it took place in a relatively confined area, so the same pages were assaulted time and time again. It took me back to being a spotty adolescent learning that a copy of Lady Chatterley's Lover had found its way past the guardians of public morality into the lending library. Of course I wouldn't have dreamed of taking it home, where embarrassment at its discovery would have caused far more discomfort than my parents' disapprobation, but there was nothing to stop me reading the smutty parts whilst secreted in a quiet corner of the library. Most of the book would be pristine, but you could always find what you were after by looking for the worn and dog-eared pages. So it was with my street maps, though the level of titillation they offered was somewhat disappointing. But the number of shifts completed before my latest bibliographic victim needed a replacement was increasing, and occasionally I would work for an entire hour without the need to contribute to the dismembering process of the next casualty. The improved knowledge, both of local geography and of the system by which work was allocated, resulted in a steadily improving income, and I rarely returned home with a sum that made a clergyman's stipend seem generous.

I had lost count of the number of people who, discovering my former profession, had quipped that being a vicar only involved working one day a week. The truth is that since most clergy have a strong sense of vocation they work longer hours than most, but over the previous year or so I really had been almost part-time, as each personal attack on my integrity undermined both self-esteem and motivation for wading through ecclesiological and religio-political treacle. The effects of driving for anything up to 75 hours a week, and adding commuting time onto that figure were profound, though by no means universally negative.

Most people who work at relatively mundane jobs spend at least some of each working day looking at the clock, lamenting the tardiness of the hour hand by comparison with its sprightliness during week-ends and holidays. By contrast I can recall being bored driving a cab only on the very rare occasions when work was as hard to find as a chilled beer in the Sahara. Perhaps this was simply the reverse psychology of fighting the clock, wishing for the day to go slowly in order to be able to complete more jobs and take more cash. Perhaps it was the constantly changing urban scenery, the idiosyncrasies of the customers and the curiosity so often aroused by those who rang for a cab. In any case the days and weeks flew by.

The tiredness generated by my work pattern often left me with little energy to do much more on my days off than rest and recuperate for the next shift. But this lack of spare time, in turn, had its advantages. A day would come when I could reflect on what had happened to me over the previous two years, but that day was most certainly not yet, and the anaesthetic effects of learning a new trade and feeling constantly tired whilst doing so blocked the synapses where memory and reflection interacted, and created an environment for healing, leaving the analysis to wait for the person who once inhabited my body to be restored to his familiar place.

# 9

## UPPER ARMLEY – 26B

Teatime with the family was always entertaining in those days. Now regarding ourselves as honorary northerners we decided that "tea" was to be our main meal of the day, eschewing posh terms like "dinner" in the true spirit of the Yorkshire working class thumbing their noses at softie southerners. We didn't go in for whippets or ferrets down the trousers but a quarter of a century on the ecclesiastical merry-go-round that had deposited us seemingly randomly in different parts of the country had left us feeling like cultural nomads. By birth Brummies, we now felt no affinity to Britain's second city, and Yorkshire was as good a place as any (and indeed better than most) to say we belonged.

It was a rare day when I returned with no "story of the day" with which to regale the family. This was usually heavily edited for the ears of my youngest two children, for whom bizarrely having a father who drove a taxi was far more of a status symbol than having a clergyman, and certainly less embarrassing in the school playground. Without doubt most of these seedy narratives were drawn from the first couple of hours of my shift. Sometimes it would be merely a narrative relating to the surreal conversations generated by the anomaly of this being the start of my day but the end of the customer's. Their long-delayed and frequently guilt-laden journey home would be coincidental with the start of another shift; they would be planning for "tomorrow" and I was already there. Moral lapses and excesses were often made glaringly obvious by the circumstances of the pick-up location, but whether or not this was so I seemed to be regarded rather bizarrely as a kind of Father Confessor. Souls were unburdened of almost every carnal sin imaginable, and some almost beyond the imagination. Gambling the rent on a one-armed bandit whose other unseen limb held a vice-like grip on the victim's dreams of jackpots; all-night orgies fuelled by performance-enhancing drugs and high-caffeine liquids; drinking bouts resulting in coming round literally in the gutter in the early morning, and seedy liaisons of which the spouse at home supposedly knew nothing. More often than not the breadth of my family's social education would be extended by an alluring mixture of the sordid and the comical. Perhaps this is mainly because I started work at what was generally closing time for the sex industry, be it the commercial sort or the homespun "husband pretending to be on night shift but really bonking his mistress since the small hours" variety. There was probably nothing in all these experiences that the tabloid press would pay serious money for; as far as I know I never once transported a member of the nobility, the judiciary, the Church or the government to or from houses of ill repute, and in any case to compromise the anonymity of the cab would have been the equivalent of a priest breaking the confidentiality of the confessional. But these experiences were certainly highly entertaining, and given a little moderate embellishment and judicious censorship kept all six of us entertained certainly until pudding was dished up. Perhaps the fact that these stories are lodged most securely and at the same time are the most accessible in my memory banks demonstrates with some profundity the limited scope of my own sexual encounters. I've never seriously regretted only having had one "partner" to share a bed with, but there have been moments when I've wondered what it would be like to play away from home.

Everyone knew that the pick-up point that came to be

known simply as "26b" was a brothel, or more colloquially a "knocking shop". Almost as a matter of principle every driver I met pretended to find it rather distasteful when "26b" jobs materialised on the datahead, but I only ever met one driver who refused a fare, a rather bizarre individual who was concerned that some unpleasant substance might be secreted onto his carefully valeted upholstery, presumably by some mystical process of biological osmosis. It never occurred to me to ask the girls (and I was far too polite) if they were wearing knickers – or "anal floss" as a friend of mine termed the thong that often passes for the more practical full gusset garment these days; or perhaps I was fearful of a slap across the face, or even more embarrassingly a practical demonstration that they were appropriately attired. They generally seemed too down to earth to skip on such essentials, and presumably their private parts, being essential tools of their trade, would be treated with all the care lavished by a master wood-turner on his chisels.

There were three wonderful things about 26b; firstly it was very close to Base where I picked up my car for a day's work, secondly closing time was 5.00 a.m., the time I generally started work, and thirdly there were some cracking jobs to be had that could really provide a great start to the day. Even the less lucrative fares provided good waking-up entertainment, a bit like the effect of one of those 70s sitcom repeats shown before breakfast that put you in the mood for coffee and cornflakes even if you can't believe that you once used to find it funny.

So it was that most mornings, but particularly at weekends, four or five drivers would be found in the car park tucked away out of sight of the few surviving prudish eyes still clinging tenaciously to residency in the area like eccentric limpets to the hull of a beached dinghy. Glancing round at their fellow cabbies each driver would raise eyes skywards in a pretence of claiming the moral high ground and offer tuts of disapproval at the rate of a light machine gun mowing down a line of infantry in order to convey an impression of being compelled to perform an unpleasant task out of a keen sense of public duty. This was pure hypocrisy; in truth we were all hoping for a lucrative hour or so before the early morning trade and heavy traffic kicked in.

Unusually for centres of adult amusement the clients and staff would normally leave at the same time, an arrangement that added to the entertainment value of this surreal game of taxi tombola, each driver wondering what weird or wonderful customer or destination might be allotted to his car. In this cavalier lottery the girls generally seemed completely normal compared to the punters, and were certainly better company, generally scoring over their erstwhile customers in not only being tolerably attractive but also displaying a half decent sense of humour. Randomness of customer and destination was guaranteed because the cars were block-booked and both clients and girls adopted them quite arbitrarily, so there was no possibility that the high-value jobs had been cherry-picked for particular drivers – on which subject see later chapters. I certainly had my fair share of both entertaining and lucrative work from 26b.

A trip to Huddersfield at that time of the morning was a driver's equivalent of three bells on the fruit machine, back in about an hour and at least £25 to the good. Strange to relate I also enjoyed talking to the various girls I drove there from time to time, and listening to their only slightly expurgated version of the night's work. After a while they were just ordinary people returning home after a lengthy and tiring shift. Apart from the scathing remarks about their customers' genitalia and performance (suddenly all those spam emails offering Viagra and penis enlargement treatments seemed to make a little more sense, and I wondered about retrieving one or two of them from my "trash" folder) they reviewed the storyline of the soaps, complained about their boss and affirmed one another by means of detrimental evaluations of other girls and their assets – the non-physical ones as well as those that were difficult to disguise in their industry – employing all the charm and dignity of alley cats.

The penny dropped somewhere on the M62 whilst avoiding a collision with one of the many truckers who seem to regard private hire drivers as the scum of the earth rather than fellow professional drivers and feel it their public duty to eliminate as many as possible. I suddenly understood why I could relate to these rather pleasant young women so naturally; it really all boiled down to the similarities of the working environments we inhabited. Not that the inside of a minicab bore any serious resemblance to a rather sordid looking upstairs flat replete with red imitation-velvet furniture provided for the purpose of bonking for cash; nor that the manipulation of the controls of a car was the automotive equivalent of stripping and offering the delights of the human body. In fact anyone looking at the average portly cabbie in his 50's would probably offer him something more than loose change to keep his clothes on.

Nevertheless the similarities were striking. I could have been loitering at one of the gathering places of private hire drivers, listening to a couple of night shift drivers bemoaning their plight and wondering what might have been. They too would have complained about being screwed by the people they worked for.

'I 'ad fuck-all worth doing last night. Couple of cheap hand jobs and the odd shag. 'Ardly worth bothering coming out.'

'Na – me neither. 'Ad a few decent customers but they weren't tippin' much.'

'Reckon that Czech girl Sacha's gettin' all the decent work by shaggin' the boss.'

'Yeah – what a pain in the arse. Told me last week that he'd see me alright for a free blow job.'

'You have to be fuckin' joking – I'd rather suck the shit out of the toilet.'

The common factor was that making a living in both of our worlds depended on the quality as well as the volume of work available and the appreciation, generosity and affluence of a clientele that was generally of dubious and suspicious character. So I took the opportunity of telling them about the relative paucity of my previous shift, how little work there had been around, how few of the customers offered tips, and how I wondered if there were a few drivers that were being fed all the well-paid work, and that they were not the only ones being screwed for a pittance.

So we commiserated all the way to Huddersfield, where I took their word for it that last night's takings were so paltry that they were unable to afford a tip, and believed their promise that next time they would be more generous if they had had a few decent shags with some optional extras; I enjoyed a very pleasant return journey, giving my once puritanical imagination permission to explore what these additional services might have entailed, and how my wife might feel about acquiring some of the accessories the girls doubtless carried in their spacious handbags.

A deeper and more disturbing question was whether the fact that I had just had a mutually helpful conversation with two prostitutes and allowed myself to wonder "what if" for 20 minutes or more reflected the depths to which my morals had sunk, or how painfully ignorant I had been of the real world and how much alike deep down was each member of the human race, whatever creed or religion they adhered to or scorned. Perhaps further evidence of my naivety is the fact that I was slightly surprised, though thankfully not disappointed, that payment for the trip was only offered in cash; I later came to realise that this was not true for all drivers, and recompense in kind was not infrequently offered in lay-bys on the edge of Yorkshire towns in the hours just before dawn. Whether my physical attributes left the girls feeling that such a service would have been the erotic equivalent of eating tripe for breakfast or whether I give off some kind of aura of clerical respectability that discourages such an approach I don't know. In any case the cash was more useful than the lesson in bedroom gymnastics, however much it might have broadened my education.

The 26b job that sticks in the memory like porridge to the cereal bowl involved punters rather than girls.

They didn't really look or act like 26b customers; for one thing they were compos mentis. I never did quite work out why most of the place's punters were so spaced out; I couldn't believe they were dizzily in love. I wondered if they put drugs in the drinks, but all the girls I met assured me they didn't. If it was merely alcohol I wondered if the detrimental effect this would have on the male libido was something the girls would be grateful for or not.

In any case these two men, both in their early 30s, were 20 years too young, too sober, and far too well educated for 26b, which I gather required a certain measure of desperation on behalf of its clients before they would part with serious cash for services in what were pretty squalid surroundings. Their demeanour suggested those who are used to being able to buy what they want with a minimum of fuss, but they also exuded an aura of sexual frustration that suggested they were unlikely to feature in the establishment's probably brief list of satisfied customers.

Exactly what it was about the services on offer that had caused their departure was never explicitly stated, but evidently the idea of having sex with one of the girls at 26b had been as appealing as seducing their next door neighbour's toothless granny. The sense of injured pride with which they left the premises may have left them feeling superior, but the triumph was something of a pyrrhic victory. The problem was they were still being held to ransom by their unfulfilled lust, a seemingly unfamiliar state of affairs and one requiring immediate attention or a long cold shower. Since the latter was neither readily available nor much desired the only means of alleviating this frustration was to find an alternative establishment that would satisfy both desire and taste.

So began the search for a suitable venue – a tall order at 5.00 a.m., particularly when they were being driven by someone with such a profound ignorance of the red light culture of the city – they had drawn the short straw in the cabbie allocation lottery. Picking my brains on the subject took not more than a few seconds; I knew only two houses of ill repute, and I only knew those because their premises were adorned with silhouettes of semi-naked females and advertised services including "sauna" and "massage", which I took to be code for "blow job" and "shag". Of these one had recently been shut down by the police (it was soon up and running again under a different name), and we found the other to be closed.

At this point the sensible thing to do would have been to call it a day and go home to watch one of the adult DVDs of which I was sure they had an ample stock. But testosterone was in competition with tiredness and very much had the upper hand; they seemed completely unconcerned that the search for gratification could empty their wallets as they insisted on a full tour of all the places in the city they knew where sex was for sale; compared to my sparse acquaintance with such places their database of brothels was the equivalent of a Google search, and had Yellow Pages entertained such an entry they could certainly have filled a full page. The next 45 minutes or so was eye-opening as we visited one establishment after another. These were mostly just houses or flats that to any undiscerning eye would have conveyed the impression of British respectability, though in some cases there was the traditional red light to give something of a clue as to a less savoury purpose. Each locked door or unanswered bell served to heighten the aura of sexual frustration to the point where it would have been almost possible to bottle it and sell it as one of those spray deodorants that women supposedly find irresistible. By the time we were down to the last couple of possibilities I could feel the tension gradually giving way to resignation, and by 6.00 a.m. all possibilities were exhausted. Business had either been too good or too bad for anywhere to remain open, or perhaps the advent of a bleak autumnal sunrise had urged a return to the sanctuary of artificial darkness. My education had been expanded by learning the location of a dozen or more bordellos, and my wallet was eagerly anticipating the influx of funds that would result from this ill-conceived adventure. For my customers perhaps the emerging daylight had been the necessary bucket of cold water on their ardour, as failure to find a prostitute who was actually awake and willing resulted in a meek request to be taken home – another quite long journey that pushed the fare towards the £40 mark.

Once their hormones had subsided in quiet resignation there was opportunity for more considered conversation, so I tried to find out a little about them and, as usually happened, they discovered that I was a former clergyman. Completely unfazed by this revelation, and evidently feeling little if any moral deficiency they talked quite freely about how and why they visited places like 26b. One of them was unattached, but the other was married, which prompted me naively to ask why he needed to pay for sex, and if his wife knew about it. By way of response my sexual education was broadened in a manner that would probably have made Bernard Manning blush. I was treated to a detailed description of the difference between making love (to his wife) and shagging (a hooker) and how they were completely separate activities, however similar were the techniques involved. Of course his wife knew nothing of this activity – she was away at the time – and would probably divorce him if she found out. This seemed to be a scenario that was considered worth the risk in the same way that a burglar considers the possibility of a passing policeman.

The endearing if rather seedy character of the institution known as 26b was, sadly, not to last, though it did outlive my five o'clock starts. However much most people may look down on the morals of such places, the trade offered was simple and straightforward. 'We will offer you sex in a wide variety of formats, and enough alcohol to suppress your inhibitions but not your drive, and in return you reward us with cash.' Perhaps it was simply that I was becoming less prudish, but if that was how people chose to live their lives perhaps there was something to be said for not passing judgment too readily. Most of us know what it is to be humiliated by imprudent actions initiated unbidden by hormones over which we have inadequate control – and not simply when we were in our teens. The tabloid newspaper accounts of pillars of respectable society caught with their trousers down – or, occasionally, their skirts up – provide ample evidence that given both means and opportunity most of us might make complete fools of ourselves. I reflected that it was probably the lack of both that had kept my reputation intact rather than my much-prized moral code. I had recently departed a lifestyle where motives were disguised or concealed, where understatement of true intentions hid the daggers of the eyes and plain speaking was the conversational equivalent of passing wind in public. One of the facets of 26b that gave it an endearing quality was the matter-of-fact simplicity with which business was conducted; I'm sure many of the clients and even some of the staff did feel defiled and guilty from time to time, but they hid it well, and I came to the conclusion that this was not quite on the same moral level as infanticide.

The change of atmosphere at 26b, when it came, seemed to take place almost overnight, and its endearing quality was replaced by something that seemed a lot more sinister; a group of Russians assumed control, and most of the girls seemed to be stabled in a row of terraced houses only about a mile away where they could be observed and monitored – so no more Huddersfield runs – and there was an air of brooding malevolence that seemed to hang over those who worked there. Quite suddenly it seemed to have become a place of fear and intimidation, and tears were never far away from the eyes of the girls. The little they did say gave away both their Eastern European origin and the apprehension, even fear that characterised their existence. They had been imported from former Soviet bloc countries, lured into the sex industry on the back of promises of a better life. Now threatened with eviction, deportation, violence or a combination of all three, they had opted for the acquiescent misery that was such a contrast to the happy-go-lucky approach of the former workforce.

The blind eye that the council and police had been turning on the establishment suddenly acquired near-perfect vision, and both lurched into action. About a year after the Russian revolution 26b was closed down at the request of the police; those who ran it were arrested not only for making money from immoral earnings, but also for human trafficking and employing illegal immigrants. I have often wondered since what happened to the girls of 26b who suffered under this regime.

But just to demonstrate the resilience of such places in their traditional format, the postscript to this story is that the establishment returned to the ownership of good old native Yorkshire folk, who restored the former glory of its earlier seedy but relatively harmless image. The cat and mouse game with council and police continued when it was closed down again late in 2007 and the good, honest and hardworking Yorkshire folk who ran it pleaded guilty to running a brothel under the guise of a massage parlour. But there was always something irrepressible about 26b; I doubt that we have seen the last of it – you just can't keep class like that down for long. I am almost embarrassed to say, several years after returning to work for a church, that I still have rather a soft spot for 26b.

# 10

## Harehills – Cwollifying

Early mornings at the service station where I went for my fuel were a bit like animals gathering round a watering hole in the Serengeti and at 5 a.m. it was one of the few places in the city teeming with life. Virtually every car was a taxi of some description and every driver a cabbie. Many, like me, were fuelling up for a day shift. Some would be night shift drivers suffering from a rare bout of optimism and judiciously adding just enough fuel to see them through the hoped-for lucrative fare which would add the cream to the full fat milk of a good shift. Other cabs called in at the behest of their already inebriated customers heading home after a night out in order to replenish supplies of alcohol and / or tobacco. I had previously wondered why petrol stations appeared so liberally stocked with beer and cigarettes; now I began to understand that at this time of day they were just about the only retail outlets available, the nearest 24 hour supermarket being several miles and an expensive cab ride distant. Beer, spirits and cigarettes are to the 24-hour petrol station what bread, milk and margarine are to the corner shop. Thus it is that impromptu taxi drivers' conventions take place at 24-hour service stations at such an unearthly hour; and just like the creatures round the watering holes of the veldt there is a distinct, if largely unexpressed, hierarchy among those challenging for a place at which to satisfy the vehicle's thirst. Whilst the normal British protocol of waiting one's turn was usually, if reluctantly observed, body language and verbal intercourse, or more specifically lack of it, gave the lie to any concept of true fraternity. The black cab drivers would generally avoid eye contact with anyone other than another Hackney Carriage driver, and would certainly never engage in conversation or exchange smiles. The night shift drivers of private hire cars, generally distinguishable by their worn and haggard expressions, would be busy exchanging macabre or grotesque horror stories from their shift in a bid to be the Edgar Alan Poe of the moment. Those of us who had no real experience of driving a cab through the early hours of the night and into the morning tended to regard night-time drivers with the same mixture of curiosity and respect afforded to heroes returning from wars in distant lands. The curiosity concerned the experiences they had enjoyed or endured in the wee small hours of the night, of imagined dangers and sordid encounters shrouded by the natural darkness of the night and the "closed shop" atmosphere their social interaction generated. Respect was born out of ignorance of what a night shift was really like, and the assumption that it required the skills and courage of a MI6 agent with 00 status to survive through to daylight. When I discovered night shift driving for myself I found that it was neither more dangerous nor more glamorous than working days, but the mystique still surrounded the species at this early stage.

If black cab drivers were the wild predators at the watering hole, the night shift drivers those beasts large enough to defend themselves and the day shift drivers the also-rans, at this point I was the equivalent of something to scrape off the bottom of one's safari boot. I had been driving a private hire car for a couple of months but by exploiting a loophole in the law the company I drove for had taken me on as an "unbadged" driver, operating a car as a "Public Service Vehicle" without a proper licence. The give-away was that these cars carried no licence number, and whilst most members of the public never noticed the difference everyone in the cab-driving fraternity knew that you were both new to the game and unqualified, and afforded you about as much respect as a disease-carrying tsetse fly; your existence could not be ignored and was even significant for its nuisance value, but you could be repelled by the insect spray of a disdainful look, and kept at bay by means of the mosquito net of contempt.

Whilst the practice of taking on unbadged drivers has now been terminated it was a great way for people like me to try the trade without committing the fairly significant sums of money required to gain a private hire driver's licence. Whilst the majority of those who tried failed to last more than a month, once they were established they were strongly encouraged to settle into the business with the suggestion "you should go for your badge." To the considerable surprise of the drivers' supervisor, and my even greater astonishment, it had finally dawned on us both that I could make a living at this game, and a mutually beneficial relationship had broken the surface of the murky swamp in which I was expected to drown. The busy period of the year was approaching – the lead-up to Christmas – when the nation seems to whip itself up into a frenzy of consumerist activity, and the only way to complete a list of tasks as long as a roll-call of failed English test cricketers is to have someone else driving you around. Then you can concentrate on being stressed over what to buy a maiden aunt (unseen since last Yuletide) for a tenner, what you can get for half that price that gives all the appearance of being a lot more expensive for the neighbours, and how to manage Christmas dinner now your teenage daughter has gone vegan. I hadn't made my fortune by any means, but I was making significantly more money than I ever did as a clergyman, and the pressure was being applied to "go for my badge."

The combination of a desire to hold my head up at the early morning refuelling rituals, the comfort of a well-filled purse and the warm if not entirely selfless encouragement of my supervisor, not to mention the complete absence of ecclesiastical politics in this feral world were more than enough to make my mind up. So I decided to invest time (which was in short supply) and money (which for almost the first time in my adult life wasn't) in trying to gain my licence.

London cabbies are reckoned to be the nobility of the taxi world, and are probably in a class by themselves, largely because of their mastery of "The Knowledge", perhaps the favourite topic of conversation in those aristocratic circles. Spoken of in sepulchred tones as if a key component in a liturgy dedicated to a minor deity, this is the test that all aspiring Black Cab drivers in the capital must overcome, and is the geographical equivalent of a PhD at Cambridge. If you ever feel the fare for a London cab is a bit steep bear in mind that you are being driven by a human street map who has endured a long, tortuous and costly process to secure the necessary qualification, and whose principal topic of conversation on the golf course on his day off is how to lop two minutes off a journey from White City to Seven Sisters.

By comparison a provincial private hire car driver has barely learned to read and write to gain his or her dubious status. Whilst there are regional variations the general pattern is that qualification is won by a driving test, a police check, a medical, a two-hour induction course and the payment of a sizeable sum of money to the local authority. The reward for success is represented by a small piece of plastic with a picture taken by one of those computerised cameras programmed to make the subject look ridiculous, and the right to drive for the operating company of your choice, so long as they are agreeable.

I had few concerns about the medical I was sent to undergo, being one of those fortunate people for whom a trip to the doctor is like having Great Aunt Mildred round for Christmas dinner – mildly unpleasant but quite bearable and even something of a novelty. Of the three visits in the previous ten years two had been related to the stress brought on by my recent experiences, and one was to have some injections for a trip to Mexico City where I led a team helping with relief work. Nevertheless the brevity of the medical examination was comical to say the least.

Arriving at the elegant domicile of the medical practitioner appointed by the cab company, in a village inhabited by professional footballers and lottery winners, I realised that I had opted for the wrong career and reflected on where I could have been had I worked a lot harder at school or played football every weekend instead of doing a Saturday job and going to church. I was shown into an area that looked like a general dumping ground for unwanted furniture, newspapers and bric-a-brac of dubious pedigree. Its status as a medical consulting room was justified by the strategic placement of an eyesight chart and a set of scales, offering only a mildly anachronistic contrast to the eclectic range of moderately expensive junk.

I had had a few medicals in the past, for life assurance and, oddly enough, to ensure that my body was capable of withstanding the rigours of clerical life, hardly the most physically demanding profession to pursue. A psychiatric evaluation would have been far more appropriate, though no one sane enough would probably have been sufficiently stupid to seek such a vocation. The only question that occasioned any anxiety was just how much of my clothing I would need to remove, and whether by wearing loose-fitting garments some of the embarrassment could be avoided. The overeating that was my inevitable comfort habit when facing the kind of insecurity I had endured over the previous few years had resulted in my overall dimensions reaching the point where loose fitting clothes were the only type that did not make me look like a medieval monarch; but I hoped that if sleeves and trouser legs could be rolled up rather than removed a little less naked flesh would need to be exposed. My concerns were completely groundless; I was spared the embarrassment of exposing my more than ample expanses of flab by being asked to remove no clothing whatever, and indeed such an apparent innovation would have seemed pointless given that no physical contact took place between the consultant and myself, barring the accidental touching of hands as I offloaded a cheque for £40 some five minutes after entering his residence. Having been asked to read a line of the eyesight chart probably visible from an orbiting space station and asked (loudly) if my hearing was ok there appeared to be nothing more to be said or done. A sum that took me half a day to earn had just been deposited in the hand of someone who had done little else other than sign a piece of paper after a brief conversation and an alleged examination that could have been conducted by his housekeeper whilst dusting the sideboard. A painful calculation indicated that at this rate he could earn in an hour more than I could in a week, and even allowing for the probability that some of the fee found its way back to the person who recommended him at my cab company the relief at clearing one of the hurdles to securing my licence was at least partially offset by the less savoury taste of having been ripped off. Perhaps this was the only encounter with the medical profession I have ever experienced when I felt cheated by remaining fully dressed and under-examined. For one mad moment I was tempted to ask for a full examination of my possibly infected anus and scrotum, just to make this greedy medic earn at least some of his fee, but opted to quit while I was ahead instead.

With the exacting rigours of the physical examination out of the way I could now concentrate on what was likely to be the more challenging demands of the Department of Transport when I turned up for my taxi driver's test.

Virtually all women who have achieved a state of domestic bliss, or even tranquillity with a man, know that there are two places where his performance is criticised at the peril of physical or verbal violence, or even the divorce courts – between the sheets and behind a steering wheel. Given that many men drive as if their vehicle were a penis substitute the correlation makes a lot of sense. Statistics are not always an accurate measure of attitudes, but the fact that something like 85% of men consider themselves to be "better than average" drivers, and almost none see themselves on the other side of the meridian, is not simply a mathematical impossibility but reveals a great deal about the locus of the male ego.

Of course the reality is that most of us are not nearly as good as we like to think, and the idea of taking another driving test under the emotionless scrutiny of one of those unreasonable morons who failed us the first time round is about as appealing as being marked on our performance in bed by a qualified sex therapist. I had undertaken three previous ordeals, having failed my first motorbike test and being congratulated by the second examiner with the immortal words "Well, I'll have to pass you, I suppose." My car test was plain sailing, and made less arduous by the presence of an examiner who had not yet had his sense of humour surgically removed.

Now some thirty years later I considered myself not only part of the 85% but most definitely in the higher echelons of those for whom it was a reasonable judgement. I also knew that thirty years was ample time to develop habits which, to my former tutor, would have been the motoring equivalent of fingernails being drawn screeching across a school blackboard. I feared that a raft of unorthodox habits had generated enough technical faults to result in failure long before the engine was even warm. Help was at hand, however – at a price – in the form of the approved driving instructor who had earlier confirmed my capacity to operate a vehicle without scaring elderly customers out of their wits. Recommended by the same person who had nominated the putative medic, presumably for a similar level of recompense, he would help me brush up my skills for £25 an hour, and show me the routes normally used on the tests designed for private hire and Hackney Carriage drivers.

Fortunately this was one of those rare occasions when I allowed my ego to be overruled by prudence; I later discovered that there were drivers at the company unbadged after two or three years who had failed a whole string of tests but still declined the denigrating offer of lessons; generally speaking those who knew they needed help and paid for lessons passed quite easily.

My instructor, Geoff, seemed curiously out of place arriving at the premises of a private hire company in his immaculately turned out Renault. Quietly spoken and with a sufficient vocabulary to render vulgarity or expletives unnecessary, Geoff came from the same part of the city that I lived in, and his genial presence was not only anachronistic in my new environment but also served to remind me of how out of place I must have looked to those I was now rubbing shoulders with. But Geoff was good at his job, speaking only when he deemed it necessary and only occasionally dropping his professional guard when his well-concealed but superbly developed sense of humour managed to circumvent the shackles imposed as a result of decades of compulsory restraint to offer a light-hearted rebuke at some minor misdemeanour.

It took only a few minutes into my first lesson with Geoff to understand why the failure rate for the test I was booked in for was so high. The ancient Highway Code I dug out of a cupboard, and with which I shared my life and my bed as a learner driver was as up-to-date as a Latin Mass, and as relevant to modern driving conditions as the dodo is to contemporary zoology. "Bus lanes", for instance, had not been thought of when my vehicle sported L-plates, and in common with most drivers I just stayed out of them on the assumption that they were for buses. "You've just failed your test", said Geoff as I drove immaculately down one of the city's arterial routes. I checked my speed – I was still studiously travelling at a pious 38 mph. "This is a 40 mph limit, isn't it?" I replied. He was patience personified "Yes, but why are you sticking in the outside lane?" "Because the inside one is a bus lane!" I responded in the manner of a pupil having realised he is the intellectual superior of his tutor. Ever the epitome of pedagogical indulgence Geoff pointed out the blue plates that detailed the times of day the bus lane had to be kept clear, with the exception, of course, of drivers of expensive German cars whose time is much too valuable to allow such constraints to impede either their journey to work or their need to park in the said bus lanes while newspaper and fresh supplies of tobacco are procured.

"What does it say on the bus lane sign?"

"7.30 – 9.30 a.m." I replied sheepishly.

"Precisely; outside those hours it is just another lane on the carriageway, and you have been travelling in the outside lane for the last two minutes, ('along with everyone else', I felt like replying) and the examiner will fail you if you do that on your test." Everyone knows, of course, that you keep out of bus lanes because the chances of finding one clear of parked cars – at almost any time of day or night – are the equivalent of the likelihood of a nun giving birth to triplets, and you just have to keep pulling out into a flow of traffic consisting of drivers who wonder what planet you are on, especially if you are one of those bizarre individuals who drive within the speed limit.

But this was one thing among many where, in effect, driving quite normally would result in failure to win the approbation of the Department of Transport's appointed representative. In fact the phrase "You've just failed your test" became as familiar and persistent a refrain as sitting in church reciting a piece of well-known liturgy. Geoff pointed out one mistake after another where, however properly I thought I was driving, an examiner would see it differently. Some of these "mistakes" could be regarded as a fair cop – the use of bus lanes being one of them – but others were really little other than cunning traps set at strategic points on examination routes in order to supply the test centre with its required quota of failures. "They don't take the ordinary learners down these routes," chuckled Geoff, "they reserve them for the taxi driving tests." It was no wonder that failure was so commonplace when each street and junction was such a minefield. It was difficult to resist the conclusion that those who planned the layout of the area had been sadistic driving examiners in a previous incarnation, or had a gentlemen's agreement with the local test centre to guarantee a reasonable failure rate among the taxi driving fraternity.

I will leave the story there and resist the temptation to elaborate on the nature of these traps for fear of damaging Geoff's business; suffice it to say I would probably have several failures of the private hire driver's test under my belt had it not been for his patient tutelage and the invaluable knowledge he imparted. But as a postscript I now live in a different city where bus lanes are generally clear, but it is still the case that 90% of drivers avoid using them when they are permitted to do so.

The driving test centre where I underwent my ordeal was in one of those urban areas where there is an underlying sense of both malevolence and depression, and to emerge from the centre to find all four wheels still affixed to the vehicle occasions a modicum of surprise. The waiting room was another alien world – the only people who had reached the fourth decade of life were the driving instructors, who were also identifiable as being the ones exhibiting merely mild symptoms of anxiety. Their perennial concerns about the survival chances of their vehicles at the hands of learner drivers were probably compounded by the fear that during the few minutes they were in the test centre an army of joy riders would have stolen their pristine cars and made bonfires out of their means of making a living. The rest of the room appeared to be straight out of kindergarten, and the atmosphere was replete with anxiety, anticipation and adrenaline, all apparently oozing from the spotty faces and expressed in the body language of the young hopefuls, who were clutching car keys like maiden aunts at a speed dating evening.

Entertaining the mostly forlorn hope that they were about to secure their passage to independent transport they also seemed to exhibit a passing curiosity about what I was doing there, looking as out of place as a teenager starting primary school. Youthful eyes turned briefly in my direction; only one of us – Geoff or myself – could be the instructor, so which of us was the geriatric prat who couldn't be bothered to get his licence at a sensible age, and for whom the imminent prospect of a wooden box hardly made the exercise worthwhile?

It was with some difficulty and uncharacteristic restraint that I resisted the very strong urge to pass my driving licence round the room to present my credentials, or to declaim my status as a qualified driver on a higher plane of existence than the rest of them. Instead I opted to slink into the darkest, least conspicuous part of the room and hope that attention was now focussed elsewhere.

My cover was blown almost immediately. The door of the anteroom opened, evoking memories of earlier driving tests which came flooding back with gut-wrenching clarity. Each candidate turns to see who is emerging from the examiners' room, hoping to be allocated to one of the few who do not look like they might have been Stalin's right hand man during one of his periodic purges. I barely had time to look, only to hope that my name would be the last to be called, so that I could remain incognito.

"Reverend Richards, please", rang out the strident voice, and suddenly the entire population of the room had ceased to worry about the forthcoming ordeal and was looking round to see who the bearer of this dubious epithet might be. I felt a dozen or more pairs of curious eyes observing me as I resisted the compelling urge to say "here, sir" and reluctantly extracted myself from the chair to lead my examiner out to the waiting vehicle. The confusion was almost palpable; "if this is a reverend where is the clerical collar, the bald head, the ridiculous specs and the weak effeminate voice?"

It has largely been the stereotypical portrayal of clergy in the media that has caused me to be ambivalent about using a title that is so closely associated with one particular vocation. Well known effete television vicars, such as the brilliant Frank Williams in the comedy series "Dad's Army" have generated such a compelling template for the office-bearers that the concept of sighting one in such a mundane setting is almost incomprehensible.

My entry into the refined atmosphere of clerical office had not been a reluctant one – I had had a strong sense of "call" since my mid-teens, and it was – and mainly still is – an immensely fulfilling vocation. I had been officially entitled to bear the legend "Reverend" for some 20 years plus at this point, having been formally recognised by my branch of the UK church in my late 20's, and "set aside" for the high calling of ecclesiastical oversight, as well as the performance of other vital functions like putting the urn on for tea, fixing the church heating system and clearing the drains. But if I had had a £10 note for every occasion on which, during that time, I had encountered puzzled looks and comments like "But you seem so normal" when my profession was uncovered I would be among the ranks of the owners of expensive German cars blocking bus lanes. I had become weary of golf partners who would apologise for their language on securing an answer to the question "and what do you do?" asked for the umpteenth time because they would only know how to relate to me when they could place themselves above or below me in the social order. Usually the compensation for the revelation was that their game went to pieces resulting in a better than reasonable chance of me beating them. I had endured teammates in cricket clubs who referred to me as "the vicar", a status surpassed in a former football club where I was promoted to the office of "the bishop." Perhaps the epitome of this artificial deference was exhibited by a woman who encountered me covered in grease trying to repair a church member's motorbike; having been told I was the minister of her neighbour's church I was greeted with "Good morning, Your Reverence." These experiences had prompted me to use my title and garb extremely sparingly.

In fact there is nothing to prevent anyone from calling themselves "reverend", but for most sane people it would come pretty low in a list of preferred titles – somewhere between "cat's puke" and "dog turd". During my time in ministry I had appended the title to some official forms and documents and had left it off others – perhaps at random, or possibly according to the reading on the thermometer of job satisfaction at that particular point. Clearly the last time I sent my licence off for a change of address had coincided with a warm, sunny spell.

We reached the car, and much to my relief I was still able to read a number plate at the requisite distance; I resisted the guffaw that tried to rise from my sense of humour centre after having been told that he was looking for an exceptionally high level of driving skills in order to give me a pass, and likewise refrained from asking if he had ever been in a private hire cab. Preliminaries over I started the engine, gave an exaggerated stare into the rear view mirror, looked over my shoulder, indicated right and let the clutch out, making sure not to cross my hands on the steering wheel; I felt a quite irrational sense of pride at my ability to complete the manoeuvre properly, having not done so for the best part of thirty years.

The test for a private hire licence was twice the length of a normal driving exam, and allowed for far fewer minor faults, and given the quantity of bad habits I had picked up over a couple of million miles' worth of driving success was by no means assured. I generally rate myself as a good instinctive assessor of character, and I weighed up my examiner companion as one displaying a pleasant disposition, with a genial manner suggesting that he would not be so devious as to try any sneaky tricks. I was soon compelled to re-evaluate this positive assessment. Pleasant he might have been, with a warm, engaging and sunny personality, but I believe that in the forty minutes or so of the test I was subject to every conceivable ploy Geoff had mentioned, and I have no doubt at all that without my tutor's input I would have failed miserably. As it was I almost racked up enough minor faults to fail, and in an uncanny echo of an event some thirty years previously was finally told "Well, I'm going to pass you – but…" The catalogue of minor errors that followed, I felt, were mainly occasioned by poor instructions from the passenger seat, but since I had been told I had passed decided to quit while ahead, take my medicine and bow meekly to this putative colossus of motoring excellence. I had my piece of paper – now I could get my licence.

# 11

## BRAMLEY – TWENTY-FOUR – SEVEN

The acquisition of my "badge" – the licence granted by the local council to those considered fit to drive private hire vehicles – resulted in an irrationally exaggerated sense of pride, since it was hardly the most exacting qualifying process I had ever undertaken. I had a handful of O and A-levels gained in those long-forgotten days when it was actually possible to fail an exam at school, and a fairly decent honours degree in theology; I was a published author and had been fortunate enough to be a speaker at one of the big Christian holiday weeks. It seemed odd therefore to be quite so exhilarated about a piece of paper confirming a status somewhere between a 25 metre swimming certificate and a Blue Peter Badge.

It was, perhaps, simply the product of the euphoria generated by the feeling of being able to give the finger to those who had previously rubbished both my skills and qualifications in an attempt to discredit me and undermine my reputation; so successful had this process been that I think I too had begun to believe their propaganda. I also had little doubt that there were those of my former acquaintance who, having undermined my credibility as a minister, were now prophesying my doom in this new world in the sepulchral tones of Old Testament soothsayers – and with a similar level of macabre glee. Now I had not only learned a new trade, but was making a decent living from it and had jumped through the necessary hoops to gain a proper qualification. I also realised that I had learned how to do something that could always be a fall-back in the likely eventuality that I would return to the world of the Church. There are a few professions – undertakers being perhaps among the foremost – who will always be in demand. There will always be a need, too, for people who will drive members of the public from one place to another for a decent fare when public transport, for whatever reason, will not suffice. Perhaps it is the case that it is not just that the grass on the other side of the fence looks greener, but the grazing in the field recently abandoned also takes on a particularly attractive hue. As I write this some years after a return to ministry I can honestly say that rarely a week has gone by without some kind of nostalgic desire to return to the private hire world. One of my provisional retirement plans is to spend some leisurely hours driving people round Northumberland, where my wife and I have a home for our later years, not needing to earn enough money to feed and house a family of six, but just enough to pay for my golf club membership and a ready supply of balls to feed my incurable slice.

There were a number of other advantages to qualification. For one thing I was no longer compelled to drive the "unbadged" cars provided by the taxi firm; these veritable wrecks of vehicles were kept for those who were new to the game and the most likely to be involved in collisions; most had been "round the clock" twice, and gave new meaning to the expression "a wing and a prayer." Secondly because insurance costs were cheaper for drivers with their badge I now benefitted from cheaper rates of hire, immediately gaining for myself the sum of £5 per shift before I began work.

The most significant benefit, though, was that I was now able to apply for a "Twenty-Four-Seven" car, one I could keep at home and drive at hours to suit myself. Apart from the obvious convenience there were a number of advantages to this arrangement, perhaps most notably avoiding some of the worst of the traffic. The biggest down side of driving the day shift was definitely having to tackle two rush hours, the second of these coming right at the end of the working day, when I was tired and trying to get those few extra fares that would make the difference between a merely satisfactory and a lucrative shift, or on a rare bad day turn disaster into mediocrity. I had decided that as soon as I had my Twenty-Four Seven car I would only ever work one rush hour in any shift, and the experience of coming home early – even if only for a break – just as the traffic was building to its crescendo on a weekday afternoon became a blissful luxury. It was with a curious mixture of schadenfreude and empathy that I remembered the hundreds of cabbies sitting in long traffic queues drumming impatient fingers on steering wheels in frustration in the late afternoon.

The family also benefitted from the new arrangement; I was often at home just as the children were returning from school, and able to share with them the news and scandal from the playground, to discover which friends and teachers were the flavour of the day, and who had become the scum of the earth.

An extra car was a wonderful asset too. For several months I had had to drive the family car to Base to collect my car, thus depriving wife and family of transport during the day. Suddenly there were two cars on the drive, and we were spoilt for choice and my wife no longer had to catch a bus to work. I no longer needed to travel half way across the city to begin work either, I could simply put my shoes on, sign on for work, and start and finish whenever I chose. Time, diesel and money thus all experienced entries in the credit column.

There was, of course, a down side to the arrangement; the rental cost of the car was £230 per week, a sum I had to earn, in addition to paying for fuel and other incidentals, before I could make any money for myself. I set myself a target of £500 profit per week, which meant I had to take something in excess of

£800 to cover rent and diesel; a daunting sum – I needed a game plan to work out how I would make it.

My working week always began on Friday, the day rents had to be paid, so I decided that this would be my really big day; I would begin each Friday at 5 a.m. and work through the day until mid-afternoon, when I would return home for a sleep and some food. Around 7 p.m. I would go out again, knowing that the busiest times of the week for taxi work were Friday and Saturday nights. In this way I hoped that by the time I finished in the early hours of Saturday morning the rent would be paid, leaving only fuel to be covered before I started making money for myself. After Fridays I planned to work Saturday afternoon and night, Sunday evening and then take Monday off. My week would be completed by working Tuesday and Wednesday day shifts and as much of Thursday as I needed in order to make the target figure.

The new regime was welcome for a number of reasons; for one thing it meant an extra half an hour in bed, because whilst I still began my normal day at 5 a.m. I could now enjoy the luxury of a lie-in till 4.45, before a quick shower, a large coffee and attiring myself in whatever clothes came to hand (my lack of sartorial elegance has long been legendary amongst family and friends.) Perhaps the biggest benefit was the establishment of a weekly routine with time off scheduled. For the first few months in the job I had been in the habit of working six, if not seven, days a week, and sometimes ten without a break, there being something almost addictive about the opportunity to earn money based on how hard I worked. In the more genteel milieu of my former existence I had always taken Mondays off and spent the day with my wife, usually exploring the beauty of the nearby Yorkshire Dales and putting right the world, the church, and the lives of our children; the proximity of this glorious National Park was perhaps the principal compensation for the grief which came weekly by the cartload from my ecclesiastical appointment. For months these Mondays had been merely a memory of less frenetic times; now they were reinstated, and the beauty of North Yorkshire assumed even greater prominence once set in contrast to the uniformly drab urban landscape where I spent most of my working week.

It had been depressing previously to begin each shift with a net deficit of about £50, the combined cost of rent and diesel for the day. This was a different league; each working week began with a liability of something approaching £300 by the time I had filled the fuel tank up, but I found I was able to reach my target most weeks, and sometimes even exceed it. This level of income represented something like a 50% pay rise from my previous minister's stipend, so Monday evenings were often spent at a restaurant, enjoying the luxury of eating out almost on a weekly basis, something we had never known before.

Another attraction of the new arrangement was being able to fill the fuel tank and not worry about running out of diesel. This may sound a rather strange benefit, until you understand something of how fuelling private hire vehicles used by shift drivers actually works.

Renting a car by the day almost always resulted in a game of brinksmanship with the fuel gauge and tank. It may seem a crazy system, but the way it worked was that each driver who took a car out was responsible for the diesel he used, the assumption being that he would begin his shift with an empty tank. The goal, therefore, was to bring it back with as little fuel in as possible without actually running out. Should this particular catastrophe actually occur and the driver needed to call Base for help it would cost him £45 of his hard-earned cash, which prompted some drivers to take a can of diesel with them whenever they drove. This was problematic in terms of being frowned on by management, not that management ever frowned in a literal sense, they generally bellowed and hectored; if there was an issue with a driver standard protocol was simply to blow a fuse.

It also meant having to transport the fuel to and from Base, not to mention having grubby, smelly containers in the boot of a car into which customers might want to place luggage, food or other merchandise. So most of us trusted in our ability to read even the tiniest twitch of the fuel gauge on the fleet cars, which were fortunately all of the same make and model, offering at least some level of consistency.

Of course the sin that was only one level up from running out of fuel was to bring the vehicle back with a few pounds' worth of diesel unused in the tank, representing a loss of available profit from the shift, so the work of nursing a car back to Base at the end of one's shift became something of an art form. When at the age of 21 I had passed my driving test the one fault I was advised to correct was a tendency to "coast" – allowing the car to roll along either in neutral or with the clutch disengaged. Far from being a fault in my new world, this became a cardinal virtue, and over time almost second nature, even in the early part of the shift; as the day drew to a close it became almost an obsession. Some drivers with several years' experience of driving company vehicles had seemingly so perfected the art of interpreting the tiniest movements of the fuel indicator that the person using the car next frequently ran out of fuel en route to the nearest petrol station after picking it up.

It wasn't so bad if the fuel ran really low a few hours before the end of the shift, since consumption of fuel and level of takings tracked each other more or less exactly, so having to add more fuel was a sign of a profitable shift. But deciding just how much extra diesel to top up with was so agonising. It seems ludicrous now but I recollect with some clarity standing with the nozzle of the pump in my hand fretting over the question as to whether I could manage with an extra £3 worth, or whether I should play safe and entertain the profligacy of adding an extra pound's worth just in case. What sometimes helped was to get a job through the datahead just as I entered the petrol station and then offset the cost of the additional fuel against the anticipated fare, relishing the pure, unadulterated profit that would be all mine once the job was complete. Maybe I would even have enough diesel left to complete one more job afterwards.

Fuel anxiety was one of the stresses I now enjoyed living without; since I was the only person using the car I could fill the tank in the blissful knowledge that whatever was put in would never serve to line the pockets of another driver.

# 12

## Hyde Park – The Drugs Trade

My new work pattern would involve my first experience of night-time work, and I confess to a fair degree of apprehension at the prospect, largely fuelled by stories I had heard from various night-shift drivers about just how dangerous the city was during the wee small hours. I was accustomed to horror stories by now – barely a week went by without hearing of one of the night-time drivers being attacked, abused, robbed or threatened. After a while I had come to see these tales from the dark side for what they usually were – inventions or just possibly gross embellishments. They were scattered like so much confetti by drivers who preferred working at night and who wanted to deter anyone who might think of following suit, and who consequently would be competing for the available work. But there was sufficient truth in enough of the graphic accounts to which I was treated to convince me that complacency was a luxury that I could ill-afford in driving complete strangers around after dark. During my time in the business a local taxi driver was abducted, robbed and murdered, and there were more-or-less weekly accounts in the local press of assault and robbery of cabbies.

In some respects there was little that could prevent such things happening, and the odds are stacked against the safety of the driver. No one in their right mind would drive their private car around at night picking up a string of complete strangers and taking them wherever requested, and essentially private hire drivers are doing exactly that. Black cab drivers generally have the security of a screen between driver and passengers, and doors that can be safely locked from within the cab, though even these features don't provide complete safety. Private hire drivers have no such protection, since by definition their vehicles must be ordinary models with no significant modification. The only concession offered was the dubious privilege of an exemption from needing to wear a seat belt; I discovered that the main reason for this was that a number of drivers had been mugged by means of someone holding a seat belt tight against their throats while an accomplice located and purloined their takings. So the driver is faced with the absurdity of risking serious injury through assault and robbery or putting himself at the mercy of road users at precisely the time of day when inebriated revellers are taking to their vehicles convinced they are perfectly fit to drive.

Many drivers took the law into their own hands and provided themselves with some more tangible protection in terms of weaponry. Whilst it was illegal for drivers to keep offensive articles of any kind in their vehicles a great deal of imagination was expended on the acquisition of devices that would be unlikely to attract attention. I was once in a three-way discussion with a couple of drivers who always worked Friday and Saturday nights about how they organised personal security; this resulted in a demonstration of the self-defence equipment they felt it necessary to carry. For one this was in the form of a large, and rather heavy, steel wrench ("for loosening those hard-to-budge wheel bolts officer".) The second weapon was as sinister as it was ingenious; a home-made device, on first impression it was nothing more than a five or six inch metallic tube. Its genius lay in the way it could be used, because two more tubes, the final one topped with a piece of solid lead, would emerge from the first with a flick of the wrist. From the comfort of the driver's seat, or at a safe distance outside, he could with a simple action extend the metal rod to three times its length, the solid lump of lead connected to the innermost length landing squarely on a would-be assailant's head. These devices were kept by the side of the driver's seat, within easy reach should the need arise to use them.

As a newcomer to night-time work I decided I didn't really want to be armed to that extent; I'm almost certainly too much of a coward to use any serious weaponry. But I did adopt the expedient of many cabbies by asking for a large and heavy metal-cased torch for my birthday – "just so that I can read house numbers when it's dark, officer." My eldest son dutifully bought it for me, but I'm fairly sure he had no real inkling of the secondary purpose I had in mind were the need to arise.

It was a long time before I realised through experience that night shifts posed only a slightly higher risk than their diurnal equivalents. Partly this was due to the scare stories related by night shift drivers with the gravitas of Orson Welles and the malice of a Bond villain; in addition most of us have natural instincts, sometimes whispering urgently, sometimes shouting, that darkness is the hiding place of bogey men, ghouls, witches and any number of other harbingers of death and destruction. But looking back on this time I can recall only four occasions when I felt under any kind of threat, and three of these occurred during daylight hours. Two concern encounters with drug dealers, and are worth recounting because they well illustrate the kind of world into which taxi drivers of all descriptions are thrust. Whilst the events may sound quite innocuous in themselves the sense of fear I felt was tangible, and the adrenalin that was pumping round my body at the scent of looming danger is a sensation I can recall with some vividness.

One of the more inane and random dicta that emanated from the management on those occasions when they probably felt that drivers had not been sufficiently berated that week was to the effect that we should not pick up anyone participating in the distribution of illegal substances. Unfortunately, and for reasons that evade my comprehension, the drug dealers of West Yorkshire were not obliging enough to wear shirts proclaiming "I'm a Drug Dealer; Stop Me and Buy Some." The only information we had access to was a name, a pick-up point and a vaguely-defined destination, so how were we to know what the customer was up to? In a wonderful and not untypical example of Doublethink there was one occasion during my time in the trade when we received third hand a word of thanks from the police force for our help in supplying information about a drugs gang who had been using our services. The official disapprobation of the sullying of our hands with contact with this particular underclass was by no means unwelcome; I must have encountered a dozen or more during my time in the business, and not a single one of them was the sort of character I would choose to have a drink with, and certainly not have as a passenger in my cab.

After a year or so in the business I learned how to avoid these jobs, though even then occasionally came unstuck. Any one of a score of streets for a pick-up or drop off began ringing alarm bells, and there was a fairly common type of body language of the customers, who obligingly were usually out on the street waiting, that really gave the game away. Some of the cul-de-sacs in the seedier parts of the city appeared to house only drug dealers, and any job to or from them could only ever mean one thing, though the telephone operators as far as I know never sifted these calls. There were other locations that seemed full of the people who bought and sold stolen merchandise procured by some unfortunate miscreant desperate for another fix. Seeing a customer out on the street with a computer tower or widescreen television under his arm waiting to be taken to an address that specialised in selling this kind of stuff on was a bit of a giveaway, and thankfully most of these dealers were either not intelligent enough to realise this, credited us drivers with insufficient grey matter to see what they were up to, or in some cases were too arrogant to care.

The first episode that left me in something of a cold sweat occurred in the middle of a quiet afternoon and early on in my career. Later I would have known from the pick-up and drop-off points on the screen what I was dealing with and simply refused the job; naively I allowed four young men, the eldest of whom I estimated should still have been at school, to deposit a rather expensive looking TV screen into the boot before climbing aboard for the short journey to what I was later to recognise as one of the few streets I really didn't want to find myself in by day or night. I don't think I have ever felt so invisible as they immediately immersed themselves in animated discussion about the state of "business." It would have been impossible not to have listened as, whether out of a sense of misplaced bravado or imagined immunity to the reach of the law, they discussed what was the going price for 32-inch flat-screen televisions, the state of the person who had stolen it and exchanged it for a supply of crack cocaine, the outcome and casualties of the most recent knife fight with the neighbouring gang who were trying to move onto their turf, and current profit margins on Class A drugs in general. If it was an act it was an exceptionally well-performed one. What convinced me of its authenticity was the matter-of-fact nature of the discussion, as if they were so many respectable housewives discussing the price of gooseberries at the Women's Institute coffee morning.

There were some streets I was always cautious about driving into, and top of the list were cul-de-sacs in areas of high crime. The one I was directed to by the sordid characters whose company I was currently compelled to enjoy was one such, and later on I would recognise it as one of those small enclaves that are almost exclusively occupied by people associated with the drugs trade. Perhaps irrationally I was honestly fearful for my safety, not to mention my day's takings – people with such a total disregard for both the law enforcement agencies and their own safety, and lacking any kind of moral compass, would surely think little of pulling out a knife and taking my money and any other valuables readily available. But what alternative did I have, and for that matter what reasonable grounds for stopping the car in the middle of a busy intersection and ordering them out? With a rising sense of anxiety I eventually turned into the dead-end street to which I had been directed and came to a halt.

It seems an anti-climax to say I needn't have worried, but I was immensely relieved when they extracted the merchandise from the boot before making off, their lack of acknowledgement of my presence being interrupted only briefly by the child in charge ordering an underling to pay the fare in a voice that had not quite yet broken. The brash acne-suffering deputy gave me the exact fare – clearly this was a regular trip – and whilst there was no tip I confess to being thankful to get anything and to be able to drive away. I watched in my mirrors as the gang disappeared with the TV into one of the many places in that street that handled stolen goods.

Even with experience, though, it was not always simple to sift young men who seemed to have too much time and money on their hands into those who did and didn't deal in drugs, as I found out some while later. This second experience of drug dealers was not dissimilar to the first, except this time it was later on in my time in the business, and the pick-up and destination points were not ones that rang alarm bells. This time it was three men, and incredibly a father and two sons. They were well dressed, polite and courteous, and I had not the slightest inkling about their trade as they settled in the car and chatted happily about the kind of domestic matters normally associated with family mealtimes. It was only the odd remark dropped out here and there that gave the game away. This time I felt far more comfortable – the father figure in particular exuded a sense not only of geniality but, bizarrely, an air of paternal responsibility in spite of how they made a living. That was until we reached the block of flats where I imagine they lived and dealt. The older man had allowed one of the youngsters, a youth of no more than fifteen or sixteen, to sit in the front of the car; I had noticed how he kept playing with something in his jacket pocket, but never felt at risk, his Dad seemed far too responsible to allow him to get into trouble. When they opened the doors to get out I discovered what was in the pocket of the youth as a knife slipped out and landed in full view on the passenger seat. This may sound innocuous enough of itself; rather than a switchblade coated with congealed blood it was only the kind of three or four inch bladed all-purpose kitchen knife to be found in any home, but it soon dawned on them that there could be only one explanation for carrying something that was both illegal and large enough to be scary, and that I was probably smart enough to work it out. And I knew that they must know, and given the relative seclusion of our surroundings – the car park of a high rise block of council flats – whilst I wasn't quite in fear for my life I did wonder about quite how much danger I was in and how the scenario would play itself out.

There was a moment of silence – probably only a few seconds, but it seemed an age that we all froze as everyone contemplated how to react. Should I grab the knife? Probably the worst move – the chances were that if one of them were tooled up the others would be, and knife fighting was one of the many practical courses that were never on offer at theological college. I felt cold sweat breaking out as the youth reached for the knife, and I realised just how vulnerable I was; I remember the bizarre feeling of mild relief as I noticed that as far as I could see the blade was clean with no signs of old blood stains – or fresh ones for that matter. My inner contempt for the older man in leading youngsters astray in this manner morphed to a sense of gratitude as, fortunately for me, he took charge of the situation, told the youngster to put it away, paid the fare (very generous tip – "you've seen nothing" was understood rather than verbalised) and departed.

I sat for some little while pondering the situation I had just witnessed. Perhaps for many this would have created a sense of minor embarrassment, or even amusement. But I had come from the sort of world where the most aggressive thing knives were used for was cutting up the quiche at the church tea; to know I had been next to someone who carried one with potentially malicious intent was both an eye-opener and a cause for ongoing anxiety. How many other young men – or women for that matter – had I transported who had been concealing dangerous weapons?

Once the mild panic attack had subsided I had to address the question of what I should be doing next. Was there such a thing as client confidentiality of the sort I had practiced in my time as a minister? Was I obliged to report this to the police? Could I argue that my cab was a kind of nonconformist confessional booth? If I did report it what exactly would I say to them? What had I seen that provided any kind of evidence of illegal activity? In particular I imagined wasting a valuable hour when I could be earning money waiting in the public area of a police station before being seen by a desk sergeant who made a few odd notes, took my details, and dismissed me with some non-committal and inane platitude. Eventually I decided on a policy of doing nothing; previous experiences of the county's police force had left me with very little respect for its officers, and what exactly would I be able to contribute to their intelligence database anyhow?

The deeper thought as I gathered my frayed nerves together was how a father could ever reach a state where he would even contemplate leading his two sons into such a business. I thought of my two sons, who have both made me proud from the day they were born, and my constant and sometimes failed attempts to be a good role model for them. Was it a kind of perverted moral code that somehow talked itself into believing that this was some sort of honourable profession? Was it the estate on which they lived, some parts of which had enough drugs for a Colombian cartel seriously to contemplate taking a controlling interest? Was it that since there was so much of the stuff around if you can't beat them you might as well join them? Was my moral compass set in such a diametrically opposite direction because of the privilege of my upbringing and the leafy environment in which I lived? Were I to inhabit a small corner of this high rise block might my two sons and I be in the same business? Finally in a fit state for my next job I drove off, again with enough food for thought to stock a small convenience store, but even now I can recall the awful silence that followed the dropping of that knife and can relive in vivid detail the harrowing feeling of those few seconds as if they occurred only yesterday.

# 13

## CHAPEL ALLERTON – A LITTLE KNOWLEDGE IS A DANGEROUS THING

I have mentioned the ambivalence and mutual distrust that exists between drivers and management in the private hire business, but perhaps I should also say that I found the company I worked for to be entirely fair. To some extent the relationship varied with the seasons. In winter, when work was plentiful and money easy to make, there seemed to be a harsher edge to the management directives, whereas in summer, when fewer drivers were working and rents were consequently down, there was a markedly softer tone. Nevertheless my experience was that I was always treated with courtesy, albeit a courtesy that featured some pretty colourful language, and generally honesty too. On one or two odd occasions I inadvertently overpaid my rent, and immediately received a 'phone call telling me there was £10 waiting for me in the office. On the other side of the coin I was asked to pay for damage I had caused; this totalled £800 in my two years, £500 of which was for the accident I was involved in that was entirely my fault.

The other £300 was fair but irritating and was caused by speed bumps the size of small square mountains in one particular area of the city. Within the first few weeks of beginning this work I discovered that the only way to drive down these particular streets was not for the wheels to straddle them, but with one wheel passing over the top of the speed bump and the other on the flat part of the road, because otherwise there was a strong possibility that the sump plug would catch the top of the mountain and the result would be a cracked sump. Given a straight choice between a damaged suspension which would be paid for by the company and a cracked sump that would be my responsibility the springs and shock absorbers never really stood much of a chance.

When this happened the first time I drove the car back to Base and explained what had happened. The garage manager told me the bad news – that it was going to cost me £150 (about half the cost a normal garage would charge) – and the good news that the same thing happens all the time. He took me inside the garage and indicated a pile of metal in one corner – a stack of about 20 identical sumps awaiting the next vehicles whose drivers had made the same mistake.

Of course, having learned my lesson it was never going to happen again, I vowed. Well, not for another six months or so anyway, just enough time to have forgotten the 150 reasons to avoid the offending dormant guardians of the law. Fortunately shortly afterwards I was driving a newer model of car with a higher clearance so the problem never recurred.

But on to the adage at the head of this chapter – a little knowledge is a dangerous thing. The notion behind it, one imagines, is that whilst ignorance can be bliss, to be only partially informed runs the risk of basing important decisions on limited data, and finding to one's cost that it would have been better to know nothing.

I had spent most of my life acknowledging the truth of the saying on the one hand and blatantly defying it to do its worst on the other. Tiny snippets of professed expertise would be paraded on suitable occasions when there was an opportunity to appear cleverer than I am. On several occasions I have come unstuck, usually with consequences ranging anywhere from embarrassment to humiliation. Only once have I felt under threat out of trying to be an intellectual Walter Mitty.

Whilst most of my customers were people who spoke the same language as myself, albeit with a strange accent and an extended regional vocabulary, occasionally I would find myself driving round those of other nationalities. I'm really not very good at languages – my French is not a complete disaster as I did it at school and have been taking holidays in France ever since – but other than that I know very few words of anything else.

It was always a treat driving French-speaking people around, which happened more frequently than I would ever have thought likely. I would listen to their conversation and, if I had been able to understand any of it, break in with a comment in French and enjoy the reaction. Sometimes this wasn't till the end of the journey when I would ask for the fare in French, and one of those wonderful double-take moments would occur as only after a delay of some seconds did they realise I had spoken in their mother tongue – and then of course they wondered how much of the conversation I had understood, and how embarrassed they should be. What always followed was a cheerful, light-hearted exchange, now in pigeon English, now in pigeon French, during the course of which they discovered just how little of their conversation I had really comprehended. Although it seems at times "The French" and "The British" have a tradition of disparaging each other in public as "The Frogs" or "Les Rosbifs" I have almost always found French people a delight to spend time with.

I also know a handful of Russian words thanks to the questionable benefit of attending a grammar school where the Headmaster was a dedicated Russophile who tried to make as many children as possible take Russian as a second foreign language in addition to French or German. Always one for trying to impress authority figures I had embarked on two years' worth of learning Russian, the result some 35 years later being a familiarity with about seven or eight words. But the language group is quite distinctive, so when a couple of rather burly men climbed into the back of the minicab for a pretty decent fare and started to speak to each other in Russian or a similar tongue with some earnestness, I only listened as much as one does to the back end of a late-night chat-show, hearing words but not really taking anything in. In spite of not understanding a word, though, I realised pretty quickly that they were not the sort of people I would like to get on the wrong side of.

The conversation they were having became increasingly intense until it was abundantly clear they had become oblivious to their surroundings and to my presence, though they obviously gauged, correctly, that I couldn't understand a thing they were saying. They were still going hard at it when we pulled up at the address they had given me at the start of the journey. Having paid and stepped out of the car I then decided to be clever and called out "Dos vedanya", the Russian for "see you again", thus exhausting about 25 per cent of the Russian vocabulary stored safely in my long-term memory.

In a fraction of a second the larger – and more sinister-looking – of the two was back at my window demanding to know how much of their conversation I had understood. Before I had any kind of opportunity to reply he broke into a stream of incomprehensible language that reminded me somewhat of the Pentecostalist meetings I had once attended with the young people from my church when we required a little spiritual excitement to offset the more carnal lusts of youth. But this was hardly a case of speaking in tongues, "the language of angels"; I needed no interpreter – the devil himself would have been suitably impressed with the level of threat and malice conveyed through clenched fists, clenched teeth and wild eyes – each word delivered with enough saliva to provide several medical samples. I contemplated an admission that I had understood nothing of what had passed between the two men, or the diatribe just delivered with malice and half a litre of spittle, but decided to adopt the maxim which had served me well for many years;

nothing is often a good thing to do, and always a good thing to say. In any case the message was clear – "keep your mouth shut or we'll come looking for you."

To this day I have no idea what it was in the conversation that generated such a reaction, but these were days when many Russians and East Europeans were entering the country to set up prostitution or protection rackets with a little drug dealing and money laundering on the side. Perhaps it was just my feelings of nostalgia for the Dixon of Dock Green and Z-Cars days, but the miscreants from behind the former Iron Curtain always seemed to lack the sense of perspective and fair play of their British counterparts. They simply didn't understand the native real-life version of "Cops and Robbers" that had been an integral part of my early playground experience, and gallows humour was notably absent from their verbal repartee.

# 14

## CHAPELTOWN – SEX AND DRUG CUSTOMERS

The people who made a living out of other people's addictions by dealing in drugs were nasty, without exception in my experience. I gave them a wide berth and regarded them with a wary contempt. But their victims were a different matter altogether. These I regarded with semi-conspiratorial benevolence in the case of "softer" substances like cannabis, and heartfelt sympathies for those who had graduated to Class A drugs. There were too many "Debbies", young people driven by a desperation that drew them into prostitution of the cruellest and most dangerous kind; here I felt only pity, along with a wish that there was something I could do that would help.

Most of those I encountered though were recreational users of the less addictive types of narcotic, particularly cannabis. Marijuana joints were, in some areas, almost as common as tobacco, only the distinctive smell of the substance betraying its true nature. What I found amusing, and occasionally side-splittingly hilarious, was how oblivious the cannabis smokers were to the distinctively sweet, intoxicating odour emanating from the roll-up depending from their lower lip. These were the days before it was against the law to smoke in a taxi, and depending on the circumstances I would sometimes allow passengers to light up next to an open window – particularly if they asked nicely. It was not uncommon, having graciously granted leave to smoke, for me to say "but you can't smoke that stuff in here." Often this was followed by effusive assurances – "It's just a fag, mate", which in turn led to an exchange that varied between the good-humoured and the threatening until the offending article was extinguished. On other occasions I collected customers who were almost completely wreathed in clouds of brownish, sweet and pungent smoke. The offending joints would be extinguished before they climbed aboard – usually with all the grace of a rhino getting into a rubber dinghy on a heavy sea – but if I was to avoid a potential charge of driving whilst under the influence of someone else's drugs I had to open all the windows and put the blower motor on full power.

If it wasn't drugs it would be sex, and one of the commonest jobs that occupied me in the early hours of the morning was to track down the purveyors of those who could satisfy the sort of addictive cravings that seem so potent at that time of night. On one occasion three men intent on a night of debauchery to satisfy their frustrated libido asked me to drive around one of the red light areas until they found what they regarded as suitable merchandise for the event they had in mind. I confess that most of my instincts rebelled against this, and I wasn't sure whether I might be breaking the law as a kind of proxy kerb-crawler. I decided once again that I would sort out the legality at some future point (though I never did) and accommodate their wishes.

It was a bit like walking round a second-hand car forecourt choosing a suitable vehicle as they evaluated the credentials of each working girl. What sort of engine, chassis, colour, finish, gearbox, added extras could they get for what they could afford? Eventually settling on a suitable model it was time to haggle over price. "How much for all of us sweetheart? Twenty each do it?", intoned the lead negotiator. "Thirty quid each and I'll throw in a couple of extras", replied the young woman who revelled in the wonderfully appropriate name of Scarlet. In the best traditions of British fairness they split the difference and settled on twenty-five pounds a head – or I suppose a penis, then came the moment of hilarity as Scarlet asked for the sum of £100 up front. I realised a split second before the customers that she thought I was part of the deal, and for the first time in many years went bright red and dumbstruck as I returned Scarlet's sweet smile and tried to tell her that I wasn't planning on joining the party.

Whatever the theoretical morality of the job, at the end of the process both working girl and clients seemed satisfied with the deal they struck, though I confess to driving just a little quicker than normal to their destination in case a passing police car took an interest in what was going on. An interesting postscript to this job was that a week or two later I picked up one of the men again from his workplace, a respectable office block. He thanked me for my co-operation, and commented on what a good time they had all had in his flat and what excellent quality girls there were working the streets. I suppose that goes down as another satisfied customer, though I wondered for quite a while whether I had broken some law or other, and certainly my conscience left me feeling at least equivocal about the part I played.

There was a question I often wrestled with in relation to men (there may have been women but I never met one) who paid for some sort of sexual gratification. It was the same question whether it involved picking up a girl off the street and finding a quiet spot for a quickie in the back of a car or paying for a lap-dance at one of the many "Gentlemen's Clubs" (now there's an oxymoron if ever I heard one) that began to proliferate during my time in the profession. The question was who was the victim and who the perpetrator, or whether it was essentially a victimless process. Never to be much of a fence-sitter I frequently came down on either side depending on the circumstances. The "Debbie" types were, in my view, universally victims; I can imagine almost nothing more soul-destroying than selling your body for enough money to feed a heroin addiction. At the other end of the spectrum are the girls who have passed up well-paid professional careers knowing that they can make more money out of taking their clothes off for people who for some reason get their thrills in the pseudo-respectable establishments that profit from the enterprise.

I recollect a conversation with a stunningly beautiful young woman who made a living as a lap-dancer. The journey home from the "Gentlemen's Club" was quite a long one, and she appeared both educated and friendly, so I decided to risk her wrath by asking if she ever felt demeaned by working in a place where the customers were only interested in her body. Her response was one I can recall vividly and went something like this. "I left university a few years ago with thousands of pounds' worth of student debt. In two years I have paid off my student loan, put down a deposit on my own flat and almost paid for my wedding next year. When I have done so I will leave this job, go into the legal profession I trained for and settle down to married life and hopefully motherhood."

It was hard to argue with that, though I did wonder whether the transition would be as simple as she thought. But it did make me think again about who was exploiting who in the strip-club industry. I fear it is probably politically incorrect to say so, but I came to the view that if there were victims they were probably the customers. A lap dance has always seemed to me the equivalent of entering a Michelin-starred restaurant and sitting down at a table set for a sumptuous dinner; the waitress then wafts under your nose the most delicious plate of food, then just as your salivation reaches frothing point it is snatched away, leaving you to go home and satisfy yourself with a ready-meal from the fridge. Or perhaps I am missing something.

The most entertaining seekers of satisfaction of their craving or addiction though were those whose nights out were not quite complete without sharing a joint or two with some friends, awaiting the sunrise before adjourning to a fantasy-filled phalanx of dreams. Another stereotype was added to the ever-increasing scrapheap with the discovery that most users of recreational drugs are pretty ordinary people for whom cannabis or something similar is a leisure choice on much the same level as spending an evening watching professional sport, downing some beers with mates or staying in and knitting a nice cardigan whilst watching the soaps. Slightly more adventurous, illegal and destructive maybe, but nevertheless a consumer recreational choice, so I admit I never minded my cab being used to track down some of the flaky stuff, and it did make for some entertaining stories.

I confess to being a non-consumer either of sexual favours or of illegal drugs; I am not particularly Puritanical – Cromwell would probably have me thrown into the nearest damp dungeon were he still in charge – but these are not vices of choice for me. Perhaps this is just as well now I am back in the world of vicaring. So I have no real idea of what the going rate for a couple of joints is any more than I know what one pays for a quickie in the back of a car – if that is still the correct terminology, but I would have thought you would need to be pretty desperate to spend the best part of an hour racking up a bill in a taxi just to try to find your next roll-up. That's what happened in the early hours of one night in one of the most hilarious episodes I ever had in my taxi-driving career.

The pick-up was outside a city centre bar at about 1 a.m. and the customers were two attractive young females and a slightly older man of Afro-Caribbean descent (who was clearly revelling in the company and wanted the night to go on for a long time yet.) He was without doubt one of the most entertaining and interesting people I ever had in the cab, and it was pretty clear the young women were enjoying the evening and had no desire to bring it to a premature end either. The plan was to go back to his place and continue the party, but having had as much alcohol as they could cope with for now if the night was to continue to go with a swing the only recourse was to track down his favourite dealer and buy some joints.

Some parts of the city were well-known for brothels and prostitution, some for drugs, but the particular area he wanted to be taken to was a haven for both in more or less equal measure, and probably the only part of town where a significant percentage of drivers would not go after midnight because of previous robberies and assaults on cabbies. Whether through foolhardiness or misplaced bravado I didn't have no-go areas, but I was at least a little apprehensive about where we were going and usually locked the doors when entering it. On this occasion I felt no need – I had no doubt that my customers were exactly what they appeared to be, and he certainly knew his way around. Settling comfortably in the back seat between his two lady friends he began to give directions.

The problem came when his dealer wasn't at any of the three addresses he apparently normally inhabited, and being unwilling to take a chance on being sold inferior merchandise my newfound friend insisted that we tried to track him down – he would be working one of the streets or alleyways in one of the darker corners of the area. What did I care – I had entertaining company, work had been a bit hard to come by, and judging from the look of him he would have no problem paying the bill at the end of the journey.

Somewhere between the second and third address we tried it became even more entertaining. He had spent most of the time when we were off the main roads scrutinising each one of the relatively few cars to be seen cruising the vicinity, and I understood why when he pointed to one and said "that's police." The unmarked car, which he identified as one of several used by the local constabulary, was just passing through an intersection in front of us and disappeared into the night. But I was curious – how did he know? Apparently you can just tell from the type of car in use and the way it is being driven. In any case he was familiar with all of them, and having explained how he came to be a connoisseur of unmarked police vehicles he spent the

THE COLLAR AND THE CAB

rest of the journey offering a running commentary on every car (other than taxis) that we encountered. The expedition in search of the means of cultural enrichment then descended into something approaching a motorised bedroom farce as we searched various residences, back-streets and ginnels (what people in West Yorkshire call alleyways) for the elusive purveyor of choice whilst avoiding the members of the law enforcement agency. The girls were clearly getting tired, and understood just as little as I did why he didn't just patronise one of the many dealers who were on various street corners and featuring as bit-part players in the said farce. It seemed that he was rather particular about the quality of the merchandise he bought, and to ask him to buy from any Tom, Dick or Harry hawking goods on the street corner would be the equivalent of a connoisseur of gourmet food dining in the local chippie. So the complaints from the female company in the back seat were more than mitigated by the thoroughly entertaining commentary being offered by this aficionado of recreational drugs, who also happened to be an expert on the machinations of those who were trying to keep a lid on the trade.

All good things come to an end, and sure enough in the depths of one of the darkest of the ginnels the dealer in question was tracked down, and whatever the cost of the merchandise another £25 was added to the bill for my time and effort. It should have been nearer £30 but I decided that the sheer entertainment value of the experience had been worthy of a healthy discount. The threesome disappeared into one of the thousands of identical maisonettes in one of the less fashionable parts of the city to enjoy the rest of the night's entertainment – whatever precisely that might entail. I felt almost bereft – it was as if I had made a new friend who had promptly emigrated to a distant land never to be seen again. But I had had a very entertaining interlude in an otherwise unremarkable shift and more than sufficient funds for it to have been worth my while.

# 15

## SHEEPSCAR – CRASHING OUT.
## ACCIDENTS, COLLISIONS AND SCAMS

*'Pride goes before destruction, and a haughty spirit before a fall.'*
(The Bible)

There are two things a cab driver of any description should never do; firstly be involved in a collision – and secondly be involved in a collision. This is true irrespective of where blame lies, if for no other reason than it makes the few insurance companies still willing to underwrite the risk of covering taxi drivers rather nervous. The average insurance bill for drivers who run their own vehicles is up to ten times what it would be for private motoring, and the cost for covering the fleet of cars owned by my company was reportedly not far short of an eye-watering £200,000 per annum; what was more, each claim made under the policy was subject to a hefty excess, meaning the company had to pay the first £500 of any repair bill where their own driver was at fault, or for whatever reason it was not possible to claim from a third party. This was the case all too often because in many of the areas in which we operated a valid certificate of motor insurance was as common as a winning lottery ticket. Not unreasonably the management felt that this cost should be borne by the driver concerned, and would not allow their cars to be used until a piece of paper accepting this arrangement was signed.

Finding affordable insurance is one of the main problems that result in many drivers failing to make it in the taxi driving business; it only takes a couple of own-fault collisions and many insurance companies will simply refuse to continue underwriting the risk, or will impose the sort of premium that makes it virtually impossible to earn a decent living.

Taxi and private hire drivers have a reputation for driving too fast and too aggressively, but in my experience this was only true of a small minority, mainly because the greater the speed the greater the risk of collisions, and the greater the risk of a hefty financial hit. Those who had learned the trade well had long since discovered that avoidance of accidents was one of the main keys to survival, and the small number who refused to learn this lesson were almost universally among those who did not last long in the business. As with almost any profession it is principally the miscreants who are noticed by the general public. It was much the same in the world of vicaring. Newspapers were only interested in women and men of the cloth when their greed or their lust had cast a shadow over a promising career. Even the local rag pushed through the letterbox with such clumsiness as to reduce it to almost illegible shreds by some spotty youth was likely to dedicate a paragraph or two to a scandal involving the clergy. An account of some amazing act of selfless philanthropy would be deemed unworthy of any column inches, even on the page facing the advert for the latest amazing 50% off sale at the local furniture supermarket. But if the local vicar "came out", eloped with the organist, was caught alone with a choirboy in questionable circumstances or ran off with the contents of the roof restoration fund the press would happily serve the story up as a main course for the anti-ecclesiastical brigade.

There is something about a vehicle sporting a private hire licence being driven aggressively that seems to excite anger more readily than would be the case were the offending piece of plastic bearing the legend "private hire" not present, and a significant quantity of the public appear ready to smear, with the broadest possible tar brush, the reputation of all who drive for hire or reward. In the "perception of who are bad drivers" stakes, White Van Man and private hire drivers usually run neck and neck at the head of the field, closely followed by motorcycle couriers and young men in cheap sports cars. I learned very early on that the drivers who fancied themselves as the taxi world's James Bond behind the wheel of a car usually had insurance premiums to make the jaw drop and enough convictions for speeding to make their continued existence in the business precarious to say the least. A driver once showed me three speeding tickets resulting from his ignorance of the placement of a new speed camera, all issued in the space of 24 hours. A further ticket – which was probably in the post even as we spoke – would result in potential disqualification.

Of course it would be facile to pretend that all taxi and private hire drivers are model citizens when it comes to observing speed limits; the quantity of hours they work and the distance they cover in congested areas will inevitably result in being better equipped to know how and where judiciously to expect the law to offer some breathing space. When there are jobs waiting and money to be made during busy periods the temptation to nudge the speedometer needle a little further round the dial is almost irresistible. But to drive excessively fast and in an overtly aggressive manner as a normal modus operandum merely invites the kind of survival prospects of a lemming approaching Beachy Head. There are simply too many hazards and too much time spent behind the wheel for it to be a viable approach to the job.

Whilst I was now earning a good living the thought of having to work a full week just to cover the cost of a moment's negligence was daunting to say the least. Many prospective drivers, confronted with a piece of paper they were compelled to sign agreeing to pay the first £500 of any claim, simply could not bring themselves to append an autograph and walked away.

Those that chose to comply with the company's terms lived in almost perpetual dread of a second's lapse of concentration in a vulnerable moment. Some drivers refused to learn their lesson even after a couple of collisions where they were at fault, or after collecting several points on their licence, and were still determined to carry on driving like Dick Dastardly in hot pursuit of Penelope Pitstop. Dark tales were whispered in the yard where the cars were kept about drivers who had perished from the profession because they had considered themselves immune from such dangers and had nevertheless succumbed. Some I heard of regarded the regular payment of large wads of cash as part of the rough and tumble of private hire driving. The company I worked for, always reluctant to lose any source of rental income, would allow those who had incurred a £500 excess to pay it back over time, usually at a rate of £10 per shift, or £50 per week. There were a few drivers who, having declined to amend their ways, were simultaneously paying off three or even four of these sums. In one particular driver's case the company's insurer had declined to include him in the company policy, and instead offered a separate arrangement at an astronomical rate, which had to be paid in one lump sum. The company offered to foot the bill and allow him to pay it off weekly. When I met him, about a month into this arrangement, he complained that he was now working a 75-hour week simply to pay his insurance premium, rent, fuel and excesses on three previous collisions. I don't know what happened to him, but I don't recall ever seeing him again.

I considered that I had little to worry about; I had not experienced a collision where the fault was mine for some twenty years, and my two months of professional driving had witnessed no near misses. What was more I now had a piece of paper confirming my expertise and more than ample competence to drive a private hire car, and my status in the elevated stratosphere of expert drivers was confirmed.

I could not have been more mistaken. Poignantly it was in the same week that I passed my taxi drivers' test that through a sheer lack of concentration I drove smack into the rear end of a poor female driver who wondered (literally) what had hit her. This was no minor shunt; the victim's vehicle looked a complete wreck, and my front end was like something that had competed in one destruction derby too many. There was nothing to do but have the car recovered back to Base and await my fate, which I feared could signal the end of the line. Shame-faced I arrived back to be met by one of the directors of the company who asked for an explanation for the pitiful spectacle now skulking in the shadows that had so recently been a bright shiny company vehicle. There was nothing to do other than to admit that it was completely my fault and offer to cough up the requisite £500. I then braced myself for the verbal onslaught and apocalyptic sermon on the peril in which my new career now stood. Instead I was greeted with the almost comforting "You're not the first and you won't be the last", following which he disappeared back into his office and I was given another vehicle and life continued much as before.

What was perhaps most remarkable was the speed with which the company's mechanics worked on the wreck. It was back on the road in about three days, and you really wouldn't have known it had even been slightly pranged. The lesson I learned from this – apart from the obvious one about paying attention to the traffic in front – was that this business was driven by only one concern – to make as much money as possible. Both driver and car were means to that end, and so long as the end was served collateral damage was little other than an inconvenience.

Some months later, when attrition rates in the minicab world meant that I was considered a veteran driver by the newcomers one of the pieces of advice I always proffered was to put some money aside each week to pay the excess on their accident. 'What accident?' they would ask accusingly. 'The one you are almost bound to have in your first six months in the job', I would reply. The simple truth is that crude statistics make it almost inevitable that such an event will occur. My twenty years of claim-free driving was at the rate of a few hours behind the wheel a week, and much of that in light traffic. Now I was driving 70-80 hours a week, and often tired to the point of falling asleep; this was effectively as many hours motoring as I had done in a month previously, and most of it was in medium to heavy traffic.

What makes a collision even more likely are other factors that load the odds against taxi and private hire drivers. Firstly there are a not insignificant number of drivers – particularly though not exclusively young males for whom a vehicle functions as a penis extension – who appear to collect occasions on which they have beaten a taxi away from the lights, or succeeded in cutting in front of one, as so many notches on the belts of their machismo. An inability – or an unwillingness – to exercise self-restraint can very easily lead to disaster. The second factor is more sinister, and this involves the scam artists who set out quite deliberately to cause minor accidents in which they can lay blame at the door of the third party. As I write now the "crash for cash" and "flash for cash" artists are hitting the headlines, and most drivers are aware of at least some of the methods used, but this was in the days when the crime was in its infancy, and not well known outside the fraternity. Of the three accidents I was involved in two fell into this category.

There are a number of variations on the scam, some more sinister than others, but most of them involve engineering a scenario in which the front of the victim's car meets the rear end of the vehicle driven by the perpetrator. Since collisions of this nature are almost always seen to be the fault of the victim insurance claims can be lodged worth a great deal of money, and a taxi is a safe target because it is bound to be insured.

The first collision of this nature I experienced was in the early days, ironically driving my own car, at the end of yet another long shift; at this point I still believed in the concept of people being motivated by their better nature most of the time, and that money was not the only commodity to excite the imagination. This was a pretty straightforward scam involving a private hire car from a different company, and was executed very cleverly – so much so that it wasn't until much later that I came to recognise it for what it was.

Following a line of cars through a set of lights displaying a green signal with thoughts hovering somewhere between dinner and Christmas shopping the driver in front simply executed an emergency stop in the middle of the junction. Caught unawares by this inexplicable and unexpected manoeuvre I found I was unable to stop before running into the back of his car on a road rendered greasy from recent rainfall. The record simply shows that I was following too close to the vehicle in front to stop in time, and theoretically of course that is true, but in reality the vast majority of people drive around cities on the assumption that other motorists will behave in a predictable manner.

The damage to the other vehicle was pretty superficial, just a couple of minor dents, which was exactly what was intended – I saw the car sporting the same injuries several times after this and as far as I know the dent never was repaired. Inspecting the damage I naively asked the other driver what had caused him to brake so suddenly, at which he feigned an inability to speak much English, other than such key words as "liability", "insurance claim" and "whiplash."

Of course the damage to the vehicle is incidental; the real value in causing such a collision is in the money to be gained from the insurance company of the third party for the horrific injuries caused by the collision which a friendly and compliant doctor has already been lined up to verify, and this can easily run into tens of thousands of pounds. Chatting to one of the directors of the company I worked for one day I discovered that it was not unknown for a driver to experience such an incident involving a single driver, and then to discover that the third party insurance claim was for injuries to four or five people who were supposedly in the vehicle at the time. It was for this reason that one condition of taking a company vehicle out was that the driver had a disposable camera in his or her possession and that copious quantities of pictures were taken of the cars, the road and the personnel involved. My failure to observe this rule fully was actually to work to my advantage in the next attempted scam I was involved with, which we will come to shortly, but this was really due to sheer good fortune.

In a moment of rare honest lucidity regarding my driving skills I realised I had to swallow my pride, and acknowledge that I was not nearly as good a driver as I had previously thought, and was perhaps worse than the average professional in the taxi business. The meal duly digested I began to watch other professional drivers, and particularly the drivers of black cabs, who I noticed seemed to make everything work in a far more efficient and relaxed way; professional driving for them simply didn't appear to be the frantic and stressful affair it was for me. I began, whenever I was working, to observe these kings of the road, and try to learn from how they operated their vehicles. In spite of what I had thought – and indeed the reputation most people ascribe to cab drivers of whatever description – I noticed that those who had been doing the job for a while both drove more slowly than most and, more significantly, created a much greater space in front of their vehicle by the simple expedient of falling back until there was enough space to bring the Titanic to a halt in choppy seas. This distance they would retain at all costs, making it possible to react in plenty of time to whatever behaviour the driver in front displayed. Should some moron cut in front of them, they seemed to have the ability to swallow their pride, control their anger, and simply fall back to a safe distance. It was one of those "Aha" moments as I realised that by doing this they not only prevented such scams being perpetrated on themselves, it also made the whole experience of driving more relaxing, whilst costing little if anything in lost time. All it required was the self-discipline not to play macho games with the "penis extension" driver looking to cut into the gap, and simply to back off to the required distance again.

I can't say I followed this rule without exception, but I did develop a mantra that I chanted in Hare Krishna tones every time some idiot cut me up or decided he was in the Hangar Straight at Silverstone. "It's not personal, it doesn't diminish you, he's not picking on you because he doesn't like you, he doesn't even know you, don't bring yourself down to his level." I alternated this mantra with the one that simply went "Just think about the points he probably has on his licence, and what he has to pay for insurance – if he has any."

I use male pronouns not out of any inverted sexism but because, almost without exception, the offenders were men – mostly though not exclusively under 40. Ironically when I did encounter the rare aggressive female driver they seemed to be intent on compensating for this gender inequality with the kind of reckless abandon characterising the car chase at the opening of Goldfinger.

The occasion when not using a camera to take pictures worked to my advantage took place some twelve months later, shortly after a richly deserved holiday, and was to save me £500 and the insurance company a small fortune. Having been caught by the simple version of the scam I was determined not to allow it to happen again, and it took a much more elaborate variation to catch me out. In truth there was little I could have learned that would have prevented this second attempted rip-off from taking place. Taking the inside lane to go round a traffic island with a clear road ahead, a sporty purple vehicle jumped from the outside lane just as I was arriving and then hit the brakes. I was barely able to reach the brake pedal before the impact took place, though of course I was travelling at no great speed.

My customers, models of fair play and integrity, sensed an opportunity to avoid paying their fare, decamped and made off leaving me with no witnesses and another supposed victim who spoke little English. With my brain still on its way back from Florida, where the family had just enjoyed a wonderful vacation, and seeing nothing more than a dented bumper on the other car whilst mine was unscathed, I forgot the warnings of dire consequences for those who failed to take enough photographs to fill a Sunday supplement, and just swapped details with the other driver who, in spite of his limited language skills, seemed a really nice chap, apologising profusely for his lack of consideration and forethought. 'I am, after all, a good judge of character', I told myself. The warm sun of Florida had generated a reasonable stockpile of magnanimity, and perhaps more naivety than was good for me. My vehicle was undamaged, he had apologised, we had swapped addresses, let's get on with the shift. What's the point of using my disposable camera up on this, when I will only then have to go and buy another? How stupid I was.

But amazingly this oversight was actually to work in my favour. By now I was working night shifts, and as the evening wore on into night I became increasingly uncomfortable at having no photographic evidence, so took a camera to the address of my newfound friend and used up an entire roll of film taking pictures of the vehicle from every conceivable angle. Fortunately the address was at a block of high rise flats, and my David Bailey impersonation went unseen by the very reasonable person who had earlier actually apologised for causing the collision.

Reporting the incident to the management of my company I was rather surprised to find not only a sympathetic reception, but of more practical use an induction into the prevalence of contrived accidents and how clever some of them are. I was treated to a lesson on the subtle methods used by those who made a living from this kind of exploit.

One of the more sinister variations consists of a car full of people reversing at speed into the front end of the target's vehicle, after which there are not only four or five victims claiming horrific neck injuries, but the same amount of witnesses more than willing to perjure themselves in a court of law by laying the blame fairly and squarely at the feet of the cabbie who drove recklessly into the back of their car. Knowing that cabs will almost certainly carry full insurance this has been seen as a safe way of making money for some time now, though there is evidence that the insurers are becoming wise to it and are fighting back.

Some months later this lesson proved immensely valuable in saving me money and grief. Having stopped to fill in some paperwork and to wait for another job I noticed two battered vehicles behind me and about half a dozen young men about to climb aboard who looked as if they were not members of the local church choir. It was one of those times when you know that something is wrong, and adrenaline starts pumping without you really understanding why. On instinct I started the engine and put down the paperwork. Having completed their discussion four entered one car and drove off and stopped about 50 metres in front of where I was parked. Looking in my mirror I saw the other two men creeping up slowly behind me in the second car to prevent me from reversing out of trouble.

Almost too late I realised what was about to happen – the driver of the car in front had engaged reverse and was beginning to accelerate in my direction. With a split second to spare I avoided being a taxi sandwich, leaving half a dozen potential personal injury claims staring after me in frustration. Congratulating myself on having avoided disaster my self-adulation was tempered by a rising anger at the blossoming infrastructure that exists to facilitate this industry. However much they may protest innocence and claim merely to be performing their public duty, the medics and solicitors who are essential components of these scams know exactly what they are doing, and that they are effectively willing participants in an illegal industry.

The company was perhaps justified in reinforcing an instruction I had seen every day and the reason for its existence. The office that shift drivers visited in order to pick up their vehicles was adorned with notices giving instructions and bearing dire warnings to those who chose non-compliance. From exhortations not to sound horns and slam doors in the middle of the night to warnings of the displeasure of the directors and the threat of repercussive measures should rent not be paid with due punctuality, they could have been mistaken for a form of art nouveau wallpaper. Most of these notices appeared to be worded and situated partly to inform, partly to warn, but mainly to intimidate. Assuming perhaps the most dominant position was one that drivers really did ignore at their peril, was entirely justified and really did make sense.

'Every driver must carry a camera (not a phone camera) and keys will not be issued unless they are able to produce one when asked. No exceptions.'

The reason for this dictum was simple. Should a driver be involved in a collision of some sort it was essential to record every detail of the incident on camera.

To return to my story, however, at first I did little more than mention it to the drivers' supervisor, hand over the camera, and pretty much forget about the whole affair until about two days later when if not all hell certainly a decent sized chunk of Hades broke loose.

The first salvo to disturb my comfort came in the form of a 'phone call to my mobile whilst I was driving. My wife had had the good sense to invest in a phone with blue tooth capacity and an earpiece so that she could call me while I was at work;

what I heard, however, was not the sweet dulcet tones of my spouse but the harsh high-pitched whine of a junior functionary at a putative legal firm asking for my insurance details so his client could pursue a claim against my reckless driving. Within 24 hours it felt that an entire organisation had found its perfect raison d'etre in the pursuit of compensation from the very large insurance corporation that provided cover for my company.

I was summoned to Base to meet a director who, in effect, said, "told you so", and having delivered a quite reasonable dressing down in the circumstances for not chasing the customers to find their contact details, set about planning how to mitigate the damage.

Fearful of losing the other half of a thousand pounds I was relieved to have both company and insurers fighting my corner. Fortunately for me my previous oversight now worked to my advantage. An insurance inspector came to assess the damage to my car from the impact having already seen the other vehicle. He found two almost invisible stress marks caused by the collision and encouraged me to cheer up. "There's no way this car caused the damage to the other one", spoke the voice of years of experience of seeing mangled motors. He then described the damage he had previously inspected, which essentially consisted of a completely smashed rear end with damage caused as far forward as the front passenger seat.

Then, of course, we were able to produce the photographs of whose existence the third party was ignorant that I had taken that night whilst my supposed victim lay abed with such horrific injuries that all the money in the Bank of England would provide only scant compensation for the years that had been taken off his life.

An interview with one of the senior investigators from the insurance company followed; it appeared that this was the fifth or sixth such claim they had received from the small estate of high-rise blocks in which the perpetrator of this scam resided.

That was pretty well the end of the matter. I was astonished that the insurance company, rather than pursuing the offender, simply intended to allow the matter to drop; perhaps it would have cost them more to prosecute the case than they could ever have hoped to gain in return.

I had learned several valuable lessons; for one thing my ability to judge character on instinct enjoyed the level of competence demonstrated by an English tail-end batsman facing an Australian pace attack, and for another most of the rules of the game I was in, however bombastically they were expressed, were there for the benefit of everyone. Perhaps for the first time, too, I saw if not exactly a level of compassion, the more human face of the organisation I worked for, and that it was not entirely bereft of a sense of sympathy.

# 16

## Pudsey – Getting the Hang of it

I don't know quite when it happened; I can't put a date or time on it, and its passing went unmarked and unheralded much as crossing a continental border does in an aircraft, but in the middle of one shift, just before my first Christmas as a minicab driver, I knew I had arrived. I had moved well beyond "Survival Day", and was now sure that I could make a good living at the job. This was not like one of those periods most football fans experience, where a string of promising results engenders the feeling that your team is now about to explode into the big time only for hopes to be crushed by an early cup exit at the hands of Chipping Sodbury Girls High School. This was not an assessment based on a few good days' takings and a string of pleasant customers; it was a sober assessment of everything that had come my way to this point. There were good days and bad days, days when I finished early because I had taken as much money as I wished to earn, and days when I laboured for thirteen hours for the equivalent of a minimum wage, or even less. But there was also consistency. I now knew a bad day would quite probably be followed by a good one, and that so long as I simply kept at it I now had an alternative career.

The feeling was somewhere between relief and euphoria; relief that I had ended a period of five or six years where almost everything I attempted seemed to result in disappointment or failure, and euphoria because I knew that now I had an independent means of making a living, and never again would I have to allow myself to be held ransom by a gaggle of dysfunctional megalomaniacs posing as a church leadership team. My only regret was that I had not stuck two fingers up to my erstwhile employers when the first broadside struck the hull of my then resilient self-respect and walked out, rather than waiting for the edifice to resemble a Spanish Man o' War in the aftermath of Trafalgar. But most of us would be rich and famous if we had the gift of prescience.

Some of the qualities required to make a decent living in the world of cab driving are obvious. Good driving skills, the capacity to work long hours and a reasonable knowledge of the geography of the area would occur to most people. I felt fairly confident about ticking the first of these two boxes, but when I started my knowledge of the routes through the city was at about the same level as the primary school child's grasp of human anatomy. I may have known that the leg bone was connected to the hip bone and the foot bone was connected to the leg bone but that was unlikely to earn me a place at medical school. My grasp of the interconnection of routes through and around West Yorkshire was very much on the level of a parody of the prophecy of Ezekiel in the valley of dry bones. Whilst my ignorance in this regard was probably more profound than most of those who take up the job there were other factors to compensate that enabled me gradually to make a success of it.

Discovering how to make a decent living as a taxi driver of any description requires a fair amount of determination and mental toughness, and I have always been equipped with a reasonable level of these attributes. More surprisingly, a decent level of intelligence also helps. The trail Fred Housego blazed as a "bright cabbie" by winning "Mastermind" as a London black cab driver in 1980 is now pretty much overgrown, and IQ levels attributed to operators of private hire vehicles reach three figures only on rare occasions. The fact remains, however, that having well-functioning grey matter is a massive advantage in a world where being in the right place at the right time is so essential, as well as knowing how different parts of a city are connected and which routes are best to use at what times of day or night.

The world of minicab driving is highly competitive, with firms constantly trying to gain advantages over their rivals. In the area in which my company was based there were five or six competitors, some needing to be taken more seriously than others. In the space of a month each household is likely to find cards advertising the services of three or four private hire companies on their doormat, and even our most regular customers could be lured away by one bad experience or by someone offering lower fares.

Price might have been the principal concern of regular users of cabs, but following fairly close behind was punctuality. Some journeys were booked well in advance, in which case there was little margin for error – especially if there was a train or, more importantly, a holiday flight to catch; you really needed to arrive by the pick-up time on the screen. Most jobs, though, were booked over the 'phone and appeared on the datahead moments later. The driver who was next in the queue for a job in that area, on receiving the information, knew that time was very precious. I came to realise that if the car arrived at the relevant address within ten minutes of it being 'phoned through the customer would probably still be there. If the delay exceeded fifteen minutes the chances were that they would have gone – either with another company or by other means, such as bus or even on foot. So I developed a "ten-minute rule." If I really wanted this fare I needed to be there in this space of time or be prepared to lose it. Of course there were exceptions – older people particularly had a much more principled approach, and would be less likely to call a cab and then travel by other means until half an hour had passed; others called a cab, changed their minds and caught the bus but did not bother to let us know. Generally, however, the ten-minute rule served me well.

Reaching a destination within a stone's throw when you know exactly where it is inside ten minutes is, of course, quite simple. When it is two or three miles away and traffic is heavy it is another matter altogether. The principal reason for the mortality rates of my street maps in the early days was simply that two or three of these minutes were taken up finding the pick-up address and working out how to reach it. Sometimes the route would be complex enough to require an intermediate consultation with my A-Z half way there, causing anxiety levels to rise and, at times, a wave of panic to wash me overboard. Strange as it may sound, time seemed too precious to waste in returning the map neatly to the glove compartment – that could wait until the destination was reached; for now tossing it on the floor seemed a good way of saving a few seconds.

The satisfaction of knowing that I could remain in this job as long as I chose and make a decent living was comforting. The next task was working out how I could reduce my hours by making money at a faster rate. On the face of it this seemed like a lottery since there were so many factors over which I had no control; jobs appeared to be allocated at random by the computer (though of course there was a little more to it than that, see chapters on "Paranoia" and "Feeding"), traffic was difficult to predict in advance and it was hard to anticipate always when a particular region would simply "go dead" in terms of work. But there were some things that could, and did, make a real difference. I learned which areas were really not worth being anywhere near at certain times of day, which were the best spots to wait in if there was no work on the screen and which were best avoided. I was able to memorise when certain places that had a free phone to our switchboard disgorged their customers – notably places of entertainment like bingo halls.

In particular I learned where certain lucrative jobs were

to be found at certain times of day, particularly in rush hours where a particular customer wanted to travel in the opposite direction from most of the traffic. One such fare that was much sought after involved taking a woman all the way to Halifax, in the opposite direction to most of the metal boxes on wheels that were oozing through the west Leeds bottlenecks like so much constipated excrement. It was always a bit of a gamble – for one thing there would often be four or five cars in the vicinity of her house hoping to land the big fish, and for another she did not take a cab every day.

This was one of those rare fares where not only was there a sizeable sum of money to be earned but the customer was a pleasure to share a car with. I was fortunate to be her driver on a few occasions, and was unable to resist asking her one day why she booked a cab when there was a perfectly adequate train service and, on a good day, even an acceptable bus service that would cost her something like 10% of the return fare she was prepared to shell out on a cab – and trying hard not to make the alternative sound too appealing, of course.

Her reply was illuminating and offered me an insight into a very different lifestyle. 'Well, I have a good job', she began. 'I am a senior manager at a major financial institution and I earn more money than I quite know what to do with. I am unmarried, and plan to stay that way. I have paid off my mortgage and have no dependents; I do not drive – and have no intention of learning. Some people choose to spend their money on their family, on going out every night, on home improvements, on nice cars or improving their minds. I choose to spend a fair chunk of my spare cash on being driven to and from work in comfort whenever I choose.'

It was hard to argue with that. For twenty years or more I had struggled to have enough cash to bring up a family, run a car, feed and clothe my children, take them on holiday and buy them something nice for Christmas – an occasion when even as a clergyman I struggled to make them believe that it was the arrival of Jesus that really made the occasion special. I acknowledged her right to spend her considerable earnings as she wished, whilst also thinking how nice it would be if Mr Right came along and swept her off her feet and gave her another perspective. For the millionth time in my life I silently gave thanks for the family that would be waiting for me when I walked through the door and realised that, whatever I was able to earn, that treasure alone made me obscenely wealthy.

Whilst a run to Halifax is hardly a romantic trip to an exotic location, work like this always provided welcome relief from the staple diet of cab driving; journeys of this length were as numerous as truthful estate agents or politicians of integrity. Whilst some drivers were convinced they were more widespread, and the dearth of their own allocation of good fares was further proof of their lack of favour with the company, the reality was that most trips were of less than three miles. Given that the average fare over the course of a day was somewhere between £4 and £4.50, the key to making money was not so much to find the odd lucrative job but to complete a large volume of work. My up-front costs were about £50 for the day, so twelve trips would see me break even, 24 would bring in £50 and 36 would net a very satisfying £100. The maths was quite simple; if I worked a twelve-hour shift and averaged three jobs an hour I would make a good living. The factors that worked against achieving this rate were traffic, time without work, and too much time taken to reach either pick-up points or destinations. The ultimate disaster was waiting for work, taking too long to reach an address and then finding the customer absent, a "no fare". In the early days, heavily dependent on street maps and ignorant of the best routes to take, no fares were all too common. As I learned to dispense with the former and absorbed the latter these became less frequent and money became easier to earn. I reached a point where I knew that so long as I put the hours in I would make a good living.

# 17

## SEACROFT – CHRISTMAS – THE SEASON OF PEACE AND GOOD WILL

The world of clerical ministry is hardly replete with incentives, bonuses and perks in the material sense, and no one in their right mind would seek admission to its hallowed ranks for the pay. The televangelists from the American Bible belt dripping in bling and oozing confident predictions of untold wealth should you subscribe to their anointed ministry are a world removed (thankfully) from the comparatively uninspiring English vicar's existence. "Stipends", which clergy are generally paid, are thus named in order to distinguish them from salaries in much the same way that a civic banquet is different from a bowl of stale vegetables. Many churches struggle to pay their clergy a living wage, and most incumbents accept this as part of the package, as well as an almost complete absence of tangible fringe benefits. The promise of the Bible that the reward for such selfless commitment is great – especially in heaven – and the satisfaction that comes from making a positive difference to the lives of individuals, usually suffice to keep the ordained nose to the ecclesiastical grindstone. I had entered Christian ministry well aware of this, had rarely complained, and really had found until recent years that the non-fiscal compensations more than outweighed the paucity of earnings. Likewise I had accepted quite cheerfully that I would not be the happy beneficiary of large bonus payments and inducements carefully packaged to avoid the attention of the Exchequer. I was comfortable sharing a similar standard of living to those at the more meagre end of my church's wealth range, knowing that in global terms even this relative frugality classified me among the filthy rich.

Christmas was always the one notable exception, when the promise of other-worldly rewards was supplemented by ad-hoc gifts of biscuits, chocolate, sweets, goodies for the children and even sometimes small wads of cash dropped anonymously through the letterbox. It was almost always the best time of year in the church calendar – the chapel was at its fullest, there were more mince pies and chocolates to eat than you could shake a big stick at, and even the most obnoxious and awkward members of the corpus were in a good humour. This had even been true in my most recent appointment. Hostilities between minister and those who had tried to recreate the verbal equivalent of a World War One bombardment with ceaseless salvos of criticism and the mustard gas of disinformation emerged from their trenches to pull a cracker with the minister and his family and even kick a ball around before regaining their trenches and resuming the barrage.

I was certainly going to miss Christmas as a minister; I had always loved planning the candlelight carol service, and leading the service on Christmas Day, seeing members of extended families in church, including those who came once a year just to keep Mom happy. The Christmas Day "service" had little to do with God, but I never thought he really minded. It was simply an opportunity for the children – and some of the less self-conscious adults – to show off their presents, and there was always someone with an underdeveloped fashion sense who really believed that the cardigan from Aunt Betty they were sporting wouldn't look out of place at a Paris fashion show.

This year the disappointment at not having a church of my own for the season was offset by the absence of the stress always created by having to demonstrate an apparent gift of ubiquity;

the divine capacity to be everywhere at once was required in order not to let down any individual or group who considered my presence at their Yuletide activity an indispensable act of ministerial duty. I also found compensation in the satisfying deposits I was making into my bank account, which had never been so well fed and even began to show signs of flabbiness. The arrival of bank statements without the epithet "O/D" appended to ever increasing figures in the "balance" column was both novel and affirming. My wife and I sat down to plan what we were intending to spend on the children and were able to draw up lists of presents previously undreamt of. In the private hire world the weeks immediately before Christmas were universally busy and lucrative, and with my growing understanding of how to make a good living in the trade I was set to have more to spend on the family than I had ever previously hoped for.

Busyness, however, does not necessarily equate to opportunity. One of the important lessons I learned early on was that a "plot" (the term used for an area marked out by the GPS used by the company) with a mountain of work in it does not necessarily mean that there is a lot of money to be made there; the datahead may be yelling at, or pleading with, drivers to head for a particular area via its digital readout, but the fact that there were ten or more jobs to be done from a particular location was often because drivers who knew their stuff were avoiding it.

Nowhere was this more true than the Owlcotes shopping centre on the border between Leeds and Bradford, containing a hypermarket with a free phone line to our switchboard. The shopping complex boasts a car park which, at a conservative estimate, can accommodate more than 1,000 vehicles, and normally making a trip to the pick-up point and out again was a simple job. But not at Christmas, when the entire road system within half a mile of the place suffered from vehicular constipation as tight-lipped motorists suspended their subscription to the Season of Good Will Association. A priceless parking bay could be secured only by means of cunning, aggression and all the other dubious qualities Santa would have taken into consideration when deciding what size sack to deposit by the fireplace; peace and goodwill to all men could take a back seat until the shopping was done.

Most of the work from the centre was local, to destinations certainly less than three miles distant, worth at most £5, but in the days immediately before Christmas it could take up to 45 minutes to complete a job. When there was plenty of work elsewhere drivers considered, not unreasonably, that it was hardly worthwhile hacking a path through the forest of frustrated motorists, however much they were cajoled by the datahead. This kind of "local knowledge" took a while to learn, usually the hard way at the cost of an hour or two of poor earnings, but once acquired was a permanent and almost instinctive fixture. On the rare occasions when the screen was replete with jobs which were there for the asking, experienced drivers have a kind of sixth sense which prevents their fingers from pressing the buttons that will send certain work their way.

Being used to having a few perks around the festive season I started to wonder, as December wore on, what kind of bonuses and displays of gratitude were offered by the company whose own coffers were being inflated by my dedication to duty. Would it be fiscal, edible or practical, something to eat, wear, use or spend?

Messages of a general nature were displayed at regular intervals on the datahead. This suited both those working in the office and the drivers; both groups tended to have something of a superiority complex in relation to the other and remote communication facilitated the perpetuation of this rather puerile outlook. By the third week in December I began to anticipate the announcement that would encourage me to call in to Base to receive my Christmas bonus; perhaps this would even include two or three days free of rent so I could earn a little extra for the season.

Sure enough the messages for Christmas week appeared on cue, though not with the content I had anticipated. The free handouts, bonuses and goodies failed to achieve a mention. There was, however, something about rents for the Christmas period; we were encouraged to call into the office to receive the latest missive from the directors, and I eagerly anticipated a demonstration of largesse by those whose pockets I had been so diligently lining. Perhaps on arrival I would be regaled with a range of other goodies along with news of a reduction in rents for the festive season.

The office was not decked out with boughs of holly; the mistletoe was conspicuous by its absence and the Christmas tree had either not been ordered or had not been delivered. Tinsel did not adorn the staircase nor was there any of that nice candyfloss type material that makes Christmas trees look as if they are inhabited by angelic spiders. The only thing waiting for us on arrival at the office was a sheet of paper telling us how much additional rent we had to pay for our cars over the Christmas and New Year period – and for owner-drivers how much per week extra would be levied. No word of appreciation for those who worked up to 80 hours a week to make a living, and in the process enabled the directors, had they so chosen, to change their name by deed-poll to Rothschild, and not even a few choccies to sweeten the taste of the extra cost.

In fairness, drivers were entitled to charge an extra 50% once the buses went to bed to await Santa's arrival and then over the New Year, and always made excellent money, but the complete absence of Christmas cheer still took me by surprise. Santa seemed to have decided to by-pass the private hire industry this year, and every other year for that matter, though given the avaricious moral code most of those running it seemed to live by this was perhaps hardly surprising.

This time round I decided against paying the additional rent and celebrated Christmas and New Year's Day at home. One year later, when I was working night shifts, I laboured through both Christmas Eve and New Year's Eve, and discovered that in actual fact the few pounds extra that were paid in rent – largely to recompense the telephone operators for taking those shifts – were compensated for several times over. It was not just the increased fares that generated the income but also the tips that were liberal sometimes to the point of munificence. These were, I suspect, largely the subconscious by-product of feelings of good will fuelled by gastronomic excesses and artificial feelings of wealth, the by-products of even the most unsubstantial Christmas bonus. I had long since accepted that the world of private hire driving was one of the most feral to be found on the planet, but still the completely barren and spartan appearance of the premises, as well as the conspicuous absence of Christmas cheer even of the most basic kind, was rather depressing.

Perhaps, however, this approach was simply a more honest one. The date arbitrarily set by spiritually-minded medieval oligarchs which has defined Jesus Christ as a Capricorn has increasingly become an opportunity for businesses to make some extra cash on the back of the sentimental sanctity of the message of the angels. "Peace on earth, good will to all men and a healthy bulge in the profit margin"; the wolf of avarice is deceptively dressed in a sheepskin that tips a hat to the perceived, and usually misunderstood, message and mission of the Messiah. With an outlook that was as blunt as it was in some bizarre way refreshing no such pretence was adopted here. Drivers were likely to enjoy higher takings as a result of increased fares, benefitting from the influence of alcohol and a generally misplaced sense of bonhomie among the general public; it was only reasonable for the company to take a slice of this cake with an accompanying cherry.

Santa visited our house that Christmas in spades, and appeared to have additional capacity in his well-appointed sack for all the family. My treat, though, came in an unpretentious package dwarfed by the boxes denuded of wrapping paper and containing CD players, DVD players, televisions and games consoles. It was almost too small to house a chocolate orange, but knowing my wife always saves the best till last I had cause to hope for something more practical and less unhealthy.

Opening the final present under the tree is always a nerve-wracking affair; knowing it is likely to be the thing you really hope for and fearing it may not be. Balancing hope and anticipation against the need to put on a grateful expression if it turns out to be something that has cost a lot and filled the giver with anticipation of your face lighting up but was not actually what you most wanted. Thankful grin resolutely secured in place gingerly I undressed the parcel to reveal the thing I had dreamed of – a brand new, pristine sat-nav. Now, as the cliché goes, I was motoring.

# 18

## WEETWOOD – GETTING MAUREEN TO DO THE WORK

There are ways to use a satellite navigation unit – and ways not to use one.

This was the era in which they were still something of a novelty, and of course Santa, in my view somewhat irresponsibly, had stuffed them into tens of thousands of decorative stockings across the country on Christmas Eve. By Christmas Day the roads were replete with motorists who knew the route to their destination as well as they knew the proverbial backs of their hands, but insisted on programming it into their new Tom-Tom, Garmin or Navman, and then driving with one eye on the traffic and one on the screen. The consequences were predictable; insurance companies were rushed off their feet keeping track of the claims for minor collisions, and the recipients of the new toys discovered that the voice database of their unit did not feature one that announced "You have just had a crash."

For many it took barely two or three days to realise that whilst it was a wonderful toy to own that was about all it was – yet another car accessory with about as much practical day to day value as a pair of fluffy dice, though far more expensive and certainly less embarrassing. Any practical worth would have to wait until an excuse could be engineered for a journey to unknown parts. In all probability there were thousands of neglected great aunts and uncles living in obscure parts of the country with exotic post codes who received a surprise visit from a vaguely remembered great nephew that Christmas, as well as a distinct drop in the revenue gained from speed cameras.

Nevertheless they remain one of the "must have" adjuncts to vehicle ownership, and not only "must have" but also "must have on all the time." I still see people commuting to work some three or four miles away along a route they have used for years and of which they know every pothole and traffic light sequence consulting their Tom-Tom like a ten-year-old boy with an electric shaver. Their electronic companion faithfully displays the road layout, their speed and direction, and emits friendly bleeps each time a speed camera comes within range. Like Terry Wogan and the old nodding dogs on the rear parcel shelf the toy has become part of the furniture of familiarity and whilst little practical attention is paid to it they would miss it if it were absent. The more recent advent of inbuilt navigation and Bluetooth systems makes this obsession marginally more justifiable. Of course I joined the ranks of those driving with only half my attention on the road on Christmas Day; I was particularly impressed with the soft, gentle but quite insistent feminine voice emitted from the unit – seductive without being erotic and directive without being bossy. I called my sat-nav "Maureen", simply because it sounded like someone I once knew. When some time later I took it to France and decided to use the French voice commands I decided she was more of a Michelle, and definitely more sultry.

Drivers of taxis and private hire cars are, along with furniture removal and multi-drop delivery companies, very definite beneficiaries of the new technology, so long as it is used properly. My first shift after Christmas saw the cab sporting my brand new Garmin Street Pilot i3 in the corner of the windscreen. It was probably the smallest, and certainly one of the cheapest units available, a testimony to the inbuilt proclivity to maintain frugality that was a somewhat unnecessary legacy of the non-conformist clerical outlook on life. The screen was so small customers frequently commented on its diminutive stature. My second customer of the day was the first of hundreds who would comment 'That's the smallest Tom-Tom I've ever seen.' Having tried a variety of ripostes the reply I eventually settled for was 'Are you making fun of the size of my equipment?' This sort of banter went down well in the real world but would have caused tuts of hypocritical disapproval from many of my pious former flock who would think nothing of watching TV programmes with endless sexual innuendo.

I never had any real doubt about the value of my new acquisition, but if there were any lingering reservations they were dispelled one dark and wet evening rush hour. The fare was a well-dressed young gent who had travelled from London by train, arriving just as the traffic was hitting its peak and, as always when it is raining, creating havoc on the roads with drivers who believed that a spot or two of precipitation required them to travel at half their normal rate and check their brakes were working several times a minute. My customer gave off an air of ineffable superiority, clearly regarding me as occupying the rank of something like an assistant footman, and calmly announced his hotel destination with the tone of one who assumes that since he is travelling there it must be well known to anyone who lives within a hundred miles of it.

By this time I knew almost all the hotels within five miles of the principal railway station, but this one I had never heard of, and neither had the operator who I radioed for assistance in the office. The customer had never been to Yorkshire before, and gave the impression that coming back would be the equivalent of dining out on dead dog with a side dish of fried sawdust, which from his superior demeanour he probably thought was a Yorkshire delicacy anyway. 'Do you have any idea which area this is in?' I asked 'None at all', he replied, and then fell silent as one who has passed the baton of intractability to someone else and now expects to see them run off into the distance with it. 'Do you have a street name for it?' I ventured 'No, but it's in Yorkshire somewhere' he helpfully offered. He might just as well have told me that there is a needle in his haystack, but then I remembered that he was a Londoner and may well have considered that Yorkshire was a small blob on a map roughly the size of Kensington. 'What about a 'phone number, could you ring them?' 'Afraid not', he responded with the air of one who has made a final contribution to a conversation with someone both culturally and intellectually on the level of primitive protozoa.

At this point I remembered that Maureen had a database of things like hotels in her memory; I had no idea how complete it was, but it seemed about the only hope I had short of throwing him out, which at that point was admittedly quite an attractive alternative. This was where I would find out if the sat-nav was really as good as I had hoped.

I entered the name of the hotel more in hope than expectation, and awaited the results. To my amazement there it was, the very place. Yes, I know that this is what satellite navigation systems are designed to do, and nowadays if the sat-nav couldn't handle it a smartphone would. But these were the medieval days of electronic navigation, and I was still lost in wonder that something barely the size of a tennis ball could not only know where such a place was, but even have a decent stab at directing me there. The screen displayed the location – somewhere the other side of Halifax – no wonder I had never heard of it. But for me it was a lucrative fare with which to end my shift, even if the company was to be of questionable pedigree and the conversation facile.

I instructed Maureen to navigate the way there and then just followed her instructions, leaving the city and hitting the motorway network. Twenty minutes later Maureen directed me to leave the M62 and take a road I had never used before. From that day to this I really have no idea where I went. Another twenty minutes obeying directions ensued, taking turn after turn, passing through villages and even glimpsing the distant lights of Halifax as we skirted it, ploughing on through the rainy night. I found myself fighting a rising anxiety as the arrival time on the screen drew ever nearer and all we had seen for the previous twenty minutes was inky darkness punctured by the occasional light from a remote cottage. We were somewhere high up in the Pennines, but exactly where I had no idea. Could it be that Maureen was to prove a capricious lover and dump me naked on a minor road outside an obscure village with a sinister laugh of derision? At least this would have generated conversation of a sort; the sullen silence from the back seat and a monosyllabic discouragement of all attempts to engage him in conversation only added to my anxiety.

The screen showed one minute to arrival; still no sign of civilisation. Then it displayed the picture of a chequered flag, Maureen's signal that arrival was imminent. Still no sign of life whatever, and anxiety gave rise to ill-disguised panic. The chequered flag grew closer, and a confident voice instructed me to turn left in point two of a mile. Still an inky blackness that fed my fear. What on earth was I to do when Maureen announced our arrival at a farm gate in Lower Who-Knows-Where? Point two of a mile gave way to 500 metres, then 200 metres, and my brain was turning over options about what to do next like an engine trying to start without fuel. Then out of the gloom emerged a green board bearing the name of the establishment. Panic subsided as I attempted the air of a professional who had known exactly what he was doing all along.

The customer, who was probably a paid-up member of the "Civilisation Stops at Watford Club", looked somewhat less than excited about being booked into an establishment about as far removed from the Westminster Hilton as Surbiton is from the slums of Calcutta. Muttering some vague complaint that there must have been a quicker way to reach this Godforsaken place, and probably for the first time in his life acquainting his olfactory senses with the odours of rural England, he augmented the fare with a meagre tip, which was added to the receipt he would use to claim it back anyway. But for me I had discovered how invaluable Maureen was going to be, I had a good fare to complete my day's takings, and now only had the problem of finding my way back. This was accomplished simply by choosing what became my favourite button on Maureen's "Where to?" menu – "Go Home", and she obligingly did the rest.

This kind of journey, of course, was unusual, and many people would find it difficult to understand how a sat-nav could make that much difference to the earning potential of an average cabbie. Since most journeys were within a prescribed area and to predictable destinations the question remained whether it would be of any real value for anything other than the occasional trip to some distant point not yet visited.

At first it appeared to offer only a marginal advantage. If I stopped to put an address in the unit I could waste two or three minutes doing so, and I generally knew roughly where most addresses were anyway. The secret was to turn off the "safe navigation" option that prevented use whilst the vehicle was in motion; I found it surprisingly easy to drive to the area in which the job was located and press the relevant buttons to set the machine working whilst driving, and then simply follow instructions to a precise address.

In a city such as Leeds this is invaluable because roads tend to be located in groups all bearing the same prefix; the Landseer estate, for example, has no less than sixteen suffixes, from the more obvious Landseer Drive, Avenue and Road to the more pretentious and decidedly misleading Landseer Green. Many streets are paired with a namesake adding the appellation "Back" – for instance Back Landseer Mount. Some of the drivers with a decade of experience or more had succeeded in memorising where every single Landseer was, but I found this kind of feat impossible.

Faced with an address in an estate like this the simple thing to do was to drive towards it and enter the exact pick-up point as I went. Long before I reached the estate Maureen was on the case and very efficiently directed me to the house I needed, probably saving two or three minutes of driving around or else consulting a street map, not to mention the fuel. Whilst a couple of minutes may not sound a lot, when this is multiplied by the thirty or more jobs completed in each shift it was by no means impossible to save up to an hour, which equated to about three jobs, each paying an average of £4-5. At a conservative estimate my daily takings increased by £10, equating to £50-60 over a week and £200-£250 over a month. The cost of the sat-nav was recouped, at a guess, after slightly less than three weeks.

Maureen also brought a great peace of mind; there was always a level of anxiety about picking a customer up, particularly from transit points or hotels, and being asked for a destination I was completely unfamiliar with; this anxiety was now largely a thing of the past – wherever I was asked to go, Maureen would probably know the way.

The down side of the advent of the sat-nav in the private hire world (Black Cab drivers did not have this problem) was the exponential growth of drivers who not only did not know their way around, but had no inclination to learn. Some of my regular customers told horror stories of being collected (eventually) by a driver who had had to enter their address (often several times) into his machine. Upon telling him the destination, the customer was then compelled to wait while he laboriously entered this information into the sat-nav and set it working. Generally speaking the customers knew exactly where they were going, and the best way of getting there. For some bizarre and inexplicable reason instead of allowing the customer to direct them they insisted on wasting more time entering the data – often incorrectly – and then following the instructions rigidly. This frequently resulted in longer journeys (particularly if the machine had been set up to prefer main roads) in heavier traffic, not to mention irritated customers who would then have to argue over a fare for a journey they made every week, because the driver would not allow them to direct via the quickest and cheapest route.

But I did learn that whilst a sat-nav was a valuable servant it was a poor master. Maureen was faultless apart from two errors both of which caused embarrassment rather than anything more catastrophic, and well illustrate the point. The first came in the middle of a busy day when the warning bleeps reminding me of the presence of speed cameras were especially appreciated. Following the on-screen and vocal instructions I turned triumphantly into the road I was to pick up from, expecting to drive to the far end to await my customer. What Maureen and I were both unaware of was the fact that the local council had, only a few days previously, decided to stop through traffic by placing concrete pillars across the road – barely 25 metres from the end I entered. Taking the corner fast enough to challenge the durability of the anti-roll bars on a Formula One car my adrenaline levels were rapidly heightened by the sudden realisation that there were several lumps of concrete barring my way and about to rearrange the front of my well-designed Skoda; perhaps it was the adrenaline that enabled me to find the brake pedal in time, but there was scarcely space for tissue paper between the bumper and disaster.

The second occasion was a lot more embarrassing, and was a perfect demonstration of the limitations of any Maureen.

The company I worked for had a contract with a television company, who were filming in various parts of the county and who regularly used cabs to transport those deemed worthy of something more substantial than the bus laid on for hoi polloi. Early one morning I was favoured with the responsibility of taking one of the leading actresses and the director to the on location set just outside Harrogate. Foolishly I declined to look at the printed directions proffered by the two women, and just entrusted the postcode of the location to Maureen. She seemed to struggle for a while to make sense of it, but then began confidently to give instructions, and certainly we were headed in the right direction.

What I was unaware of was the fact that the filming was taking place on a private estate and in a stately home that was not open to the public, and which lay at the end of a driveway that offered no right of way. My endearing personification of the machine giving directions as an amiable but slightly strict middle-aged school mistress disguised the reality that it was actually nothing other than a piece of clever electronic equipment which, asked to perform an impossible task, will seek the most logical way to complete it as adequately as a mere machine can manage.

My passengers were busy discussing matters of such monumental importance as the best foundation to use on the face for outdoor filming in cloudy conditions, whether the mobile canteen manager was gay, and whether one of the programme's co-stars had found her route to prominence via the producer's hotel room. There was no lull in the chatter until the point when Maureen confidently and commandingly directed me to leave the well-heeled, well surfaced and relatively straight trunk road we had taken since leaving Harrogate for a scruffy, dog-eared and impoverished country lane replete with horse manure and pot-holes.

The semi-whispers from the rear seat gave way to a slightly more strident tone that masked more than a hint of anxiety. 'Are you sure this is the right way, driver?' To doubt Maureen's competence after the famed run to the Halifax hotel would have seemed close to infidelity. 'Well, the sat-nav has never let me down yet,' I replied with a confidence I hoped was convincing to those who were used to dealing with temperamental thespians.

The anxious silence in the car increased in direct proportion to the deterioration in the quality of the road as it wound its way through a couple of hamlets and between farms whose livestock had laid substantial droppings on their way to being milked. It was around the time the tarmac disappeared completely, to be succeeded by a track of solid earth, that I realised just how absurd the sight must have looked to the thankfully sparse collection of casual spectators who greeted us with mild amusement and the scratching of sage, grizzled Yorkshire heads. A cab driven with determined, if groundless confidence, by a city cabbie transporting a brace of important-looking people through their unheralded little hamlet up a track navigable only by tractors and armoured personnel carriers would have provided an attractive additional course to a number of farmhouse dinners that evening.

I helped myself to a large slice of the humble pie now on offer, consulted the map they had already proffered, apologised profusely, assured them they would not be charged for the diversion, and rapidly found the correct entrance to the estate.

In fairness to Maureen she was simply doing her best to accomplish the impossible task she had been assigned. Presented with the postcode of a manor house that lay at the end of a private road she came up with the ingenious idea of entering through the rear of the estate via what appeared on her map as a viable thoroughfare, and was probably very pleased with her inventiveness. The customers were less impressed with this unscheduled tour of obscure and relatively uninspiring Yorkshire countryside, and were perhaps out of sympathy with the view of most natives that this was "God's own country." Their relief at finally reaching the front entrance of the destination to be waved past the "no public right of way" sign by a member of the peaked cap brigade failed to dispel completely the frustration of a late arrival. In true Yorkshire fashion, however, their primary concern was that the unscheduled rustic digression should not be charged to the company's already substantial bill.

Maureen and I had a mild altercation on the way home,

but in truth I learned an important lesson that day. Like most technological breakthroughs a sat-nav is an excellent tool but should be used with healthy chunks of common sense. There are situations where it is invaluable, and certainly after a few weeks I could never have imagined reverting to life without Maureen, but owning one was no substitute for the hard work of learning my way around. As I became increasingly familiar with the routes through the main areas my taxi firm used I would still give Maureen an address but would often choose a different route to the one she proffered. Maureen's response to my digression from her directions was (and still is) the single word "recalculating." This is articulated in a tone that seems to convey both mild rebuke and reluctant acquiescence, very much in keeping with the personality of a Maureen. I developed a conversational style which was firm but engaging with the joint objectives of making sure she knew who was in charge but that she was still appreciated. 'It's alright, Maureen, I know you want to go that route, but trust me – at this time of day there will be less traffic if we do it my way.' Maureen seemed to resume her normal cheerfulness quite easily once our routes converged and would always inform me both politely and cheerfully that we were "arriving at destination on right" (or left) as if that had been the route she had intended to navigate all along.

Over time Maureen became as much a companion as a tool, and especially on night shifts assumed a similar role to the volleyball Tom Hanks called "Wilson" in the film Castaway, though my companion at least had a voice. Somehow the cab was never lonely so long as Maureen was switched on, and imaginary conversations with her were some kind of substitute for human companionship.

# 19

## HUNSLET – PARANOIA – FEEDING AND SHITE

Certain mild forms of psychiatric disorder appear to be almost essential requirements for particular professions. Currently dentists and farmers are the most likely to suffer from levels of depression severe enough to precipitate suicide. Politicians experience periodic bouts of narcissism and delusions of grandeur, depending on their popularity ratings. Football managers and players seem to suffer from manic depression, their place on the bi-polar scale determined by the results of their team and the perceived merits or otherwise of the match officials. But if the conditions known as "housemaid's knee" and "tennis elbow" relate in any way to those occupations there should certainly be a condition called "Taxi Driver's Paranoia."

I encountered quite severe forms of the illness not so much from day one but from hour one in the private hire world. Several drivers arriving at a similar time to collect a car seemed to share the common objective of outdoing one another in relating accounts of how awful a hand they had been dealt. Whilst the main area of contention was either the quantity or quality of jobs they were allocated – or both – other unreasonable victimisation they allegedly bore included the "pile of fucking shit they gave me to drive", "the fucking arrogant way those bastard operators spoke to me" and "the fucking fortune the idle wankers of directors make out of me."

For the first week I assumed that I had just come across a few disgruntled drivers who had for whatever reason not enjoyed a very good shift; three months into the job I realised that this kind of attitude is endemic, and in some perverse way acts as a kind of soothing balm to anaesthetise them from the more unsavoury aspects of the job. In the same way that some children develop comfort habits that are quite destructive or bizarre (I knew one young girl who found solace in systematically pulling all the hair out of one side of her head whilst sucking her thumb and watching television) those who drive for hire and reward seem to acquire a variety of persecution complexes that provide succour for their distressed souls. These are expressed in a variety of forms; from the Mazurka of Martyrdom through the Sonata of the Scapegoat to the full-blown Symphony of the Sacrificial Lamb with full highly-strung orchestra. The detail of the score would typically contain several stories demonstrating to any reasonable listener that they had been picked on to perform a succession of thankless tasks adding up to a shift that not only failed to keep the wolf from the door but positively welcomed him over the threshold and into the kitchen. Only by working their butts off could they prevent the rapacious invader from ascending the stairs to devour their families. All such jobs and periods of work were known collectively as "shite", the final "e" affording the opportunity to lengthen the middle vowel and thus facilitate the expression of a greater level of disgust than the simple monosyllabic "shit", though the two terms were used more or less interchangeably.

The root causes of the persecution complex are to be found in the thought patterns encouraged by the isolated nature of the job on the one hand, and the value attributed to the work allotted to them on the other (shite). For now I will say something about victimisation and return to the value of jobs that came through the anonymous medium of the datahead and the concept of "feeding" in the next chapter.

The relative isolation the driver experiences from anyone

else working for the company during a shift was, for me, one of the most attractive aspects of the job. It is impossible to survive two decades in clerical ministry without being a decent "people person" and being able to cope with the often unreasonable demands of the average churchgoer. Twenty years or so of constant pressure from people with problems and needs – some real, many imaginary – had, however, left me with a powerful longing to hold the human race in general at arm's length. At one point in my life this had resulted in an attempt to buy an isolated croft in the Outer Hebrides and move there lock, stock and barrel. The attempt was thwarted in the end by the owner, one of Stornoway's loyal army of Free Presbyterian churchgoers, pulling out of the contract at the last minute when she was presented with a better offer. I have since come to regard this episode as divine deliverance; I would have loved the barren landscape of Lewis, and could even have coped with the weather, but would have very rapidly despaired of this particular brand of Puritanical hypocrisy. So when I began to drive a minicab for a living the discovery that once ensconced in the car I was unlikely to have to speak to anyone with any kind of call on my time and attention, and indulge only in the superficial conversation typically held with customers, was one that made my heart feel very light indeed.

Given that most taxi drivers register at least half way up on the schizophrenia scale, however, the apparently arbitrary manner in which most work arrived via the datahead was almost certain to result in some measure of paranoia. There would be few problems when work was plentiful and profitable. Shifts like these allowed very little time for thinking about anything other than work. When a job was completed the driver was required to enter a code into the datahead which cleared the vehicle for the next assignment. In busy times this would appear instantly, to be replaced by another when that job was completed. This non-stop flow of work could easily last for several hours, and messages would appear on the screen pleading with drivers not to take a break until it died down. Occasionally this state of affairs would last all day, a twelve-hour shift would pass in the eponymous twinkling of an eye, and there would be little or no opportunity for reminding oneself that we were a persecuted minority oppressed by the arrogant plutocrats who believed they owned our souls.

Most days, however, there was at least one sizeable lull in the flow of work, providing ample opportunity for exercising one's paranoid imagination. No amount of staring at the inactive screen would induce it to cough out another piece of work, however much willpower or hypnotic effort was applied to the uncooperative electronic circuitry. When such periods of enforced idleness extended upwards of fifteen minutes, and still no work emerged, it became increasingly difficult to attribute the dearth of earning opportunities to anything other than some malevolent individual who had decided for whatever reason that this particular driver on this particular day should be deprived of a decent living. These attacks of paranoia would begin in quite a mild way, with perhaps just the odd stray thought about a recent conversation with one of the telephone operators that could have been misinterpreted, but the longer the wait without work the more frequent and the more intense they became. The victim complex would be fed by various factors; it was possible, using the datahead controls, to see what was happening in other areas, and perhaps noting that other drivers were finding work; a driver who was next in line for a job in a particular "plot" might see the number of cars in the queue diminishing and believe that he was being overlooked whilst other drivers were receiving work and jumping the queue. Should he see a succession of company vehicles driving past with customers, or possibly on their way to collect one, the attack could reach frenzied proportions. I heard of one or two drivers who were so convinced they were victims of a conspiracy by those allocating work that they drove to the company offices and tried to assault the telephone operators. It was not altogether without justification that the offices were off limits to drivers except by invitation or appointment.

In spite of the irrational sense of being picked on or overlooked shared by many, if not most drivers, the question is whether there is any justification for this all-pervasive paranoia. To say something about this it is necessary to risk the patience of the reader with a description of the way the system of job allocation in a large private hire company like this works.

The city and surrounding region was divided up by a grid into small areas known as "plots". To all intents and purposes there were about fifty of these, although I am told that this number has now expanded to nearer sixty. The size of each "plot" varies, depending mainly on the volume of work generated in that particular region. Some plots cover ten or twelve square miles since other companies are dominant in that region and work is sparse. At the other end of the spectrum one plot covered a few hundred square metres, but housed a casino which provided prodigious amounts of work at certain times of the night.

Each car was tracked using GPS and its entry and exit into and from each plot would be recorded by the computer at Base. The datahead, the in-car computer, would display this information as the driver's status in the format "Plot... Position...' The first car into a particular plot would assume position 1, the second position 2 and so on, and the driver's place in the queue would improve as jobs came in for that particular area, or one that was immediately adjacent if there were no cars within its boundaries. Thus "Plot 1 Position 1" was a good place to be because Plot 1 was the area immediately around Base, where a lot of work was generated, and being first in the queue generally meant that work would arrive within a minute or two. Conversely "Plot 52 Position 6" was about as bad is it could be since this was the very large plot in East Leeds that generated almost no work and waiting there for the sixth job to come up would probably take all day. Thus "Plot 1 Position 6" was probably a better status than "Plot 52 Position 1". One of the significant keys to making a decent living was knowing the value of any particular position in any particular plot, and understanding the other variable – how this was affected by what time of day it was. There would be little merit in waiting for work in the plot dedicated to the casino at 9 o'clock in the morning, for instance, but it was an excellent position to be in some four hours earlier when taxis were booked to take the staff home. There were certain plots that were best avoided in rush hour because, in spite of work being plentiful, congestion stifled any opportunity for making serious money, and there were others where commuter traffic was almost non-existent.

The other end of the operation involved the telephone operators who were responsible for logging the work onto the computer system. Calls would be taken from customers who were asked to give a name, a pick-up address and a destination, and once this information was entered the job would, generally, simply be fed into the computer. Once placed on the system the job would automatically be allocated to the car at Position 1 in the plot containing the pick-up address. If there were no cars in that particular plot it would be allocated to the driver at Position 1 in an adjoining plot. If these plots were empty it appeared on all drivers' screens and they were then entitled to ask, or "plot" for it using the controls on the datahead. Pre-booked work would also be logged automatically onto the computer at the appropriate time and then go through the same process.

Claims of victimisation were frequent. These charges were usually made by drivers who had had an altercation with one of the telephone operators, and were convinced that their life was being made a misery by a vengeful spirit, ensuring that they had little work, and what did come their way was of very poor quality, or "shite". In truth it is almost impossible to see how this could have happened, given the volume of calls that were taken and the freedom of each driver to go to any area of his or her choice and to "plot" for any work that appeared on the screen. A particular operator would have had to track the vehicle involved, and arrange the order of work for each plot the car entered so that anything that did come the driver's way was likely to be unprofitable. Even if this could be done it would often be impossible for the operator to know whether a particular job would pay well. As automation became more prominent it was increasingly the case that work was transferred straight from the 'phone line to the computer, and no destination would be stated. Pick-ups from clubs and casinos were often requested by staff for customers without asking for their destination.

Much of the paranoia arose from a mistaken belief that the greater the distance travelled in the course of a job the more it was worth. Short trips that paid less than £5 were often labelled "shite" and completed with a scowl and a sense of injustice. "Minimum fare" work, consisting of journeys of less than a mile, was consigned to the excrement receptacle, whilst anything that paid in excess of £10 was the stuff of dreams.

I say it was a mistaken belief because in fact small jobs were often the most lucrative form of work. It was not unusual to complete six in an hour, and not unknown for a driver to complete eight, resulting in income of £15 – 20 for an hour's work, consuming little fuel and leaving the driver in an area where more work was readily available. A fare of £10 could involve negotiating much traffic, using more fuel and finishing at some remote point 30 minutes later. To find more work the driver would often have to retrace most of his steps to regain an area replete with customers.

It was doubtless true that some assignments were more profitable than others, but the simplistic view that long distances necessarily meant high earnings did not bear serious scrutiny. One of the most sought-after jobs, for instance, was a run to Manchester airport. If the journey was made when traffic was light, and customers were being taken to the airport, or alternatively were out on time to be picked up from the terminal, a driver could return within two and a half hours about £60 wealthier, a very worthwhile sum in spite of the additional fuel used. On the other hand if the journey was through rush hour traffic and the pick-up was from the airport where the flight was delayed the same trip could take four hours or more, in which case the driver would almost certainly have been better served staying closer to home. It appeared that many cabbies were either unwilling or unable to think through this simple arithmetic.

Generally speaking I concluded that victimisation did not take place, and work really was allocated by and large at random. Of course there were shifts when a driver seemed to have a succession of poorly paid jobs, or "no fares" (a term used when there was no customer at the pick-up point) but conversely there were shifts when it seemed that everything that fell into one's lap was worth having. In fact I noticed that in spite of my perception of whether the shift had been good, bad or indifferent, my takings over a twelve-hour period varied only by about £20-25 at most, and usually fell into a bandwidth of about £10. So long as I completed all the work that appeared on my datahead whether it was busy or quiet, whether the jobs were short or long, my takings were about the same each shift, and on a weekly basis achieved an amazing consistency.

There was another reason why so many private hire drivers used the vocabulary of the sewer so vocally to describe their lot, and this displayed a subtlety that one would not easily attribute to members of the sub-species "taxicus driverus." One way of seeing the total workload of the company was as a large cake that had to be divided between all those seated at the family dining table. The more family members there were the smaller the slice of cake. Each new addition to the family was thus viewed with a certain level of avaricious resentment as another mouth to feed, with the result that there was slightly less for those who had been seated at the table for some time. If a new addition could be frightened by tales of misery and squalor to the extent that one disappointing shift would convince him that there was no money to be made from the job, he would be likely to abandon the dining table of his new family and go to scavenge in some local refuse tip before he became established. He might have gathered a few crumbs into his mouth by then, but there would be fewer mouths to feed at the next sitting. I noticed that as I became established as a regular driver the airing of grievances did not diminish, but was interspersed with complaints about how many drivers were being taken on. Because there was a belief that new drivers were "fed" – on which see the next chapter – what little work remained was likely to resemble the contents of a toilet pan before flushing.

I was left with the impression that however profitable a day most drivers had they would retain their paranoid sense of injustice as a toddler clings to a comfort blanket at bedtime; if there is a profession with a stronger sense of unjustified victimisation I have yet to encounter it.

# 20

## FARSLEY – FEEDING FRENZY AND FLIGHTY FICKLENESS

On the face of it the procedure for allocating work was open and fair, but inevitably no system can ever be quite that simple. There were a number of jobs that never reached the computer system but which, for various reasons, were allocated to specific drivers, and this was where the difficulties mainly arose over the practice of "Feeding." Sometimes, for instance, a driver would do a favour for the company by picking up a member of staff, or taking a sick vehicle to the main dealer for analysis; a driver might have suffered a breakdown (mechanical that is – the company had no time for psychological inadequacy) on a previous shift and have been prevented from making a decent sum for the hours he had worked. Rather than reducing his rent he would be offered a particularly profitable fare that would effectively make up the difference. When these lucrative jobs were received by the operators they were usually placed onto a different computer system to be allocated to drivers who were "owed a favour." In my experience this allocation of plum jobs was pretty fair – I received my share, and found that respect and politeness towards those who were responsible for allocating work paid dividends. Other drivers were almost constantly moaning about the "shite" they were getting compared to those they believed were willing to curry favour with the management and offer an oral cleansing service to the appropriate anal region. More often than not they belonged to that breed of human being that finds courtesy and good manners as easy to master as supersonic bicycle travel; lack of civility led to being overlooked for good fares, which in turn fed the paranoia, and a spiral of self-fulfilling prophecy was the result.

Sometimes jobs were kept for experienced drivers, or those with a good track record of completing work, because they were part of a lucrative contract or involved transporting a particularly important customer. Not unreasonably the company felt these jobs were best allocated to drivers whose clothes did not provide random additional ventilation at the knees, elbows and feet, and whose cars were not the vehicular embodiment of a council landfill site. Such preferential treatment was, in any case, a mixed blessing. Several times I was called upon to drive half way round the city centre to collect an executive from a television company only to deposit him at the train station five minutes later for a minimum fare, reduced because the job was part of an account, and rarely received any kind of gratuity.

The system was, of course, open to abuse. Towards the end of my first year I learned about a telephone operator who had an agreement with a particular driver; he paid her £50 a week, and in exchange she ensured that there was a fairly constant stream of well-paid work coming his way; both were deprived of their livelihoods once the scam was discovered, but as far as I could tell this was a rare occurrence. Occasionally a romantic relationship would develop between a driver and an operator, resulting in a more subtle level of favouritism. Since most operators were under thirty – and some quite attractive – and most drivers were a safe distance on the wrong side of any mid-life crisis such liaisons were not particularly common.

More contentious, and more reasonable, was the complaint that new drivers were "fed" with well-paid work in order to help them through the first week or two so they could become established. Whilst this undoubtedly happened it was not unreasonable to point out that all of those impersonating the whine of the average company car's gearbox were once new drivers themselves, and almost certainly received similar preferential treatment. Selective memory was seemingly employed to erase the recollection of just how precarious the first few weeks were, and how much difference the odd favour makes to a new driver's odds on survival. The shock to the system in those early days is something akin to abandoning a cruise ship in the middle of the Atlantic and having your breath taken away by the icy water. Being tossed a life jacket may not guarantee survival, but at least it gives you a fighting chance.

When all the paranoia, ritual grumbling and self-inflicted misery is stripped away the real complaint revolved around the policy of the company to take on as many drivers as came through its doors looking for work. This resulted in a belief that there was an ever-diminishing portion of the collective cake for each driver to consume. There is some truth in this; it was difficult at times to resist the conclusion that the company would have happily offered work to the entire population of West Yorkshire given the opportunity, since the more drivers there were the more rent they would be able to collect. Many of us would have liked to think that we were the favoured few engaged only after a rigorous selection process to sift the wheat from the chaff, but the kind of selection that really took place was only of the commercial Darwinian variety. Success in the gene pool went to those fit enough mentally and physically to make a good living; the majority, I suspect, became victims of natural deselection. Like so many salmon struggling to fight their way upstream the careers of most lay lifeless at the bottom of a ladder designed for the benefit of those who controlled it. They were not mourned, either by the company, who knew there would be another batch along presently, or by the survivors, who were too busy with their own struggle for luxuries like sympathy. Only when one had proved its capacity to survive would there be more than a passing interest in keeping it in the fish farm. Thus an endless stream of recruits seemed to process through the yard and offices. Unless a potential driver was likely to cost the company money in wrecked cars, increased insurance premiums or lost customers it made sense to have as many as possible. With something in excess of 400 drivers, each one representing an income of up to £1,000 per month, it was not difficult to see why the company would oppose any kind of control on the recruitment process.

So it was that most weeks when for one reason or another I found myself visiting Base I would catch a glimpse of the same middle-manager who offered me the opportunity to drive running through the induction process with yet another potentially lucrative unit of production. I could almost visualise my slice of cake being trimmed at the edges and losing a couple of sultanas and a cherry. It wasn't as simple as that, of course. The newcomers were visible; those leaving did so through the back door to a symphony of silent indifference from all concerned, drivers and management alike, to be mentioned only by disgruntled cabbies as members of a putatively large group who had left en bloc to join a rival company.

I discovered that there were a number of cycles affecting the supply of work – the proximity of the shift I was working to the end of the month's payday, the time of year and the prevailing weather conditions being obvious examples. One of the less obvious cycles took much longer to understand. This was the cycle created by the number of drivers working for the company, and it generally took about three months to complete. At the top of the cycle would be a short spell when for a week or two there would be no breaks in the flow of work. This time of plenty would usually lead to a period of gradual decline, until work was quite hard to come by. The final week or so of the pattern was always difficult, and occasionally a minimum wage job in a fast food restaurant fleetingly appeared an attractive alternative to driving for a living. Then just as I was wondering how I would go on making a decent living it was as if a dam broke and we were back at the start of the cycle.

I later came to associate this with the simple laws of supply and demand that determined how many drivers were working; it appeared that when work was scarce a large group would leave for what may or may not have been more luscious pastures and an inundation of work would flood the datahead. The increased flow of work encouraged more drivers, until saturation point was reached, when the cycle would restart. I learned over time to recognise this pattern, and just sit tight during the periods of drought. Even then I always managed to make some kind of a living, and my most common mantra became "put the hours in and you will make the money."

These vagaries function in the context of the curious relationship that exists between the director of a private hire company and those who drive for it. The company I worked for was by far the largest for a long way around, and had two directors, who were reputed to be very skilful at running the "Good Cop Bad Cop" routine. The former was diminutive, dapper and easygoing – at least on the surface, whilst his partner could have had a starring role in the McDonald's "Go Large" advertising campaign. He had a belligerence and overt ruthlessness that sat comfortably with both his physical stature and his gravelly voice. They had built the company up from being a three-car operation run from a small basement office into what was undoubtedly the envy of every other outfit in the county. With a fleet of 400 or more cars and even more drivers they had secured contracts for work with just about every hotel, casino and night club in the city, as well as servicing the needs of the major television company, the principal theatre and even, during my later days, the local hospitals. Almost every large organisation, public and private, was among their clientele and, like Don Juan eyeing the maidens of his village, they regarded it as only a question of time before the rest succumbed. It was this colossal quantity of work that attracted so many drivers to the company, particularly at the "respectable" end of the business – all such terms being relative.

So far I have used the terms "private hire driver" and "taxi driver" almost interchangeably, but to describe the relationship of mutual suspicion, dependence and hostility between directors and drivers it is important at this point to explain a distinction that was lost on me previously and, I have since discovered, most of the population as well.

Taxis, or Hackney Carriages, and their drivers are distinguishable by the word "TAXI" which will adorn some part of their vehicle. In the area I worked they were either the shape, though not necessarily the colour, of London's black cabs, or coloured black and white with an illuminated "TAXI" sign on their roof, but they can take many different forms and are sometimes otherwise almost indistinguishable from private hire cars. A licence to drive a Hackney Carriage is generally more demanding to acquire; some demonstration of local geography and principal routes may be required, along with a more rigorous driving test and a more expensive licence as well as higher insurance premiums.

The benefits of being able to drive a car with a sign reading "taxi" are many: the right to use most bus lanes, being able to pass through bus gates, having a meter that runs constantly, even when the vehicle is stationary, higher fares and, most importantly, being able to pick up anyone at any time who flags the vehicle down.

By contrast private hire drivers are not entitled to adorn their cars with the word "taxi", are generally paid purely on distance covered (the car's trip meter should be reset for every journey and charge made according to a set scale), have no privileges in terms of road usage, and are not allowed to pick up customers who have not booked with the operating company.

Nowadays private hire cars are not infrequently required to state specifically on the vehicle that they are allowed only to take advance bookings and / or that any journey not pre-booked is uninsured; members of the public would do well to heed the warnings.

This two-tiered system generates a fair amount of friction; Hackney Carriage drivers usually maintain a superior air as better cabbies than their private hire counterparts, a claim that is, in general, justified, if for no other reason than they will on average have been in the trade for longer and have learned how to stay out of trouble. Private hire drivers tend to resent this snootiness, and have little intercourse with taxi drivers. I witnessed some quite comical episodes at all-night petrol stations when I worked nights and taxis and private hire cars were almost the only vehicles on the road. There would be up to a dozen cabs of either variety at pumps, with drivers either filling tanks or paying for their fuel, and it would be possible to tell the two types of driver apart from the smug superiority or the sullen resentment of each driver's body language. Just occasionally, when work was really plentiful for both types of vehicle, I struck up something of a conversation with a Hackney Cab driver, but still almost felt compelled to touch my forelock before and afterwards in deference to a member of a superior caste.

The mutual resentment is caused by a number of factors. Hackney cab drivers felt – not always unreasonably – that their private hire counterparts lowered the tone of the profession and gave all the drivers a bad name. In our turn we resented the air of superiority and at best the grudging condescension offered by our illustrious colleagues. But by far the commonest cause of tension is the practice of some private hire car drivers to ply for trade (asking people on the street if they would like a cab) and to "flag" – pick up customers who try to hail them and who may not understand the difference between the two types of vehicle.

Not unreasonably the Hackney cab drivers feel that this creates an uneven playing field when the cost of running their car is so much higher than their minicab counterparts – as well, of course, as being illegal.

These practices were, and still are, not uncommon, particularly at night near centres of entertainment, and continue to cause tension. In spite of its illegality and the risk of losing one's licence as well as prosecution, many private hire drivers continue to regard the risk as one worth taking. The licensing authority and police deploy officers from time to time to ask drivers to take them somewhere, and catch countless miscreants in this way, but the practice has not diminished, perhaps because the risk of being caught is still relatively small. I never risked my licence in this way – and honestly never needed to, but I did experience one such sting operation during a night shift.

Midnight had come and gone, and business was slow as it usually was till about 12.30; I'd stopped for a coffee at one of those fast food establishments that make a small fortune in the early hours of the morning by dolloping large quantities of cardboard strips in a piece of bread and calling it a kebab. I was still about number three in the normally busy plot as I was finishing my coffee when a young couple approached my car and offered me a lucrative fare. After a year in the business I could recognise those who just didn't fit; few people in this area at this time of night were stone cold sober, and none I could recall were ever smartly dressed. Articulate to the point of refinement and without a hair out of place they were the last people on earth who would ask a private hire driver to break the rules.

I did what I always did anyway – check that I wasn't yet number one (in which case I could have radioed in the job and taken them) smiled politely and said that I regretted I was unable to help, but could radio for a cab for them. Offering apologies for disturbing me they said not to worry, they would find another one. I took the liberty of calling them back, assuring them that I was one of the drivers who didn't break the rules, but that if they wanted to catch the people who did they needed to do something about their clothes, language and appearance that prevented them from looking like a Rolls Royce in a scrap yard. This was followed by one of those wonderful moments of mutual but unspoken understanding; both smiled, before the rather pretty woman police officer (I was pretty sure they were part of the constabulary rather than the local authority) was unable either to maintain eye contact or suppress a burst of laughter. The man simply smiled, winked, and waved as he led his colleague away.

The air of distrust, antipathy and hostility with which the management regarded drivers arose largely out of the abuses of the rules by some of the drivers, and reflected a not totally irrational paranoia. A number of drivers would pick up their car and "sign on", then go touting for business. Should they be flagged down they would register that they were having a break using the datahead and earn a nice wad of cash – usually charging well over the odds for the journey. Some owner-drivers would not even bother registering for work, but would simply go out in their car bearing the company's logo and tout for business. Not only did the management complain that drivers were not available for the company's work when they were doing this, but they were also tarnishing the good name of the business. Good reputations are, of course, measured in relative terms; my company was held in generally high esteem in much the same way that Mussolini would be compared to Hitler, Stalin or the Khmer Rouge; pretty nasty but not without a modicum of decency.

Given the promiscuity of the recruitment policy of most companies and the congenital paranoia exhibited by almost all drivers it is, perhaps, not surprising that marriages between them are rarely made in heaven, and have about the same survival prospects as a match between two particularly narcissistic celebrities. It will not be very long into a driving career before most drivers have cause, sometimes justifiably, to feel slighted, unappreciated or neglected by their partner. Reports and rumours of another company securing contracts guaranteeing rich pickings circulate with as much accuracy as the tabloid press speculating on the secret vices of soap stars, but if the rumours are even a little convincing, the previous days takings were disappointing, and there has been a minor altercation with the management, or even one of the office staff, it is quite likely that the driver will feel tempted into infidelity. Given that the process of changing to another company is quick, simple and cheap, the cabbie who feels slighted or unappreciated may well move on to another firm who he is sure will treat him with the appreciation his loyalty deserves. More often than not those who choose second marriages are simply starting on a veritable career in serial divorce and remarriage.

The management of the jilted business is soon able to dry its collective tears, place another couple of adverts in the local press, and wait for the next round of speed-dating. As often as not the vagrant sheep will return to the fold – perhaps not so much wagging their tails behind them as grasping them firmly between their hind legs. The fatted calf will live to see another day, but the welcome back to the fold will be warm and genuine, further evidence that this is the best flock to belong to and that the competitors are really not doing nearly as well as their publicity would suggest. The vigil for the first glimpse of a particularly lush piece of pasture just over the next fence will soon herald another completed cycle of frustrated optimism, crushed hopes and inevitable disappointment.

# 21

## DAWSON'S CORNER – ANSWERING BAIL AND RETAIL THERAPY

Most dogs, it is said, grow to look something like their owners. I had always thought of this as one of those things people say to compensate for lack of intelligent conversation, until I noticed that it actually seems to be true. Not merely the physical appearance of the animal, but even its temperament, all too often for coincidence seemed to reflect that of the person on the other end of the lead. The truth, when it finally worked its way into my cerebrum is, of course, that there is a simple explanation; dogs don't necessarily change at all. People who go to choose a canine companion, either from a breeder or a rescue centre, very often (perhaps largely subconsciously) pick the ones that most resemble themselves. It's handy to realise this if you are trying to work out someone's personality and they have a dog. Study the look and nature of the animal and you will probably have a pretty good idea who you are dealing with. The truth is that more often than not the dog picks the owner, not the other way round.

The taxi-driving business operates on a similar governing principle; many of the people who take up the profession are really there by default – it is the next, if not final, step along a career path that was always going to lead them to this point. The collapse of large-scale British manufacturing and other traditional industry and the increasing reliance on financial and service sectors that dominated our economy in the 80s and 90s was something most of us thought of in terms of a victimless crime, and who needs steel, chemicals and coal anyhow when they come at such a cost to social cohesion? Delve into the world of cab driving and there you find several strata of manpower who found themselves unemployable and generally surplus to requirements. Perhaps with too much pride to claim unemployment benefit for the rest of their lives, and with a little too much initiative for work in the retail or fast food sectors, as well as insufficient familiarity with the computer age, taxi driving provided at least a niche that could be occupied pending a resurgence in the fortunes of the industries that once provided a living.

Most cabbies are, I would judge, of above average intelligence, and have to be in order to realise anything like reasonable earnings. There are thousands with degrees at bachelor level or above who have found that the skills that were once in such demand are now about as sought after as central heating in Ecuador. These were the men I felt a particular sympathy for – erstwhile engineers and technicians whose skills and expertise had gone out of fashion in the same way as the steam engine and the horse and cart. It was difficult to see how anything for them would change between now and the date they were able to draw whatever pension they had been able to provide themselves with. Nearly all the drivers I met wished they could have done something different, and drove a cab because the only work they could otherwise have found would have failed to pay anything more than a minimum wage.

There were exceptions to this rule, though, and many of them were to be found in their cabs in the supermarket car park at Dawson's Corner on weekday afternoons. The drivers who I came to call "The Flask of Tea Brigade" had other reasons for spending hour after hour sitting behind a steering wheel on this gigantic piece of tarmac that sits on the cartographical dotted line that separates Leeds from Bradford. These characters were unlike any other type of driver I encountered; they were bemoaning neither the quantity nor the paucity of available work, and the term "shite" belonged to a foreign language. Nor were they trying to squeeze as many fares as possible into each hour they were at work. They were the gentlemen to our players.

The Dawson's Corner plot suited them down to the ground. Installed within the entrance area of the supermarket was a freephone link to the company offices, and since there were hundreds of people passing through the store each hour this provided a nice steady stream of work. Almost adjoining the supermarket was a branch of a very popular department store, one of the largest of its kind in the country, providing another constant stream of customers. With the exception of the week before Christmas, on which see above, on a busy shopping day this could be a lucrative plot to work. Fares were normally small – usually less than £5, but customers could be picked up along with their shopping, deposited at home within a mile or two of the retail centre, and having "cleared" (the process of announcing one job complete and availability for more work) by the time the return journey was made another would have come through the datahead, ready to be picked up immediately upon arrival outside the supermarket. This pattern of work I came to label "Dawson's Corner Loops", and after several months in the job I was capable, on a good day, of completing five or six of these in an hour, generating takings in excess of £20.

That was how most of us saw it, but not the Flask of Tea Brigade. These men had every appearance of those who have recently retired, don't play golf, and have wives who complain about them being under their feet if they are at home too much of the time. They would position themselves at the far end of the car park and after pouring their first cuppa make themselves available for work. When a job came through they would spend the next five minutes finishing the tea, rinsing the cup and carefully packing their mobile canteen away before making casual progress down to the pick-up point where they would exhibit attentive, if somewhat dilatory, assistance in aiding the laden shoppers into the vehicle. Typically they would reappear some 20 minutes later, pour another cup of tea, make themselves available for work once again, and repeat the cycle. On the odd occasion I happened to be passing through the area and found I was number three in this plot with a high turnover. I would pull into the car park and join these gentleman drivers, regarding being number three here as preferable to taking a punt on one of the empty adjacent plots. On more than one occasion having been third in the queue for a job I arrived at the pick-up point outside the supermarket before either of the preceding car drivers had finished their tea, invoking the wrath of shoppers who could not understand why having been there first they were still waiting for their car after a newcomer was well on their way home. This was gentlemen's cab driving – a refined circle of older drivers, pedestrian in pace and as likely to discuss the weather and the state of the economy as the parlous state of the taxi driving industry. When they complained about their work it was usually because instead of being allowed to spend their shift running local shoppers home from the supermarket they had been dragged into an adjacent plot and forced to undertake a journey of five miles or more; horror of horrors once or twice they had even been expected to drive someone from a nearby housing estate to the city centre – a job most of us would relish, involving a fast dual carriageway and a good fare with the decent prospect of more work to be picked up at the other end. For the Flask of Tea Brigade this simply meant having to risk their immaculate vehicles to the questionable mercy of the congestion of city-centre traffic, and suffering the olfactory deprivation of not being able to sniff their next cuppa for a good half hour or more. Even these drivers were not immune to the paranoia that afflicted the profession; they would complain about being "dragged off their plot" as if there was a malevolent telephone operator who had decided to see how far she could pull them away from their preferred orbit of existence by stringing together a series of jobs that would keep them from their next hot beverage for hours at a time. The truth was that even had there been an operator with such a desire the sheer volume of calls that passed through the switchboard would have rendered such a scenario impossible to manufacture. Telephone operators, even had they felt the inclination, certainly didn't have the time for such puerile games. But the sinister conspiracy theories thrived unabated by these palpable realities, and almost seemed at times to rival those surrounding the assassination of Kennedy.

I came to regard the Flask of Tea Brigade with a mixture of amusement and quiet envy, and began to look forward to a day in the future when I would be able to drive a cab at a leisurely pace for pin money, and alleviate any irritation I might risk causing to my long-suffering wife simply by being around too much.

The area known as Dawson's Corner boasted only one major additional feature to the shopping complex that generated steady if unremarkable income for the Flask of Tea Brigade, and that was the local police station, serving a significant area of West Leeds at the border with what most saw as its poor relation, the city of Bradford. But work to and from this establishment was a world removed from the haven for retail therapy that was its immediate neighbour, and almost always significantly more interesting. The more mundane, though always pleasant jobs, involved taking police officers to or from the station; the key to this work was to encourage less than discreet disclosures about recent shifts both because such tales were generally fascinating – if sometimes toe-curling – and because it discouraged the passenger from looking too closely at the speedometer. I have little doubt that these worthy public servants had far better things to do than concern themselves with the minor violations of speed limits of their transport, but I often entertained a bizarre nightmare fantasy of an officer paying his or her fare whilst simultaneously serving me with a speeding ticket. Not that I drove excessively fast – I had discovered that stress and anxiety levels were significantly reduced by keeping to a reasonable speed, but it would be a little too creative with the verities to pretend that I abided rigorously by the posted speed limit. In truth it would have been difficult to earn a good living were I to have done so, particularly when travelling to pick-up points.

Even more entertaining than transporting officers of the law, however, were those jobs involving taking people to the police station as part of their bail conditions, providing a gateway into what seemed like a parallel universe in which almost anything could happen.

Before I found myself in the world of taxi-driving almost the last people I would have expected to find in the back of a minicab were those without jobs, homes or obvious means of earned income who subsisted in a hand-to-mouth fashion on the fringes of anything resembling respectable society. Such notions are seriously misplaced, and one of the more frequent thoughts that would go through my head in the course of a shift was "how can these people afford a cab fare when people like me generally can't?" Perhaps this was really a manifestation of the innate Puritan drive for austerity that eschews such extravagance when public transport, bicycle or legs are available. On the other hand it may have something to do with many of my customers having shares in an alternative economy, and the simple fact that there were good reasons that compelled so many of them to answer bail on a regular basis.

The first fare to this particular police station involved one of those "I'm in a hurry and stuff the consequences for your driving licence" conversations. The social miscreant, "Dean", according to my datahead, sported an ankle tag that clearly caused him no embarrassment whatever and was accompanied by a girlfriend of the "Stacey" type ("I know it won't last, you know it won't last, but we'll have a kid together then try something different.") He barked his orders peremptorily. "I'm going to Dawson's Corner nick and I'm in a fuckin' hurry. Shit – is that the time. Can you get there in ten minutes mate? O yeah – we'll be coming back again afterwards so can you wait for me?" This sense of urgency appeared not to be contagious – his female companion embarked languidly with an air of having seen it all before – probably with a number of different men. With heavy traffic and a couple of speed cameras to negotiate I did well to arrive barely five minutes after the announced deadline, and Dean disappeared into what was probably for him the equivalent of a hornets' nest assuring his girlfriend and myself that he would be out again in a couple of minutes.

Waiting time was charged at 20p per minute, and proved a mixed blessing depending on how much work was coming through the datahead. If it was difficult to come by then 20p a minute for doing nothing was not bad. But if the screen was full of jobs waiting for drivers then the hourly equivalent of £12 represented a poor return, and there was always the possibility that once this job was finally cleared all the work would have disappeared. Of course the other hazard was the small matter of communicating the need to levy this charge to people like Dean. This was scarcely a problem if it was a couple of minutes, no one would really notice the difference in fare. But a ten-minute wait involved an additional levy of £2, and this usually required some form of explanation which would in all probability be greeted with all the enthusiasm of a premier league footballer scoring the goal that won the cup only to have it disallowed by the seemingly arbitrary flag of a linesman.

The two minute deadline came and went without event, and after ten minutes the female companion, who had demonstrated her anxiety by making and receiving 'phone calls and sending text messages to friends and family alike with the dexterity of a double-jointed touch-typist, seemed suddenly to come round and express at least passing curiosity as to the fate that had befallen her man within the confines of the "nick." At fifteen minutes it occurred to her that the simple way to find out might be to darken the door of the establishment to make enquiries, so off she went in leisurely pursuit of Dean while I tried to work out how I was going to break the news of the waiting time charge. The "Stacey" emerged quickly with an air of relative indifference tinged with chagrin that she had been put to the inconvenience. 'They've nicked him, love. Turns out there's another three warrants out on him, so he's in the cells. Take me back home.'

I confess to being at a complete loss to know what I should have said to someone who had just witnessed the incarceration of a partner and was exhibiting about as much disappointment as she would in ripping up this week's losing lottery ticket. It seemed as if recording one's presence at a police station to answer bail was one of those regular hazardous pursuits like learning to ice-skate. You know you are going to fall over, it's just a question of when and how much it's going to hurt, so you might as well get on with it and deal with the consequences as they arise. Fortunately I didn't have to attempt any linguistic feat of interested concern in her lingua franca because she spent the return journey letting half the world know that "Dean's been nicked again"; I was not privy to the responses to this bland statement of fact, but had the impression that it was received on much the same level as being told the cat's been sick on the doormat. 'Oh alright luv, thanks for letting me know. Must dash, I've got a cake in the oven.'

I'd read the statistics and watched the sensationalist television programmes designed to shock us into the realisation that such a sub-culture as this can and does exist in our land, but had probably passed them off as isolated and very small pockets of anti-socialism scattered about like so many mud flats in a sea of law-abiding respectability. In actual fact I discovered an entire world of housing estates where the three-bed privately-owned post-war semi with net curtains and aspidistra were regarded with the same level of bemused incomprehension as I experienced in trying to get my head around the world of Staceys and Deans. The dominant topics of conversation were housing benefits, soap operas and ASBOs rather than stock markets, second homes and the price of petrol, and the inside of a minicab was one of the few places where the two worlds could exist side-by side with something approaching companionship rather than mutual incomprehension. Over the course of the two years I drove the population of West Yorkshire around I must have had hundreds of Stacey and Dean combinations in my car. Once I was desensitised to it such work was always interesting, entertaining even, simply because of not knowing how the real-life soap in which I was now playing a drive-on part was likely to end.

# 22

## RODLEY – TIME TO TAKE STOCK

It was that time of year when Spring finally breaks free of the shackles of Winter – even if only to succumb periodically at any point up to the end of May. April was giving notice to quit, and the air was rich with the scent of nature reasserting its immortality. Much the same was happening to my mental health. The psychological injuries I had previously sustained had given me some idea of the trauma experienced by those involved in serious road traffic accidents and unprovoked assaults. My life had never been threatened physically but my sanity had; even the odd suicidal thought had crossed my mind on more than one occasion. I had come out of the operating theatre, done my time in intensive care, and was now officially off the danger list.

Easter had passed by in a blur. This of course was nothing unusual for me, but the manner in which it had passed was, to put it mildly, unfamiliar. I had made a special effort to be in church on Easter Sunday – something I managed on most Christian Sabbaths, though rarely before the service started. But Good Friday had merited its epithet this year only in the sense that it had been exceptionally profitable, and there was something about the triumphalism of the familiar hymnody of Easter Day that seemed strangely hollow.

The period from Maundy Thursday to Easter Sunday had hitherto been a maelstrom of frenetic clerical and ecumenical hyperactivity with little or no variation in pattern for the last 20 years or more.

Thursday evening generally witnessed a respectable and insipid re-enactment of the Last Supper, with small cubes of bread and individual glasses of sweetened, non-alcoholic communion wine that assuaged the thirst of the sensitivities of traditional nonconformity rather than connecting with one of the most dramatic episodes in the gospels. The real Last Supper featured large chunks of roast lamb and an almost limitless supply of decent red plonk, and took place against the backdrop of looming disaster and certain, agonising death following the spineless betrayal of a friend. Too much of that kind of atmosphere would have been considered inappropriate, and very likely put the good churchgoing folk off their late night cheese and biscuits.

Good Friday had always provided the opportunity to do something with other local churches, the argument being that if we could not work together on the occasion on which we remembered the death of the Saviour of us all, how could we even pretend to claim a common heritage and purpose? For at least one day of the year we laid aside petty resentments over recalcitrant former members who were now part of another local flock, allowed theological disputes over the correct quantity of water to use in initiation rites to lie dormant, and almost reached the idyllic state of wanting all churches to do well. Typically this exercise in ecumenical camaraderie took the physical form of a march down the local high street. We would pass bemused onlookers exhibiting modest levels of admiration at our courage and perhaps just the tiniest trace of guilt that they were out shopping on such a sacred day; over the years the guilt seemed to diminish and the bemusement to morph into incomprehension about the whole exercise. We would walk more timidly perhaps past diverse hostelries hosting the sort of people I had always convinced myself were not having nearly as good a time as they appeared to be, and was certain that they knew nothing of the deep joy of the faithful such as I.

Everything culminated, of course, in the triumphant assertion of each Easter Sunday that "Christ is Risen, He is Risen Indeed" never again to die, the gift of God to assuage sinful mankind's guilt and provide a guarantee of eternal life to all who believe. Perhaps it was familiarity rather than a loss of faith, but it seemed to me that the power of that simple message to change lives, indeed to alter the course of human history, was largely lost in the background. Thoughts of Sunday lunch and the anticipation of plans for the Bank Holiday assumed centre stage after the second verse of "Thine be the Glory", or five minutes into a sermon reinforcing the same eternal conviction with varying degrees of certitude.

My wife and I had far too much of our lives invested in the institution that is Church to be able to stop attending on Sundays, though our children's disillusionment was to result in at best spasmodic churchgoing until they were able to process their feelings more thoroughly. We had made our spiritual home in one of the relatively few lively churches in the city where I was not a familiar face to more than two or three people. By now I was working almost every Sunday and certainly every Bank Holiday, opportunities to navigate the relatively traffic-free arteries, veins and capillaries of the city being far too good to miss. The morning service at St. Matthias was about half way through what was for me a working day and I was, and always will be, thankful for the people there who made us so welcome without asking too many questions. The fellowship provided some very comfortable mental and spiritual furniture with which to augment the somewhat battered pieces that survived our previous experience. Nevertheless I had to face the harrowing truth that along with the dismantling of my self-confidence and professional reputation my carefully constructed spiritual hermitage had also fallen around my ears, and now lay like so much rubble at my feet. I stood leaden-footed, exposed to elements that had previously battered unavailingly on the walls of my carefully constructed house of faith. Leaden-footed I might have been, but it would be erroneous to mistake lack of movement for any kind of stability. I realised just how efficiently I had worked to keep the arguments against my faith at bay using a combination of pseudo-spiritual semantics and recalling memories of the few occasions when the presence of God had seemed so palpable as to dismiss doubt as so much chaff to be blown away by the wind of a single line of a familiar chorus.

The quest to delve into my soul to look for the remains of a belief system amidst the rubble was neither an academic exercise nor a leisure pursuit. More than six months had now passed since I had relinquished a pulpit in favour of the driver's seat of a private hire car. Whether out of a sense of puritanical masochism or because I had still failed to learn my lesson I was meeting leaders of different churches to look at the possibility of returning to ministry by the autumn – a process called "settlement" in my denomination – that usually takes at least three months. There are doubtless clergy who have lost their faith in a God who has become anything other than a metaphysical image and who are still able to trot out Christian dogma quite happily with fingers crossed behind their backs; I have never been one of them, believing that St. Paul was stating the bloody obvious when he commented "If for this life only we have believed in Christ we are of all people most to be pitied." It was time to ask hard questions about how much of the faith I had spent almost all my adult life propagating I still believed.

One of the first tunnels dug under the foundation of my belief system came as I spent time reflecting on what had actually taken place in the church which I had previously led. Lulls in work during the day shift tended to come after the morning rush hour had died down and in the early afternoon, and the odd spell of enforced idleness would not infrequently provide opportunity, often unbidden, for a somewhat maudlin spell of reflection during which I would try to make sense of what had happened to me. As the months passed and the immediate trauma eased these times became more frequent. One particular question kept arising: – 'How can a Christian church behave like that?' This question twisted and turned its way through my brain like one of those computer screen displays that appear to present a particular pattern making predetermined progress backwards and forwards, up and down, till the realisation finally dawns that actually it is simply the product of a piece of computer code that generates only meaningless repetition. I was simply at a loss to understand how putative followers of Christ could indulge in such destructive behaviour, and pursue their own agenda at any cost – particularly if that cost was someone else's livelihood and reputation. How could we possibly claim to be a church and find ourselves in a situation where two sets of people were willing to go to almost any lengths to undermine the credibility and morale of the "other side?" How could they allow the church to become a place where the ruthless carnage of attrition would be maintained until they emerged triumphant on the ecclesiastical battlefield, where pillaging, looting and gloating would take the form of hypocritical prayers of concern for the dead and wounded of an enemy that had now demonstrably fallen into disfavour with the Almighty?

The answer, when it came, was as simple as it was profound, and twice as devastating to my erstwhile naïve faith. One day I simply tried to imagine that instead of this being the story of a church it was the recent history of the committee of the local golf club, and that God had nothing to do with it all. Amazingly absolutely everything fell immediately into place, and appeared with such clarity as to render superfluous any further analysis. The truth was that whatever these people had professed with their lips whilst in church the belief system they claimed devotion to had no impact whatever on their behaviour when it came to church politics. The issue was a desire for power, a need to be in charge that arose from a range of personal issues – psychological insecurity, frustrated ambition, suppression of views that challenged flimsy foundations and so on; the church was simply the particular domain in which they worked through their petty neuroses. It could have been the local sports society, working men's club or parent-teacher association; it happened to be a church where the game is identical even if the rules and language have to be adapted slightly. In a breath-taking example of doublethink they were capable of holding in their heads one set of religious beliefs whilst at the same time behaving in a way that denied their application to ordinary life, and never allowing themselves to see a contradiction between the two. Whilst not claiming to be anyone's version of St. Francis of Assisi, and acknowledging my occasional dabbling in the same game I could begin to see that a major part of the difficulty had been my desire to bring biblical teaching into the conflagration, something that many had previously worked so hard to prevent. In effect so long as I tried to bring biblical principles to bear on an institution that only used such luxuries on a theoretical level I was never likely to enjoy a great deal of success. The teachings of Jesus were for meditation, reflection, theoretical acquiescence, and to accompany sentimental liturgical ditties, not to be sullied in the grimy world of church politics. The judicious use of religious language in this conflict was carefully calculated to give an air of credibility, if not of piety, to the proceedings.

But if this was true of the church that had so summarily dispensed with my services, just how accurate was it for the rest of the Christian world, and if the practice of studiously ignoring the teaching of Christ on anything other than a theoretical level whilst running a religious institution was as endemic as I suspected, was there a church anywhere that was any different? More pointedly, how much of my previous ministry that had, by anyone's estimation, been fairly successful, was really down to the practical application of the teaching of Jesus, and how much was due to my capacity to manoeuvre other people in a way that suited my purpose? What of previous conflicts from which I had emerged in a stronger position and felt my judgments vindicated? Put simply just how much genuine faith was there in the Church, and if it was as common as a winning lottery ticket what did that say about my own belief system?

I began to think about different churches with which I was familiar from a variety of strands and traditions – liturgical churches, established churches, "swinging from the chandelier" type churches, "happy clappy" churches, liberal churches, conservative churches, radical churches – and reached the conclusion that whatever the cosmetic differences in the way things were done, they exhibited quite remarkable similarities of behaviour and outlook. I considered the people in different churches that I had led with whom I had crossed swords and inflicted minor to moderate wounds. Those who wanted to keep the pews rather than have soft chairs even though sitting through a service in one was enough to keep half a dozen chiropractors in business; those who refused to sing anything that was written later than the mid-19th century even if the words were unintelligible and the tune made the local ice-cream van sound like a well-balanced symphony orchestra; those who had been sitting in the same pew and doing the same job in the same way using the same equipment for half a century, complained about it as the cross they had to bear but steadfastly resisted any attempt to relieve them of it or apply modern technology to its execution; those who insisted on using a version of the Bible written nearly 400 years ago in a language incomprehensible to anyone under the age of 150, themselves included. What was really going on in the lives of these people and the institutions they sought to dominate? Time to face up to some real answers, because if I had decided nothing else I had determined that I was not about to re-enter clerical ministry in order either to play games or to pander to the whims of those who chose to live on a different planet once they passed through the portals of the church.

A few years ago the British churches were forcibly confronted with the news that something like 2,000 people a week were leaving, in most cases never to return. The humanist lobby gloated over this apparent loss of belief in an old man in the sky with a beard that people were now recognising as a fantasy, but in most cases these supposed apostates had not lost their faith in God, and still saw themselves as practising Christians; they were simply choosing not to do so from within the institution of a church. I had encountered several such reprobates in the course of my taxi driving life to this point; the conversation typically followed the usual pattern of asking me what else I did because I didn't much sound like a taxi driver, and on finding out I lost track of the number of times I was greeted with the response "I used to go to church." The conversation generally reached its terminus with something like "I had to leave, I just couldn't stand it anymore" or, even more devastatingly "I was losing my faith, and the only way I could stop it happening was to leave church." There was really no way of answering, particularly after hearing accounts of what had taken place in the institutions to which they had belonged, ranging from a level of megalomania that would have made Julius Caesar blush to paranoia rivalling Stalin at his most insecure.

Some of it made my own experience seem like a walk in the park. If it wasn't the power struggles that caused the mass exodus it was likely to be paranoid clergy or lay leaders whose insecurity made life unbearable. This insecurity could be either in their position or their faith – or both – but produced similar symptoms, usually manifesting itself as an almost psychotic need to be in control. This would extend to the minutiae of church life, even down to the level of deciding which brand of paper clips should be used in the office. Mondays would be spent on the 'phone berating any member who had failed to appear at a meeting for which a three-line-whip had been prescribed. Many spoke about not being permitted to think for themselves, and being squeezed into a mould from which they feared they would emerge one day set for life in a shape not of their choosing. Once the erstwhile victims of these regimes saw them for what they really were the genie was out of the bottle; any residual respect soon evaporated and they joined the ranks of those who were prepared, to mix metaphors, to face the fact that the emperor had no clothes. There were a significant number who had decided a while ago that they were more able to worship their creator and communicate with him more effectively by themselves somewhere in the wonderful countryside with which Yorkshire is replete. It was not so much that they had fallen out with their church, lost their faith, descended into the dreadful mire of apostasy from which screeching demons were dragging them into hell, but a completely rational choice that there was a better way for them to practice their faith.

It was an alarming truth to discover at first hand the extent to which Christianity and the Church had ceased to be, if they ever were, co-terminus. The extent of this anomaly was reinforced by the discovery of an entire sub-class of believers for whom church was a distant irrelevance.

What was also fascinating were the conversations I had with such folk; the revelation that I was some kind of vicar masquerading as a private hire driver would not infrequently be followed by an enquiry as to how this state of affairs came about. I adopted a policy of being quite open about this, and had the two-minute summary of my late ecclesiastical life off pat after a month or two in the job. Those with no real church background would typically respond to the story with a mixture of amazement and even horror that such things went on and express sympathy for me as the victim of it all. Those who had been, or were, members of churches, however, tended only to nod, shrug, tut, offer some brief words of condolence and change the subject – they had seen or heard it all before.

Reconstructing my faith was to take much longer than I expected, and in many ways is an ongoing process, but in those early spring months at least I made a start, even if what I learned resulted in the creation of more rubble from walls that had been laid on false foundations. My encounters with the ordinary folk of West Yorkshire were also to be an important part of the process.

# 23

## LOWER BRAMLEY – GOD BLESS

Like respectable Edwardian families, who were inclined to have them institutionalised, most of us have a relative who is embarrassing in company. The draconian options open to our ancestors are no longer available, so we have to find other means of marginalising their potential effect on respectable company. Those who plan and govern major cities are faced with a similar predicament; there are whole tracts of land that are an embarrassment, usually featuring a fairly wide, but entirely predictable array of local authority housing. These are the estates that survived the great sell-off of council housing during the Thatcher era, or failed to benefit from them, depending on one's perspective. The generally preferred means of coping with these substantial bunions is a combination of denial and disguise, the latter largely being a means of facilitating the former.

My own head was removed from the concrete desert when my neck was yanked effortlessly by the force of sheer necessity. It was simply not an option as a cab driver to avoid this reality since so much of my work took me into the kinds of urban landscape I thought had become extinct during the slum clearance programmes of the post-war era. Most of these dwellings were erected long after the Orwellian "flying aspidistra" semi in the plush suburban districts that had been the domestic staple diet of almost my entire life. My maiden foray into one of the labyrinthine, arthritic byways that wound its way through a bewildering and depressing topography was a jaw-dropping experience; how did people go about constructing anything like a decent life in these surroundings? Row upon row of once-identical buildings containing any number of dwellings, sometimes configured together like one of those wooden puzzles given as a gift on Christmas Day, dissembled, and laid aside after an hour's futile manipulation. The original uniformity of appearance was distorted only by the largely, but by no means universally, cosmetic scars, some inflicted by time and weather, others by frustrated or malevolent residents, visitors or the local criminal fraternity. The parts of the landscape set aside for what was comically called recreational use were adorned with the discarded detritus of broken-down domestic appliances and redundant technology – fridges, washing machines, video recorders, cassette players and the like that had once lured underemployed credit cards from reluctant wallets. Whilst on one level this provided plenty of hardware to function as makeshift goalposts or cricket stumps, any sporting activity would be the equivalent of a game of hopscotch in a minefield. Were there any youngsters with the inclination or courage to venture onto the putative recreational areas they would often have had to brave not only the dangers of abandoned appliances but the likelihood of coming to grief on a used hypodermic syringe.

Some of the damage suffered by homes designed to give ordinary people a decent and wholesome habitat almost beggared belief. A tiled roof once the accomplished product of a skilled artisan that had somehow been crushed from above; craters in gardens that would not have done injustice to the reputation of a decent Luftwaffe bombardier, and holes in walls that might have been inflicted by a medium-sized wrecking ball.

Homes that exhibited this sort of damage were generally unoccupied, but not all of them. Those that did not quite make the premier league of structural disarray usually housed families whose precise relationships were somewhat indeterminate; a family tree would probably look like one of those molecular diagrams with odd spherical shapes on the ends of rods protruding at grotesque angles from an amorphous core.

It was these bloated blotches on the landscape that I, like so many others, had previously been cheerfully ignorant of, that now caused me a sense of profound shame. How could such streets and blocks of housing and the people who inhabited them be so unknown to me when I had lived within a few miles of them for the last six years? Where was the Christian presence that might have made some kind of difference to the erosion of morale and hope that surely must be the by-product of being brought up and trying to secure some kind of an education in this setting? I surveyed one particular street whose principal feature was a rather large pylon, and wondered why anyone agreed to live there. Let them try to put that in a respectable private estate where house prices were steadily rising and provided one of the most popular topics of conversation, and where most residents knew at least one city councillor; the mountain of mailbags of protest from Yorkshire's 'Disgusted of Tunbridge Wells' (perhaps the 'Horrified of Harrogate') retinue would have resembled Kilimanjaro.

The simple truth is that these sordid estates are an economic and sociological necessity. The cost of rebuilding them could probably only be met by the discovery of a major oilfield in West Yorkshire, and even then the price of crude would probably need a hefty rise. Even if the money were found to level them, the units of distinct sub-culture they bred would have to be relocated, and even the most generous social commentator would be disinclined to attribute all the ills running rampant to the quality of housing stock. In truth the problems would simply follow the rehoused population, much as happened in the slum clearances in my home city of Birmingham with the creation of the Chelmsley Wood estate in the 1970s.

How much the disguising of these streets, tower blocks and houses that Picasso might have designed on a particularly eccentric day is attributable to a collective subconscious denial I would not like to guess. The policy, however, seems to be one of keeping most people at a respectable distance, far enough away from the bunions to prevent the kind of exposure that might result in significant numbers declaring "something should be done" in tones reminiscent of post-war socialist idealism. From the ring road round the west of the city, for instance, some of the estates can be seen, but not closely examined whilst travelling by car, as they are set back and hidden by more presentable architecture. The traveller may be aware that a power line supported by pylons is passing overhead and seems to go through the middle of a housing estate, but would have no real notion of the level of intrusion into the neighbourhood this creates. The filthy walls, cracked windows and vandalised community facilities are beheld only on a much closer inspection, and the truth is that this kind of scrutiny is not perceived to be in the interests of either council or commuter.

Quite early in my venture into the world of minicab driving I was directed to what I was sure must have been an incorrect address, as none of the houses looked as if they could possibly be inhabited other than by small rodents; most had windows boarded up, hardly any front lawns had seen the business end of a lawnmower for some years, and even were some kind soul to make the attempt at such a feat they would have to clear enough jetsam to fill a Cornish beach. A major excavation with an industrial digger might unearth an eclectic mixture of weeds and the odd blade of grass in the last throes of terminal illness.

The car's geriatric anti-roll system creaked arthritically as I negotiated streets adorned with prime examples of built-in obsolescence – once state-of-the-art sound systems with no current resale value and fridges with broken compressors, still proudly bearing their makers' monogram– abandoned in the street as a cheaper and less inconvenient option than arranging environmentally-friendly disposal.

Even if the address on the screen was correct, I surmised, there was surely no one living in this kind of estate who could possibly afford a taxi. Just in case there was someone around, however, I decided it might be expedient to reverse down the cul-de-sac to which I had been directed, steering carefully through the slalom course of discarded white goods and builders' rubble. The further down the narrow road I drove the more it resembled the East End of London in the blitz. Just in case I really did have a customer I entered the code on the datahead that rang the intrepid commuter to announce my arrival. I prepared to lock the car doors and prepare for as rapid a departure as the worn piston rings in the old Skoda would allow in the event of an all-out assault by the living dead who must surely be the only possible inhabitants of such a desolate landscape. It was far more likely that I would shortly be radioing Base to report a no fare.

I hadn't been waiting more than 30 seconds when with a screech of protest what appeared to be the only door still in proximity to its frame was yanked through about 30 degrees – just sufficient to allow the egress of what were surely the only survivors in the devastation that surrounded me. They made for the car with a nonchalance that recalled stories of Churchill sitting on rooftops during German air-raids and challenging the Luftwaffe to do its worst.

Overcoming the shock of the realisation that there might actually be a fare in this foray into no-man's land I wondered what kind of person might inhabit such an environment, imagining something like the human equivalent of the sewer rats of medieval Paris. The sight of an apparently normal human biped with a seemingly well-nourished infant in tow was a welcome surprise, as was the jovial "Hello luv" with which Sarah greeted me, feeling no apparent need to make any reference to or apology for the surroundings which she called home.

Sarah looked like a woman in early middle-age, but I suspect she was younger – a year or two either side of 30; slightly overweight, with a careworn face etched with the pain that was the inevitable companion of survival in her kind of world. Her light brown hair was interlaced with prematurely grey streaks and had probably not been styled for many a year, but her smile was engaging, genuine and generous; in fact she was rather attractive. Most of her clothing, from her threadbare jacket to shoes that I suspect had holes in the soles that more or less matched those in the uppers, would have failed to grace the shelves of a charity shop. Her voluminous bag, like most such receptacles, was a living example of Murphy's Law of women's fashion accessories – the amount of paraphernalia carried will always expand to fill however much space is available. Nevertheless, whatever else it contained I knew what little cash it could boast would be regarded by most people as pitifully inadequate for the acquisition of enough food to feed a family – before the taxi fare was paid – and the worn but anorexic purse would not be replete with the array of plastic most of us regard as essential to survival in the modern world. But as I was to learn Sarah was actually a fairly typical customer.

Of all the surprising facts I discovered working in minicab driving one of the earliest, and most startling, was that the bread and butter of my work would not be from the outer city suburbs taking the well-heeled middle class executive to catch his early train, or affluent families to the airport amidst an excited babble of anticipation of the fortnight in the sun that lay ahead. These jobs did exist, and provided welcome relief, as well as more substantial fares; anything in excess of £10 for a fare, with or without gratuity, was considered rich pickings in an industry where the minimum fare was about £2.50 and most were under £5. Taking the Sarahs of this world to the local shops for under £3 was, in fact, to be the work I relied on from day to day to provide a steady income. Airport runs, or trips from outer suburbs to the city centre, were little more than the jam that made the bread and butter more satisfying.

Being self-employed agents of the company, drivers were entitled to turn down any job that was offered, though this was strongly discouraged to the point of being provided with no other work for anything up to an hour afterwards. I adopted the policy from the start that I would take any job that was offered (other than picking up people I could easily identify as drug dealers), and see if the rough and the smooth together combined to provide a decent living; I never regretted doing so, though there were days when I had more than the odd doubt.

The five-minute trip with Sarah was to the local shopping precinct, which was replete with proprietors who knew that the restricted mobility of their customer base allowed them to charge inflated, and in some cases outrageous prices, and the brevity of the trip curtailed our conversation. I couldn't, however, resist the desire to find out what prompted someone so apparently normal to live in such an environment. The difficulty was in finding a way of doing so without raising her defences, insulting her or committing some sort of sub-cultural faux pas.

'Lived here for a long time?' seemed a reasonable opening gambit.

'All my life, luv. My Mom lives in the next street, and that's where I was born and brought up.'

'Ever thought of moving somewhere else?' says he who was desperate when growing up to put at least 100 miles between him and his family at the earliest possible opportunity.

'The council are building some new houses off Wyther Park Crescent. One of those might be nice.'

The epithet "Wyther Park" conjures up images of almond blossom wafting gently in the breeze whilst chaffinches swoop in from nearby meadows with the sun on their backs chirruping their glee at the beauty of a warm spring day, whereas the emphasis should really be on the "Wyther". The area known as

"The Wythers" was not infrequently used as a euphemism by the cab-driving profession for all that was most sordid and run-down, though it has to be said there were worse places to live within a couple of miles of the estate. How could the limit of such a pleasant individual's domestic ambition find its boundary at Wyther Park Crescent?

Whilst this unspoken question remained unanswered by Sarah and beyond my ability to articulate in a non-offensive manner, I silently thanked divine providence for the comfortable suburban semi to which I would later return. But something else was going on in my mind at a somewhat deeper level; the truth was that this woman did regard her existence as something like normal, was grateful for what she had and was, by and large, content with the hand fate had dealt her. Rather than complain about her house, her neighbourhood and the ever-widening gulf between herself and those with cars, computers and mortgages, she was grateful that she had a family, somewhere dry to call home and people that cared for her – four generations living within walking distance of each other and sharing together all they considered important. All in all a woman who owned less, had fewer advantages and far more limited prospects than most of the churchgoing folk of my acquaintance, and who I knew instinctively would consider church almost the last place on earth to consider worth wasting a good Sunday morning on.

We reached the shopping precinct, and I unloaded her buggy and shopping paraphernalia almost with a sense of privilege; this was not caused by the size of the fare – a little over two pounds – or the tip, which whilst modest by any standards represented a more significant sum than it would have for most – but because I realised that I had had the privilege of transporting someone who had fought the odds stacked against her and had come out on top. We exchanged smiles, her daughter and I waved goodbye, then she simply said 'Bye, luv; God bless.'

God bless? What did she mean "God bless?" Expressed with

apparent warmth and sincerity it seemed such a strange thing to say, like an echo from a far-distant land.

This wasn't the first occasion on which I had heard these words of friendly farewell; but previously when such a benediction had been offered at the conclusion of a brief foray to or from places like "The Wythers" to an area where most buildings at least enjoyed the luxury of complete roofs and intact window panes I had passed it off as a meaningless gloss on a moderately pleasant conversation. It was only over the course of time that I came to recognise it as something more, and it was perhaps this dawning awareness that put paid to what remained of a belief system previously designed to produce a ready-made answer for any encounter that challenged it. I had spent decades polishing generalities and platitudes, shaping them to provide answers to awkward questions that would easily be swallowed by anyone with a respectable measure of gullibility; sometimes I even managed to convince myself that there were no holes in the arguments. Now after a few months of relentless contact with people for whom the idea of occupying a pew in a church building rivalled a serious contemplation of a leap from Beachy Head I had become adept enough at semantic gymnastics to reconstruct my former systematic theology on something of a miniature scale. This fragile antique I kept hidden in the recesses of consciousness I had always reserved for those cherished notions I could not bear to part with, to be brought out and dusted off when the odd awkward question managed to emancipate itself from its carefully constructed stockade. Generally the strategy served me well, but encounters with the Sarahs of this world tended to generate enough honest soul-searching to compel me to examine it more closely and ask whether what I was really holding was nothing more than an item of bric-a-brac fit only to be sold off at some banal village bazaar.

This was always a perilous undertaking because of the fear

that the whole edifice of faith might crumble under serious scrutiny, and what would then be the value of this lifetime spent trying to attract people to my version of absolute truth? And if I had wasted my life what would stop me from joining the queue at Beachy Head? So long as I had a system that held enough water to irrigate my religious survival instincts I could convince myself that it had all been worthwhile. The water was sparse, and for years had had to be severely rationed and directed very carefully down irrigation channels to avoid wastage, but there had always been just enough. Each meeting with decent people like this, irreligious and impious on the one hand and seemingly on nodding terms with God on the other, punched a small hole in the aqueducts, and now the seepage was threatening that which had sustained me for almost half a century; take away my carefully nurtured seeds and Despair was the name of the crop I would be harvesting.

Fortunately the Sarah trip was followed by a whole string of more mundane jobs, and the leaks were plugged; the patching up strategy would suffice until a few months later when I switched from day to night shifts.

# 24

## BURLEY – PERSONAL FUEL SURCHARGES AND OTHER MEANS OF MAKING A BIT EXTRA

At least one section of the "notice wallpaper" with which the drivers' office was decorated was permanently devoted to the retribution likely to be visited on those who were willing to line their pockets at the expense of hapless customers. A typical example ran something like this: –

> ANY DRIVER CAUGHT OVERCHARGING WILL BE
> DISMISSED IMMEDIATELY. NO EXCEPTIONS.

These bleak pronouncements of certain and terminal retribution for miscreants almost always followed the same pattern; printed in large capital letters, accusatory, intimidating, all-inclusive and usually containing at least one error of grammar, spelling or syntax that served to encourage the moderately literate to take them with a pinch of salt. One such notice adorned the door from the area drivers were allowed in to collect keys to the main offices where they were less than welcome: –

> NO DRIVER'S ARE ALOWED PASSED THIS POINT
> UNLESS THEY HAVE PERMISON FROM THE
> MANAGMENT. NO EXCEPTIONS.
> YOU HAVE BEEN WARNED.

Some words, like "warned", "dismissed" and "exceptions" were such common verbal currency that those who typed the notices had learned the correct spelling, but someone in the office with a GCSE in English language would probably have been a worthwhile recruitment move.

Such auguries sometimes rivalled the descriptions of the plagues that befell Egypt at the behest of Moses, portending dismissal from the bosom of the company as if it were on a level equivalent to being evicted from a plane half way across the Atlantic with nothing more than a large handkerchief and a bit of string for a parachute. No shift would be complete without encountering at least three or four pronouncements of this nature, provided courtesy of another piece of rain forest or on the datahead. For the average new driver they were intimidating, but given my state of mental health at the outset of my new career they made me feel vulnerable in the same way I did when undergoing my vasectomy. Over time, however, they were to become sources of mild amusement rather than anything more sinister, and I would even experience a sense of mild disappointment had I completed a shift and not been threatened with something that felt like summary execution.

Most of these threats, if not entirely empty, were as likely to be carried through as the promises in a political party's election manifesto; containing the broad thrust of the intentions of those who ran the show possibly, but likely to represent little more than a vestige of practicality. For one thing it was technically impossible for the company to dismiss a driver since they all worked for themselves; the worst damage that could be inflicted was a refusal to allow access to company vehicles, radios and dataheads. If the management felt particularly vindictive they might make the odd 'phone call to other companies to warn them against taking on this particular individual should he materialise on their doorstep; not that that was likely to make much difference in anyone's recruiting process.

On the odd occasion when draconian action was taken and drivers were removed from the company's books by far the most common cause was because they had been trying to charge customers too much. Of all the complaints made by both customers and management against private hire drivers this is by far the most common. At a conservative estimate at least 50% of private hire drivers indulge in this practice, some to the tune of 10% and some far more. The absence of meters, of course, makes it easier to be creative about fares, and customers rarely ask to see the car's trip meter and compare it with a fare chart. In any case those who habitually overcharged invariably suffered a sudden bout of acute but temporary amnesia just at the point when they should have reset their mileage. I was frequently treated to stories of overcharging by customers keen to tell me that they knew what the fare should be and "don't try it on."

Of course on one level this practice did no direct damage to the company, but indirectly it had the capacity to cost them a great deal. In an age of diminishing brand loyalty private hire companies tend to lie in the relegation zone of the lowest division in the league. Customers who were overcharged would frequently take their business elsewhere, and a drop in the customer base led to a fall in the quantity of drivers wanting to work for the company and a consequent fall in rental income. Conversely a private hire firm that could establish even a modest reputation for employing honest drivers was likely to be on the receiving end of a steady flow of new custom from victims of previous sharp practice.

I resisted the not infrequent impulse to add a bit onto the fare of customers who made my life difficult, or as one of my colleagues put it, 'include my personal fuel surcharge.' To be truthful this was less out of any sense of moral principle and more out of a fear that once I started such a practice I would probably find it difficult to stop, and would one day find myself having to account for it on the carpet of a director's office. Perhaps the most satisfying statistic from my time in the profession is that on not a single occasion did I overcharge a customer, even on occasions when it would have been ridiculously easy to do so, or when the fare was difficult or unpleasant.

Some of the stories of passengers being overcharged made me angry, particularly when they involved elderly folk or those on a limited income who had no option other than to use cabs. Many accounts, though, were hilarious, and caused me to wonder about the place on the evolutionary scale of the brains of some of my fellow drivers. The most vital ground rule if you intended to add a few quid to the fare was to pick carefully the customers you victimised, and particularly to make sure they didn't know what the fare should be. One woman I picked up quite regularly to take to a bingo hall a little over two miles from her home had been using the same company for ten years, took a cab at least twice a week, and knew the fare to all the destinations she frequented. She told me one day that the new driver who had picked her up a week previously had tried to charge her £2 extra for a trip she made every week. She presented him with the normal fare, and added to it a mouthful of choice verbal abuse and a whack with her not insubstantial bag, reported the incident to the company and asked not to have that driver again.

One of the more jaw-dropping attempts at overcharging I heard about was during a night shift towards the end of my time in the business. I was fortunate enough to pick up the manager of one of Leeds's manifold nightclubs catering for the student market at the time of night when work is quite hard to find. It was a good fare – out beyond the boundaries of the city, and worth a good £12, but reachable in no more than fifteen minutes at that time of night courtesy of the M621. Not only was it a decent fare, but the customer was sober, engaging and interesting – attributes that were all at a premium after midnight – with a wealth of entertaining anecdotes. It was the kind of job you really appreciate in the middle of a quiet night shift. He paid happily, added a small gratuity in appreciation of my promptness, making it even more worthwhile, and then told me about his previous driver, whose stupidity really beggars belief. Having completed the same trip he announced the fare as £26; he had picked on the wrong customer. Instead of arguing about the fare he told the driver to hold on a minute and called the company office on his mobile 'phone. Having been put through to the night manager he simply asked why it was that for a journey he made two or three times a week at a cost of about £12 his current driver had asked him for more than double that sum. The manager promptly asked to speak to the driver, told him not to collect a fare, and return to Base immediately. The customer had a free ride, and the driver lost both his fare and his livelihood.

I had no sympathy with him whatever – or others like him; not only was he giving the rest of us a bad name he succeeded in exhibiting amazing stupidity in his choice of stooge. It also made life for the honest drivers more difficult. Almost every customer I collected had at least one story of extortion at the hands of a private hire driver they wished to divest themselves of, and I always knew that the subtext of such conversations was either a plea not to rip them off or a threat of non-payment should I try. The announcement of an intended destination was not infrequently the prequel to an intimidating 'and I know how much the fare is' or, more plaintively, 'it's not going to cost more than £10 is it?' Confirmation that they would not be overcharged was often greeted with the cautious relief of the semi-reassured and a horror tale from a previous experience of calling a minicab. Frequently this narrative related to one of the ubiquitous 10-cars-or-less outfits the owners of which were likely only to attract more unscrupulous drivers and who adopted a policy of non-regulation of fares. In the long run this method of operating a business simply represented another means by which the big fish gradually swallowed up the minicab mackerel of West Yorkshire.

There were two directors of the company I worked for in the early days – both of whom I got on well with on the odd occasions our paths crossed. I found them straightforward in that they offered no pretence of altruism; they were in the business of making as much money as possible for themselves, and were completely up-front about it. Anything that promoted this cause was welcomed and any driver whose actions cost them money was liable to experience their wrath. Drivers caught persistently overcharging were definitely in the "bad for business" category, and were likely to be on the receiving end of a severe bollocking. One of the more notorious legends concerned the director who adopted the "Bad Cop" persona mentioned earlier. The story goes that he summoned six or seven members of an informal price-fixing driver cartel, whose creative fare structure was legendary, into his office. Having given them barely seconds to explain themselves he announced their summary expulsion from the bosom of the company. The leader of the miscreant band had the rank stupidity to threaten legal action for racial discrimination and had not even had time to pause for breath before he and his colleagues found themselves summarily driven from the premises in a scene putatively reminiscent of Christ's eviction of the moneychangers from the temple courts. Any similarity with the Saviour of Mankind was, of course, at best coincidental. As far as I know there never was any legal action, but even had there been those who ran the show had long since recognised that retaining and cultivating relationships with highly competent professionals such as lawyers and accountants more than repaid the effort and expense involved.

Like most personal accounts of economic exploitation there were often two sides to a story, and it was not infrequently the case that awkward customers brought misfortune on themselves through negligence, lack of forethought or even sheer stupidity. For the driver a scheduled pick-up of 3.00 p.m. meant three o'clock rather than five or ten minutes past, and if we were there punctually it was not unreasonable to expect the customer to be ready for the time they had booked the cab, or else to pay waiting time. Most of us were prepared to allow a little latitude, particularly if the journey was a decent distance, but a ten minute wait for a five minute journey was unlikely to benefit from a waiving of these costs. Customers did not always appreciate that in the time they had kept a driver waiting he could have completed another job; in fact it sometimes felt as if some of our clientele believed that taxi drivers, unlike other homo sapiens, were charged only half price at supermarkets and department stores and received free utilities. This was one of a number of similarities between this and my former profession.

Memories of jobs that caused friction with customers over fares are numerous, some amusing and some yet retaining the capacity to bring an unpleasant taste to the mouth. Early one very busy April morning I was summoned to the address of a Mr. Forsyth to transport him the short distance to the railway station, a journey that would normally incur a fare of about £3.50. Arriving while it was still dark some five minutes before the appointed pick-up time to ensure he would not be late for his train I could observe him and his wife through the un-curtained front bay windows preparing to leave. Rushing around to very little obvious effect like a pair of demented hamsters in a cage full of exercise wheels something like fifteen minutes elapsed; it was now ten minutes after we were scheduled to leave and there was still last-minute packing to perform; five minutes later Mr. Forsyth emerged from the house to signal to me to wait as he would not be long. I seethed with impatience; my screen was full of work waiting to be done, much of which was probably significantly more lucrative.

Twenty minutes after we should have left, and now running the risk of missing the train the hapless duo emerged from the house complete with suitcases, small rucksacks and various items of miscellaneous outerwear that would probably have catered for any climate from the Kalahari Desert to Siberia. Luggage duly stuffed into the boot Mrs. Forsyth then remembered that she had "forgotten something", and upon her return Mr. Forsyth thought he ought just to run in and make sure the back door was locked before they went on holiday.

The Forsythian compulsive-obsessive disorder having been temporarily quelled we were able to set off; of course by now Mr. Forsyth had realised that it would be touch and go whether we reached the station on time. 'I think we're a bit late, driver. I know there are speed cameras on this road, but can you really put your foot down or we will miss our train.' With an apparent abdication of responsibility for the plight he and his wife had brought upon themselves he clearly hoped that the train company would not choose this particular day to run their trains on time, that those who examined the evidence in the speed cameras would understand the predicament, and that I would be willing to risk my licence in the interests of seeing him safely off on holiday. Hurtling along at a rate slightly faster than I really dared, partly out of exasperation and partly out of a desire to prevent the possibility of this particular customer missing his train and requiring a cab in the opposite direction, further despair materialised courtesy of the realisation dawning from the back seat that they did not have the means to pay me when we arrived. 'O, sorry, could you stop at a cash point on the way please, driver?' Screeching to a halt briefly before tearing away with cash accrued Mrs. Forsyth appeared to be in a world of her own, oblivious to everything but the condition of the varnish on the nail at the end of the middle finger of her left hand.

Miraculously we reached the station in enough time at least to give them a sporting chance of reaching the train if it was only five minutes late, so long as they had the pace of an Olympic 100 metre sprinter. There still seemed to be a chance as I single-handedly removed the carousel-sized complement of luggage from the boot; until, that was, Mr. Forsyth proffered a £5 note and with the condescending tone of a Victorian philanthropist advised me to keep the change.

'Sorry, mate,' I duly advised him, the fare is £7.50.

'But I do this journey all the time, and it's never more than £3.70', protested the flustered Mr. Forsyth. '

'I'm sure you do, but you were 20 minutes late, and then we had to stop at a cash point machine on the way', I responded. 'You can't charge me for that, we were just finishing our packing', protested the hapless traveller. 'Sorry, mate, it's 20 p per minute waiting time, and your fare comes to £7.50.'

Whether it was the indifference of Mrs. Forsyth, who had now at least extracted her not inconsiderable form from the vehicle and was busying herself with the important task of adjusting her high-heeled shoes, the imminent departure of their means of transport, or (less likely) the reasonableness of the argument that prompted the agonised extraction of a further £2.50 from the vault of his jacket pocket, I can't be sure. Perhaps I should have offered a small discount for the somewhat entertaining sight of Mr. Forsyth propelling his wife's substantial frame through the station entrance with as much grace as Mr. Blobby on stilts. I returned to the driver's seat and made a rapid exit just in case the Forsyth's remembered something else.

# 25

## SWINNOW – NIGHT SHIFTS

The first anniversary of my departure from the world of clerical gentility and pseudo-spiritual thuggery was almost upon me. The tentative plan for me to move back into full-time church work whilst my wife stayed for a year in the Leeds area with children completing their GCSEs and A-levels had foundered on the rocks of simply not wanting to live our lives apart for such a length of time. It took the leaders of a particularly interesting and attractive church to make us realise this in saying how much they liked us, but could not see how we would survive for twelve months living separately for most of the time. I hated them for it, but reflecting back some time later we both realised they had understood the situation better than we had.

So another year of cab driving beckoned, not that I approached it with any sense of dread. A local church was looking for part-time ministry for which they were willing to provide a house the size of a small chateau set in its own grounds, and a modest salary. This was a wonderful treat for us, being able to sever the last ties with our former church by moving out of the house we jointly owned and settling in the wonderful urban village of Farsley. It may be fanciful, but it felt as if heaven was providing us with the perfect setting for our final year with all four children at home. Each child was able to have their own separate room (by this time one was working and one was studying at Durham university during term-time) and since the house was set in its own grounds our younger son was able to play his drum kit along with recordings from his favourite band, Iron Maiden, which he had assured us was an ensemble with an extremely varied repertoire of slow, lilting airs played pianissimo.

It was with a mild sense of anxiety that I gave up my 24/7 car in order to reduce my hours to three twelve-hour stints a week as I took my first tentative steps back into what was now the decidedly odd world of Christian ministry. I became a shift driver once again, and almost on a whim responded to a suggestion from my wife that I try a night shift since I seemed to get by on so little sleep and there was a lot less traffic around then. Since my wife is almost invariably right about such things I decided tentatively to give it a go, and soon discovered another world opening up that at times bore little relation to the daytime experience. My previous Friday and Saturday night shifts were preparation to some extent, but I chose to work Sunday, Monday and Tuesday each week as a general rule. I never had cause to regret the switch; these shifts were almost always entertaining, and sometimes a veritable education.

With almost a year's experience under my belt I thought I knew my way around pretty well, but whereas day shifts had involved taking people to and from work, shops and health centres, these rather run-of-the-mill venues were far less likely to be frequented in the wee small hours. Only a few venues were held in common, and this was true also of Friday / Saturday nights compared to weekdays; in fact it was something of a surprise to discover that each night shift seemed to have its own particular pattern. There was always something different round the corner, and in spite of now being considered something of a veteran in the business, I was still capable of being surprised by some of the more extraordinary behaviour I witnessed.

I think it was a Tuesday evening a little before midnight that I was called to a pick-up from a respectable bar in the more salubrious end of town, and Sandra emerged to occupy the front seat of the cab. Sandra was one of those women whose age is almost indeterminate – could have been in her twenties or her forties, slightly overweight, with nondescript hair of a vaguely blonde hue and modest make-up that looked like it had been applied in something of a hurry without the benefit of a mirror.

But two things were immediately obvious about her; firstly she had had a little too much to drink, and secondly she was cross – and cross in spades. 'We're going to Swinnow, love', she remarked in a tone that made it clear that her ire was directed at some individual other than myself. 'But we've got to pick up my old man first.'

The 'old man' was, for some unarticulated reason, in a bar at the other end of the city centre, a venue noted for its association with the seedier side of life. Fights were almost nightly occurrences, and illegal substances were available for a modest price. Sexual favours were also on sale for a reasonable consideration, but the chances were you could just pick someone up for a night's bedroom gymnastics so long as you weren't too fussy.

I decided the safe thing to do was not to try to make conversation, and in any case she was soon on her 'phone calling the recalcitrant partner so that he would be outside waiting for us. I could identify the equally inebriated individual from the sheepish look on his face and the sense of foreboding at the unpleasantness to come written on his features and in his posture.

No sooner had he climbed into the back of the car than it started. The first volley of verbal musket-shot directed from the front passenger seat had no sooner made its mark than an answering tirade of alcohol-fuelled abuse flew in the opposite direction. I never was able to work out what the row was about, but with the possible exception of performances in the kindergarten we call the House of Commons I don't think I have ever witnessed quite such an amazing episode of two people shouting at each other at the tops of their voices without hearing a single word the other was saying.

I managed, during a brief pause for reloading of weapons, to extract the address for which we were heading and set off with a certain amount of apprehension on the fifteen-minute journey, fearful that the verbal exchanges would graduate into a fist-fight with all the risks that would entail. Once we were on our way the war of words resumed with renewed vigour, and I decided to hope for the best and drive slightly faster than normal.

The route out of Leeds city centre took us on an inner ring road which, for reasons I never really understood, was classified as the M64, so the rules of motorway driving applied. The volume and level of abuse steadily increased until their vocabulary of profanities seemed to be exhausted. Where to go from here? It was around this point that the gentleman in the rear of the car hit upon the novel idea of "upping the ante" by opening the window and, with a casualness clearly calculated to engender reciprocal incandescence, tossed his phone out of the window. The effect on the woman was to spark an eruption the equivalent of Vesuvius in full flow. It became clear that the 'phone had been a costly present from a happier era in their relationship, and he had just demonstrated, in the most dramatic way he could imagine, in just how little regard he held her.

If you can imagine a human earthquake and volcano all rolled into one you will have some idea of what happened next. Removing her seat belt she erupted in a rearwards direction preceded by a torrent of language that would have caused a navvy something more than slight embarrassment. Fortunately I was able to keep the car in a straight line and shout loudly enough to read the proverbial riot act to them both. The fighting subsided almost immediately, though the verbal exchanges remained just as vitriolic.

After a couple of minutes the man asked if we could go

back to pick the 'phone up, and I was thankful to be able to explain that this would involve breaking the law, as well as being exceedingly dangerous. An expensive lesson, but perhaps one they both needed to learn.

After that it became far less exciting. Whether it was the soporific effects of the alcohol they had both consumed, whether they had forgotten what it was they were supposed to be arguing about, or simply that the arsenals of abuse were exhausted I'm not sure; I do know that for some couples regular fights – verbal or physical or both – provide the cement that holds the relationship together, and perhaps this was an example. In any case the verbal volcano subsided and general sulkiness – a tactic I am far more familiar with, being one of the nation's leading experts – took over. There was even a certain meekness apparent by the time we reached their home. She stomped off, making abundantly clear whose responsibility the taxi fare was, and in what now felt like an oasis of tranquillity we had a short conversation: –

'Do you ever have that kind of row with your missus?'
'No, not really.' (mainly thanks to the longsuffering of my wife we have a row about once a year just to keep our hand in) 'We've been happily married for 28 years.'
'So what's the secret?'
'Apart from being married to the most incredibly wonderful woman in the world, perhaps also that we're Christians.'
'Do you think that makes a difference?'
'I think so.'

I recommended a local church I knew that would be perfect for them both, he thanked me and went his way. I have no idea what happened to them both, but this kind of informal way of sharing my faith was pretty common, and I often wonder if over the course of those two years I contributed more to the Kingdom of

God than at any other time in my life.

It is not altogether accurate to describe the hours I worked as a night shift; some drivers liked to start at around six in the evening and work through till the day shift came on some twelve hours later. But there were usually cars available once the school runs were complete on Mondays and Tuesdays – sometimes earlier, though Sunday afternoons could involve a short wait for a returning day shift driver. I always liked to start as soon after three as possible. Although this meant bearing the full brunt of the evening rush hour for two of my three shifts there was also plenty of work, and often by the time most families were finishing their evening meal I had covered my costs and was starting to "work for myself", thus taking much of the pressure off the remainder of the shift. I aimed to make enough money by a little after 2 a.m., be in bed before 4 a.m., and up again by mid-morning.

The Sunday night shift very soon became my favourite time of the week to drive a private hire car. Perhaps it was partly because I was accustomed to this being a busy working day, and my clerical responsibilities now only required my presence before lunch. Undoubtedly it was in part because there was no rush hour to endure, but I think I enjoyed it most because of the combination of the routine and the unexpected it offered. In the course of a Sunday night shift I would usually encounter some familiar faces driving some very familiar routes, whilst later on almost anything could come my way, particularly once the buses stopped running.

Sunday night, for some reason I could never altogether fathom, seemed to be the time when a significant proportion of West Leeds conducted their weekly pilgrimage to their "club." This term should not be confused with its equivalent in Pall Mall or Soho – they were the sort of venue frequented neither by the plutocrat nor the hedonist in pursuit of sexual gratification. The legend on the outside of the building might betray its origins but was generally unlikely to reflect the socio-economic nature of its clientele. Thus, for example, there was steady trade to the clubs with putative political allegiance – Conservative or Liberal, and often the former were in areas where it was difficult to imagine anyone casting a vote for the blue party. Working Men's clubs were frequented by families from all walks of life and were almost indistinguishable on the inside from the Conservative and Liberal versions.

Another category of "club" was one associated with a particular industry or trade; in particular there were establishments associated with the railways, located in places that looked as if tracks once ran through the area before the savagery of the Beeching cuts, but those who went had little or no connection with the modern rail industry.

What all these establishments seemed to have in common was reasonably-priced alcohol, and decent companionship with friends who had known each other most of their lives and with whom they spent Sunday evenings either putting the world straight (an exercise that seemed so much simpler after a few beers) or discussing the latest developments in the Soaps. I had the impression that many of the folk I took to or from these social clubs had been using a cab to travel to and from their favourite watering-hole at precisely the same time for decades, and would continue to do so until they finally shuffled off the mortal coil probably ten minutes after returning from a Sunday night out.

But there was something very civilised about seeing the same faces on the same journeys and having similar conversations each time I drove them – not infrequently about the driver who took them the previous week and tried to overcharge them for a journey they had made for half their lifetime. I came to respect this urban yeomanry a great deal – the kind of people who accept the reality of living on a limited income, budget carefully and decline to live beyond their modest means. These are the people who make it possible for a largely law-abiding community to function in the face of a fair amount of factors that mitigate in favour of anarchy, and it seemed that a Sunday evening at the club was their weekly treat.

So the first half of a night shift was generally quite predictable on Sunday or a weekday, picking people up from school, work, shops, sports venues, taking them to clubs, the cinema, the theatre, restaurants or to and from visits to family with children in tow. It was really around ten o'clock that the fun began, for this was the time that the students would emerge from a hard day in the library or the bar depending on their level of diligence.

# 26

## KIRKSTALL – STUDENTS

Leeds is a city with a significant but incredibly varied student population, some of whom move there in order to achieve a first degree and some of whom regard this objective as an optional but by no means essential by-product of their first time away from home. The division is, to some extent, dependent on which university is attended, one being of the old-fashioned sort with a strong traditional academic base and the other being a former Polytechnic, a scenario played out in many British cities since "Polytechnics" were allowed to rename themselves as "Universities." Of course it would be a gross oversimplification to label all students of one as academic underachievers out to have a good time and little more, and the others as serious, conscientious and clean-living young people seeking only academic excellence, but in broad terms my experience certainly suggested that such a distinction could be made to some extent; at least that was the case when it came to using private hire cars.

Students were one of those groups of people I expected to see on bicycles, jogging to lectures or waiting at bus stops at respectable hours of the day if they were going out to socialise, rather than 'phoning for a cab. Perhaps this image was cultivated by all those episodes of Morse, featuring an Oxford where even the professors meandered between the dreamy spires perched precariously on contraptions masquerading as bicycles that looked as if they had been handed down from father to son for the last six generations. Maybe the hilly terrain of West Yorkshire didn't really lend itself to any form of self-propelled transport, but I recall seeing very few bikes around the city, even on the university campuses.

Surprisingly the use of private hire cars to travel around the city made rather a lot of sense. A return cab fare from halls of residence to the city centre might be somewhere between £10 and £13, but if shared four ways would be more economical than the bus, and usually more reliable.

I was fortunate in my choice of companies to work for, because my outfit was the one recommended by the universities and the only one with unfettered access to all the halls of residence. Whilst there were a few horror stories told about cabbies who were optimistically lecherous, greedy or both, by and large I worked for what was a trusted, reliable and economical brand. We even had an agreement that a student who was stranded in the city centre without cash could travel home in a cab, leave their student union card as security with the driver, and pay the fare the next day. All of which meant that on night shifts in particular student work was plentiful.

My favourite journeys were from a halls of residence complex labelled "The Brewery" – a place where the eponymous "piss-up" was successfully arranged in dozens of locations on a daily basis. I gather the building was once home to a famous beer manufacturer, but whether it was this dubious heritage or a sense of irony that justified the epithet at the design stage is now a matter of conjecture. In any case, and predictably, there was never a shortage of new students heading for the hallowed cloisters of Leeds Metropolitan University (the Polytechnic as was) who opted to make "The Brewery" their home. One of the perks of being the cab company of choice for LMU was that the apartment complex was a sealed unit, and we were the only drivers of minicabs allowed to enter by the security guards who, strangely enough, seemed relatively efficient.

Some weeks into the night shift leg of my time in the business I discovered that once students were accepted by the university they were sent, among other things, a questionnaire about what sort of accommodation they might like for their first year; most moved into private accommodation if they survived the first year exams and went on to complete their course. The various halls of residence were graded in terms of quietness, much as holidays in Spain might be graded from the secluded beauty spot designed for families with small children to the all-action world where drinking and entertainment of a morally dubious character would last all night. In terms of this scale The Brewery was anchored securely to the hedonistic, Club 18-30 extreme, which made for some wonderfully entertaining trips of about four miles between the apartment complex and the city centre.

The waking day of The Brewery was in a kind of time-warp, and on one level was a little 24-hour city cordoned off from the rest of the world. I had visited before I started nights on several occasions, often at the start of a day shift when students who had had an especially long night were returning after 5.00 a.m. The first time I did the trip at this time of day I tried to drive slowly enough for the car's arthritic joints not to make enough noise to disturb the peaceful repose of the sleepy residents who were doubtless dreaming of a day crammed full of lectures, private study and essay-writing. In actual fact the geriatric rattles of my old Skoda were totally drowned in the cacophony emanating from the scores of parties that had begun the previous night and if not still in full swing were barely beginning to pay any attention to the sky gradually lightening from the east. The tax-payer and father of students in me resented the waste of an educational opportunity, whilst the ageing man was forced to admit how envious he was now that such stamina was well beyond his reach. Increasingly I was inclined to the view that everyone has one life to live on earth and how we spend it is our own affair.

I enjoyed many surreal experiences as a night shift driver in relation to student residences, but one of the more comical was undoubtedly the ritual of speaking to my wife each evening somewhere between ten and ten-thirty, when more often than not I was driving to or from The Brewery. One of the practices we have adopted, to the amusement if not incomprehension of many, and to "oohs" and "aahs" from the more sentimentally inclined, is to speak to each other every night if for one reason or another we are apart, usually around bedtime. My wife's bedtime almost invariably coincided with the time of night the students were about to go out to the clubs and bars of central Leeds, and calls took place in transit between student residences and the fleshpots of the big city. Whilst my headset kept my hands free and one end of the conversation private, of course my end was public property. So there I would be, wishing my wife a good night's sleep and sweet dreams and telling her I loved her (another daily ritual) whilst for the customers the night had only just begun.

This exchange gave rise to some interesting conversations about everything from faith to sex and marriage, particularly with the girls. In ascending order of how difficult things I said were to believe it went something like this; that I was a former clergyman who still believed in a God you could talk to and have a relationship with was just about credible. This was especially so if the evening had begun an hour or two previously in the student residence bar, where the drinks were much cheaper than in town, leading to many students becoming somewhat lubricated before venturing out. That I had been happily married to the same woman for the best part of 30 years and was still so absolutely in love with her that I could never imagine being with someone else was pushing credibility up to, and perhaps slightly beyond the limit. That I had only ever had one sexual partner and only intended ever to have one was on the level of asking them to believe in fairies at the bottom of the garden, and that I firmly believed that developing a sexual relationship with one person was far more satisfying than sleeping around was sufficient to have me committed to the Funny Farm. Nevertheless countless conversations with female students finished with something akin to "Ahhh, how sweet." After that I tended to be regarded as a somewhat avuncular figure to whom all sorts of confidences would be entrusted; this in turn brought out in me the instinct of a parent with children of similar age, and most trips into town ended with my admonition to my charges to "stay safe."

Student work wasn't confined to nights of revelry and sexual opportunism, of course. There were countless jobs during the day transporting the next generation of the intellectual elite to or from lectures, exams, sports fixtures, and transit centres at either end of term for the journey to or from home. The diurnal student jobs were some of the most enjoyable work for me; the students were generally sober, chatty and interesting. I was always fascinated to know where they were from, what they were studying and what their interests were. My own son was at university in Durham at this point, which almost invariably impressed my young passengers. "Oh God – he must be clever to get in there" was the typical response, which always made me feel proud. We would discuss the place the students came from, the subject they were studying if I knew anything about it, and what was a job of work would almost inevitably become a pleasure.

Just occasionally I had to bite my tongue and be diplomatic with the student population; I had thought young people went to university to study proper subjects like Maths, Physics, History, Geography, Philosophy and Modern Languages. I will never forget the first time I was entrusted with the revelation that the undergraduate occupying the front seat of my cab was reading "Events Management." I didn't like to be rude, but couldn't help wondering how on earth such a subject could be something that someone studied as an academic discipline. The conversation went a bit dry as I tried manfully to think of something intelligent to ask about a course in "Events Management" that would not cause this aspiring organiser of Rolling Stones concerts to feel patronised, but drew a blank. So my mind wandered and I began to ask myself how many managers of events the nation could usefully employ; might there be as many as a dozen people who had set out on this course of intellectual improvement, I wondered?

When some five or six weeks later I realised I must have transported at least a score of readers of Events Management to or from one of the centres of academic excellence where worthy purveyors of this discipline entrusted their pearls to the eager youths in their care I began to understand the scale on which it operated.

I never tried to be an academic or intellectual snob – my BA in theology from a government-sponsored organisation set up to award degrees to small academic institutions they didn't quite know what to do with hardly gave me grounds for that – but I did start to speculate about what would happen to all these eager young adults who were learning how to organise the population of the United Kingdom so as to ensure their safety and enhance their enjoyment at any event they chose to attend. I wondered whether in order to satisfy the need to find jobs for them all once they graduated there would have to be some kind of National Service imposed on the population by means of which every UK resident would be obliged to spend at least two weeks a year at an "Event" that was managed by a specialist in the subject.

Not that Events Management was the only academic discipline that caused the elevation of the eyebrows or the quiet chuckle; disciplines such as "Tourism", "Sports Psychology" and "Public Relations" were also much in vogue amongst the young people who so helpfully provided such a significant percentage of my work.

Eventually I found a line of enquiry that satisfied both my scepticism about the idea of studying such subjects and the integrity of the students. "How did you come to take an interest in that subject?" generally elicited a response that told me all I needed to know. Occasionally I would discover that the young person really did want to spend their working life learning how safely and efficiently to herd human beings into disparate venues to enjoy the feast of cultural delights that had been prepared for them. But in the vast majority of cases the simple truth was that they had chosen the subject because they really didn't know what else they wanted to do. In many cases they had not performed very well at A-Level and there were usually enough spare places on these courses to take those who had achieved modest results or who went through the "Clearing" process. This latter group then divided into two further sub-sets – those who had tried their best but were not very bright, or were perhaps let down by poor teaching, and those who simply wanted to go away to university to enjoy three years of independence from home and have a thoroughly good time of it, needing only the fig leaf in the form of academic advancement as a pretext to justify their prodigality.

# 27

## HEADINGLEY – THE WORLD OF CASINOS AND BINGO HALLS

My first introduction to the sub-culture of the three casinos that operated in central Leeds at that time was as a day shift driver, with the 5.20 a.m. lottery of "Napoleon's". This always seemed to me a particularly apposite name for an establishment whose driving forces were greed, acquisitiveness and the exploitation of ordinary people's vulnerability. On a day shift the first task was to provide life support for my cab at the petrol station so that it was no longer running on fumes. The second was to see how many cars were waiting for work in the plot covering an area replete with hotels, clubs, lap-dancing establishments, the main railway terminus and Napoleon's. If there were fewer than six it was worth heading there with all possible speed, slowing only for the speed cameras on Tong Road, to try to pick up a job taking the casino staff home after their night's work. Because buses were not operating this early the casino block booked a number of cars for their staff, and each one would be allocated a reference number. When the staff came out each driver would call out his number, and the relevant passengers would climb in. Some of these jobs did not pay particularly well, just a couple of drop-offs to local areas, but some went well outside the limits of the city, and would provide a very satisfactory start to the day's work. Of course the lottery element involved in allocating work of varying value fuelled the ubiquitous paranoia of the drivers about who had scooped the best paid jobs, but in reality it was probably completely random – whoever was dispatching cars had far better things to do than see who was driving each vehicle and then make an assessment of how much favour to bestow on whom. I had my fair share of "shite" and more lucrative trips, for which, perhaps poignantly, there seemed to be a dearth of adjectives in the cab driver's thesaurus.

Night shifts were different, though, because jobs almost invariably involved taking customers home rather than staff, and by the time I had completed a hundred or more jobs from the casinos to various residences I had a pretty good idea of the sort of clientele they attracted and the kind of losses people would sustain during an average visit.

The first question, naturally, that one would ask once a fare was on board was how successful their evening had been. It may, of course, have been part of a general ploy to be as meagre with fare and gratuity as possible, but of all the people I ever picked up from a casino I only recall a handful who claimed to have had a good evening and made anything like a profit on the night's venture; almost inevitably the tale was one of frustration, disappointment, woe and even anger.

Many losses were, of course, quite modest, and provided good value for money in terms of a night's entertainment; these customers took their losses with a mixture of good humour and Stoicism. But there seemed to be an equal number that were of an altogether different nature, who brought into the cab an atmosphere of anger and resentment. At times almost palpable, it was sometimes focussed on the management or staff of the casino, but more frequently it was directed inwards, at their own stupidity and lack of self-control. Many of the journeys from one of these establishments were almost literally down the road to an area of the city where few people would choose to live unless they were martial arts experts or else armed to the teeth. Some gentle probing not infrequently revealed that many such customers earned enough money to rent or buy property in a much less volatile neighbourhood, but their gambling addiction consumed a significant percentage of their disposable income, as well as demanding proximity to the means of gratifying it.

There were also some comical stories of trips from casinos; there was a student who, at the start of term, and with a bank balance loaded with several thousands of pounds to pay for the cost of a term's lodging, food, books and general spending, had gone into the casino on a Monday evening. By the time I collected him in the early hours, he had managed to strip his bank balance naked – though thankfully still kept enough petty cash in hand to pay his fare. On enquiring what he would do now he had no money he replied that he would think about that in the morning, but seemed unruffled and Micawber-like at the predicament in which he had landed himself.

The star prize in this category undoubtedly goes to the middle-aged oriental couple I picked up around 1.00 a.m. who directed me to return them home to Harrogate – a nice job worth around £25 that, given a fair wind, could be completed at that time of night with a return to Leeds in around 40 minutes. Their English was perhaps only one stage up the evolutionary scale of articulation from the proverbial pigeon, but they were sober, pleasant, and clearly well-to-do. It transpired that they owned a restaurant in Harrogate which made for them a very nice living, and the weekly trip to the casino was one of the pleasures of life they allowed themselves to offset the long hours and stress that are an inevitable and prominent feature of such a trade. This particular evening they had been especially profligate, and had spent all the money they had taken with them, trying to recoup losses with ever larger bets and with entirely predictable results.

The journey as far as the outskirts of Harrogate was spent, as far as I could discern from the fragments of conversation in English, berating themselves for their lack of self-control and wastefulness, and at their age they really should know better, and would I mind waiting when we arrived at their home while they went in to find some money with which to pay their fare. Then it went quiet for a while, before a fresh line of dialogue opened up to which I was not at all party but sounded more positive and hopeful; they seemed to reach agreement on some decision as we arrived at their front door, where I was told there had been a slight change of plan, and would I wait whilst they went in to get some more money and then take them back to the casino? Of course had I been a responsible member of the clerical profession I would have urged them to stay at home, nurse their wounds and learn the error of their ways, but I was rather attracted by the fare for the return journey, and if they were stupid enough and all that... So I offered them a special reduced rate on the grounds that I had to drive most of the way back to pick up work anyway, thus making them even more upbeat and even salving my conscience just a little. I have often wondered since how they did at the tables they challenged to a rematch, but suspect the return leg of the fixture ended in a not dissimilar result.

You might be tempted to think that compared to the heady world of televised professional poker, and the gambling of large sums of money at the serious casinos of a major city, the humble bingo hall on the edges of the densely-populated council estate would be strictly minor league; you would also quite probably be mistaken.

There were a vast array of bingo establishments operating in the city; whilst it is true that some were generally akin to the amusement centre on the traditional British seaside pier where quite manageable sums were generally lost and occasionally won and the atmosphere social and convivial there were also the big chains. These counted their assets in hundreds of millions and their profits by perhaps moving the decimal point one numeral to the left. The establishment that generated most revenue for the private hire profession was just off the Leeds Ring Road and sandwiched between two huge housing estates rising up on either side. For some of the punters their weekly, twice-weekly or in some cases daily trip to the establishment bore some resemblance to worshippers making their way to a shrine where they hoped to receive the favour of the gods of fortune. The possibility of a minor goddess looking on in benevolence would be enhanced by various quasi-religious rituals, from the use of "lucky bingo markers" or mascots in the form of small furry toys to repeated habits such as wearing the same clothes and sitting in the same seat that they had occupied the last time the deities of caprice had selected them as objects worthy of grace.

Typically there were two major bingo sessions, one in the afternoon and one in the evening. The thirty minutes or so during which the faithful would travel to the shrine were happy hours (or perhaps happy half hours) for us; almost all the journeys would be minimum fare jobs, but an experienced driver could rattle through several in a short period. Because the journey was so short it was possible to clear yourself for work the moment a passenger entered the car, because five minutes or so would be all it would take to transport the customer to the bingo centre and arrive at the next customer's house, when the exercise would be repeated and in a short time a very healthy sum would be generated.

What astonished me when I discovered it, though, was the quantity of money that was gambled during the course of an afternoon. I began by thinking I was taking some middle-aged ladies (and the occasional gentleman) for bit of fun and relaxation with the possibility of winning a few pounds but no great harm done, whereas in fact the stakes could be massive. True some of the customers did spend barely a few pounds, having only one bingo card and playing maybe seven or eight games, but there were those for whom this was a real addiction. In the most extreme cases three or four cards would be operated throughout the session by those who had learned to search out numbers and close them with the dexterity of a multi-limbed oriental goddess. This would be followed by feeding a fruit machine to bursting point in the generally vain hope of some kind of return. Because particular outlets were linked to others run by the same chain across the country there were times when the potential winnings ran into several thousands of pounds, luring the punters into committing more and more cash to the venture in the hope of scooping the big prize. It was not uncommon to drop people off after a session at houses in areas most folk would choose to live in only if a cardboard box in a shop doorway in the city centre were the only alternative, and hear that they had lost fifty, sixty or even seventy pounds.

The addiction was fed by memories of a time when they experienced a run of good luck, or even scooped a Snowball or something similar. Whilst the casinos seemed more efficient at extracting every last penny out of customers than the bingo halls, it was not unusual to feel a lot of pity for folk who were addicted to this supposedly more respectable form of gambling. There also seemed to be more winners than the casinos generated, and most customers had had some good fortune in the not too distant past. But nearly all spoke of "the lady in the blue cardigan who sits at the next bank of cards who seems to win every time she plays." I put this down to the same phenomenon as perceiving that the checkout queue next to yours in the supermarket or the next lane in the traffic jam always seems to be moving quicker than the one you are stuck in.

# 28

## MOORTOWN – DOING A RUNNER AND OTHER WAYS OF ABUSING TAXI DRIVERS

One of my friends is a police officer who does a fantastic job on her beat in making the community a safer and nicer place to live. She once told me just how difficult it is for a beat bobby to catch a villain intent on running away, unless inebriated literally to the level of leglessness. 'The problem is the amount of gear we have to carry', she complained. 'By the time I've attached my stick, spray, handcuffs, whistle and all the other paraphernalia we have to carry, then put on my stab-resistant jacket, hat and boots at the start of a shift I weigh a ton and can hardly break into a trot'. Private hire drivers just wear ordinary clothes, though in later times my particular company did begin issuing uniforms (when I say "issuing" I mean selling them to the drivers at a profit having made them compulsory.) But inside the cab is likely to be money, sat-nav, 'phone, wallet, and various electronic gadgetry for which the driver is responsible. So when a customer does a runner to avoid paying it's nearly impossible to do anything at all about it, because it would mean leaving the car unattended, often in dodgy areas, and then chasing some yob who is likely to be half your age and racing through ginnels much like diarrhoea through the large intestine; come to think of it this is not at all a bad analogy.

Of course drivers of Hackney carriages are protected from this kind of deception thanks to the simple expedient of being able to lock the rear doors to prevent egress. There were times when I quite envied them this capacity to seal their customers in the rear of the taxi whilst remaining safe in the driver's compartment. The additional protection was reasonable because Hackney cabs were always liable to be hailed in the street, and the customer anonymity this provided rendered them more vulnerable to assault and robbery.

So when this happened to me for the first time in the middle of a night shift half way through my second year in the job, I confess the only surprise I felt was that it had never happened before, when I was in a position of such vulnerability. These particular customers were in their late teens at a guess, two girls and two boys, picked up from a twenty-four hour supermarket around midnight and asking to be dropped off on one of the dodgier estates in West Leeds. With a level of intelligence I would not have expected they sensibly arranged for the girls to be dropped off first, then when I stopped outside their supposed address they simply opened the rear doors and disappeared into nowhere.

What was I to do? I couldn't leave my car unattended and chase them for fear it would be standing on bricks when I returned, even had I been able to catch up with them. Call the police? But then what? Even if a miracle happened and a patrol car came to my rescue, and then the unthinkable happened and they caught the lads, what would happen then? The best case scenario, and a pretty unlikely one, was that I would be paid my fare, but would have lost half an hour or more waiting for it. By that time I could have completed another two jobs, so the exercise would have incurred a net loss, however much I would have enjoyed the satisfaction of seeing them caught. So I simply cleared and looked for the next job, and put it down to experience. But having realised how easy it was to do this I was astonished that in two years of driving it only ever happened to me twice.

What's more I was able to have the last laugh over this

particular incident, because amazingly some three or four weeks later I went to a pick-up from the same supermarket and encountered the same group of youngsters. I couldn't believe they would call the same cab company having pulled the previous stunt, but there they were, two girls and two boys in whose mouths the eponymous butter would not deign to melt. Fortunately they didn't recognise me, and this time I jumped out of the car in time to grab them should they try to run off. I rather enjoyed what followed.

ME: – 'Not your lucky day this is it?'

YOUTH: – 'Wot?'

ME: – 'You don't remember me do you?'

YOUTH: – 'No idea mate.'

ME: – 'I'm the driver you ripped off a few weeks ago – remember now?'

YOUTH: – 'Oh fuck...'

ME: – 'Well there's two ways we can deal with this; I drag you off to the police station round the corner and let them deal with you or you can pay me the fare you owe, and if you pay me double, and a bit extra, I'll take you home.'

Youth: – 'OK mate – will £20 do it?'

How I was going to effect the process of getting one or more of them to the local nick and then convince the police they had avoided paying their fare weeks previously when I had never reported it I don't know, but fortunately they never called my bluff, paid the fare up front (about double what it would have been) and sat meekly in the car while I explained how nice most of us drivers were and how we didn't deserve to be treated like this. Amazingly I think we parted almost friends, and certainly there was no hint of a grudge in their language or demeanour.

The only other customer who ever tried this was a young

woman who exited the cab at a respectable address and went inside supposedly to get some money for her fare; five minutes later when she hadn't emerged I rang the bell. There was no response, but a neighbour put her head round the door and told me that this was her mother's house, and she had pulled the same trick before – walking through the back of the house and hopping over a fence into a park and disappearing. Once again I realised that to find some way of reporting this was likely to be both futile and cost me money in aggregate terms.

A far more common practice was calling a cab and then finding an alternative means of travel. Some customers would do this, for instance, and then change their minds and catch a bus instead, or even walk to their destination, but not bother to call the cab company to explain. The worst abuse of the system of all was the practice (usually carried out by students) of calling anything up to six private hire companies and then simply getting into the first cab that arrived, leaving the other five to pursue a wild goose chase. The hazard with this particular practice was that they ran the quite distinct risk of two cars arriving at the same time and the drivers both refusing to take them, though this only ever happened to me once; but not infrequently I would arrive at a student residence to discover it empty and potential customers long since gone. On one particular night I had no fewer than six such no fares on the bounce, and spent the rest of the shift as far away from student land as I could possibly manage.

Another not uncommon practice was to entertain one's guests by calling half a dozen cabs to an address across the street and run a book on which one would arrive first. Most companies use a call-back system which alerts the customer when the car is about to arrive, so participants in the entertainment can organise a kind of lottery or just simply gamble on which company's car will be first, second, last and so on. Then a further game will be guessing which one gives up and leaves first having realised this is some form of hoax.

Given how vulnerable taxi drivers are to this kind of nefariousness or costly prank the only surprise is that it doesn't occur more often. You might expect the taxi firm to make a note of the 'phone number of people who pull this kind of stunt and refuse to send drivers should another call come in from the same source. This doesn't happen for two reasons; firstly they are almost always mobile 'phones that cannot be pinned down to an address and often not to an individual either, and secondly the company has no real interest in having a blacklist any longer than is strictly necessary because it is in their interests to have as many calls coming in as possible. In all these situations it is the self-employed driver who bears the loss and the cost in time and fuel, not the company. The only risk to the management is that drivers will become so fed up with being messed around that they will change to another firm, resulting in lost revenue; in practice what usually happens is that the inbuilt taxi driver paranoia is fed, there are more moans about the "shite" that they keep getting fed, feel much better for it and move on to the next job.

The worst thing that could happen to a cabbie was to be assaulted and / or robbed, and during my time in the profession this happened to a small number of Hackney Carriage and many more private hire drivers. Tragically in one case this resulted in the death of a cabbie, and made us all a lot more aware of the dangers of the profession.

Whilst the Hackney Carriage driver is to some extent secure in his sealed cab, the private hire driver has no such protection. Recognising this vulnerability the law allows minicab drivers to operate without wearing a seat belt, and most of us chose to do so for much of the time, especially working night shifts, or in areas where we were likely to pick up characters of dubious provenance. This change in the law was brought about after a spate of incidents where private hire drivers were assaulted and robbed by two people sitting in the back seat, one of whom pulled the driver's seat belt tight against his throat to prevent him moving while the other robbed and often assaulted him. Whether the risk of serious injury in a collision was offset by the lower risk of assault and robbery has not, as far as I know, been statistically analysed, but it is certainly a question of choosing the lesser of two possible evils.

I was never robbed or assaulted, though I was constantly aware of situations in which this could have happened. The most bizarre incident arousing fear and a sense that perhaps the God I believed in was somehow with me and protecting me occurred on a night shift; it was curious for a number of reasons, but mostly because only days before it occurred I had heard a vivid account of a minicab driver being robbed at knifepoint having been taken down an unlit street in a remote area of one of the city's many satellite towns. Put briefly he was asked to pick up a fare late at night who directed him to a cul-de-sac shrouded in darkness in what was normally a bastion of well-heeled Yorkshire respectability. Here the "your money or your life" scenario was played out and thankfully the cabbie did the sensible thing and lived to drive another day.

There were some jobs that appeared on the datahead that aroused a level of concern, usually based either on the pick-up or destination point of the journey, and this was definitely in that category; regular customers who called from a home address and travelled well-worn routes were easily the safest – the short runs to school, doctor's surgery or shops from a known address in an area much frequented by our company may have been humdrum, but were in many respects the bread and butter of the job – on day shifts in particular. Unknown pick-up addresses, unspecified or non-specific destinations and a vague sense that this job was "unusual" aroused suspicion. When the pick-up point was neither a home address nor one of the many hotels, casinos or shops that had a direct line to the booking office, I was always on my guard about who I might be picking up and what they may want a cab for. It was as well that this happened well into my second year in the job, when I was far more conscious of the potential hazards involved in being a minicab driver.

So it was about 11.30 on a Sunday evening when I was directed to a shop doorway opposite one of the numerous leisure complexes that had been springing up all over the country for a number of years. The customer was a youngish man of slim build but both sober and with a pleasant disposition, which partly disarmed the suspicion aroused by the destination on the screen, "TBA – to be advised."

But when do coincidences cease being coincidences? The area he asked to be dropped off in was the one I had recently heard about, and there were things about him that didn't quite add up – not least why he wanted to be picked up from a shop doorway when he could have been enjoying the delights of one of the many centres of entertainment at his disposal across the road. Was he trying to avoid potential witnesses?

When he announced his destination I would cheerfully have opened the door and put him out, but I couldn't do that on the grounds of just not feeling comfortable; in any case it was a £15 fare at about £1 per minute, and it would take me away from the seedy pubs that dotted the area I was in just as kicking-out time was in full swing. But I was feeling distinctly nervous as we drove from the moment he told me where he wanted to go. We travelled down the main roads, well-lit and with plenty of people still milling about, as well as a steady flow of traffic, and his conversation was pleasant and engaging. Surely it was just coincidence that he fitted the description I had been given and lived in the same area.

But the sense of security began to diminish when he directed me off the main route – insisting on giving me directions because no one could ever find it, and 'Tom-Toms never have it in their database.' The conversation was still pleasant, but he began to take me down roads I scarcely knew where street lights were rare and heavy curtains were drawn across living room windows. The similarities to the story I had heard began to create a sense of sinister apprehension. Soon the hairs on the back of my neck were standing on end.

Finally he asked me to drive down a cul-de-sac ('my house is right at the bottom') where there were no street lights and no discernible life whatever. Too many alarm bells were ringing – I told him I needed to drop him off where we were, and waited with ever-increasing anxiety to see what might happen next.

Whether I had a guardian angel that night I'll never know, but it was at precisely that moment that a group of people emerged from a nearby house and began to walk down the street. My customer reached for his wallet and (apparently cheerfully) paid up. I will, I guess, never know whether I had a narrow escape that night, whether the coincidences were all part of some heavenly plan to keep me safe from danger, or whether he was simply what he claimed to be, but I don't feel disappointed about remaining in ignorance.

The most unpleasant form of abuse I experienced was as meaningless as it was unexpected and illustrates so well the vulnerability of drivers. I suppose I should probably have known better than to be sitting in a stationary car in the early hours of the morning in an area that was infamous for most forms of criminal and anti-social behaviour, but I had just dropped off a fare and was contemplating the end of my shift and where I might find the last two or three fares I needed to bring my takings up to a level where I felt happy to call it a night. Scrolling through the screen to see where most cars were working and to see if there were any jobs I could plot for I simply did not see it coming. The only thing I heard was a dull crashing sound followed by the crisp rattle of laminated glass falling onto the rear passenger seat. Utterly taken unawares I turned to find the cause and saw them for the first time – a group of young lads the eldest of whom couldn't have been more than sixteen, who clearly having committed the deed, since there was no one else even in the street, were now continuing on their way. One glance at the back of the car told me the story – a rather large piece of concrete had been hurled through the rear window and was now adorning the rear seat where it was surrounded by the remains of the rear window, complete with strands of its heating element. I think the worst thing about the whole incident was that the young men who had committed the crime were not even bothering to run away but were simply casually sauntering down the street.

I weighed up my options and realised I had none. To chase them would have been futile and potentially dangerous – I couldn't help but wonder what people who could do this kind of thing might be capable of when there were half a dozen of them and only one of me; I could take my heavy-duty torch for protection but that might not be a lot of help against six young men who might well be armed with knives or something equally unpleasant. I could call the police, but to what effect? They would arrive (eventually) to find the perpetrators long since gone. The only thing I could think of was to follow them for a while at a safe distance, but when they split up and dispersed in a variety of directions through various ginnels into the sort of housing estate where I would not readily leave the car I realised the futility of the situation. Discretion proving the better part of valour I called the office and was advised to bring the car back and simply take out another. With a vague but misplaced thought that they might be concerned for my welfare I took the trouble to reassure them that I was unhurt and had not been assaulted. The absence of any expression of relief and thankfulness filled the slightly embarrassed silence that follows someone answering a question that no one has any real interest in asking. Such incidents, it seemed, were the common currency of night shifts.

# 29

## WEST PARK – SCARBOROUGH FARE, BAKED BEANS AND THE JUST PLAIN BIZARRE

It was in my first few weeks as a cabbie that what would be seen by most of the profession as the dream job came through the datahead. These were the days already referred to when I enjoyed a certain level of preferential treatment (known in the trade as feeding) to try to persuade me that the life of a private hire driver in West Yorkshire was second in significance and pecuniary reward only to CEOs of FTSE 100 companies, and pretty much up there with David Beckham and Tom Cruise in terms of glamour.

The first thing most private hire drivers do when a job comes through the datahead is to note the pick-up address and then scroll down to see where they are taking the customer; this probably reflects the fact that in spite of the universal deprecation of the mundanity of the work the optimist in the majority of drivers has never quite been extinguished. Nine times out of ten the immediate consequence of this exercise is the emission of an audible sigh of disappointment followed by an expletive or two expressing the sentiment that all they get these days is "shite."

I had little sympathy with this kind of perennial paranoid depressiveness. It was a simple fact that the great majority of our work was of the short-distance, low-fare variety; you made your money by working hard and completing as many of these jobs as possible and when the odd one came along that paid £10 or more it was really little more than a pleasant change from the humdrum, and not necessarily as lucrative as it seemed. The ideal fare in my opinion is one that is a distance of several miles along roads that are fast and easily navigable and which ends in an area from which more work is likely to be forthcoming. By no means did all of the relatively well-paying fares fall into this category, and some were to be avoided if at all possible. Work from football matches at Elland Road or test matches at Headingley are good illustrations; the grounds would frequently disgorge customers who wanted to travel quite significant distances, but on match days most drivers with any experience avoided these plots like the plague, because it could take half an hour or more to pick your way through the traffic, locate the customers and extract yourself from the general melee of people and vehicles that proliferate on such occasions. Music festivals were another bad idea – The Who had reformed for a nostalgia tour during my time in the business and were performing at Harewood House, a stately home near Harrogate. Late one evening I was offered a pick-up once the concert had finished. The drive there took seemingly forever, not only negotiating traffic, but on arrival finding a hundred or more people all wanting me to take them home but none of them being the people who had actually booked. Eventually locating the customer and emerging from the vehicular and pedestrian scrum I managed to deliver the intrepid concert-goers to their home in something a little over an hour after setting off. Since we were paid on mileage – and only when people were in the car – the amount I took at the end of the job was about what I could otherwise have made in a little over half an hour had I stayed in the city. Many drivers on this sort of run just picked up the first person they came across who wanted a cab and pretended it was the customer whose name appeared on their screen – and charged mileage both ways. This was a hazardous thing to do, firstly because it is against the law and secondly because the time would come when the original customer would ring the office and ask "where's my bloody car?" This would in turn result in a radio call from Base and an earful from a frustrated operator or manager.

But pretty well every driver I met still greeted each job that appeared on their datahead with a mild frisson, usually vaporous and short-lived, betraying a deeply submerged but not completely extinguished hope that the gods had smiled on them just this once. If they were real optimists they might wonder whether their innate significance and value to the interests of the company had finally been recognised by the allocation of work which would elevate them to some fictional status in the aristocratic stratosphere of taxi-driving.

But generally all they got was "shite."

After a while I dropped the habit of looking at the destination until I arrived at the pick-up address – especially once I could say I really knew my way around the areas we worked; most likely it was a bread and butter job, and so long as I refrained from looking I could entertain the remote hope of something more lucrative, and it was quite good fun not knowing where I would be going. But this "dream job" came in the early days when it was of the utmost importance to see the destination as early as possible in order to try mentally to plan a suitable route – assuming I had the first idea where we were supposed to be going.

So when the datahead gave me a nearby pick-up late one weekday morning and I scrolled down to see the destination as "Scarborough" I could barely credit the possibility of a job that would take me the rest of my shift to complete, assuming the customer wanted a return ride later that day. In fact I assumed that "Scarborough" must refer to some local pub or other venue – I later discovered a pub known exactly by this name in the city centre. On the other hand if I really was taking someone to Scarborough who could possibly want to go to the expense of a cab when there was a perfectly good rail and bus service for a fraction of the price?

I discovered later that there is actually quite a lot of this kind of work, usually for people with mobility or other health difficulties for whom the use of public transport is particularly hazardous. I know an elderly couple who are members of my current church who booked a taxi to take them from Leicester to Hunstanton because they can easily afford it and are too frail either to drive or to use public transport. These jobs very rarely see the light of day on the ordinary cabbie's datahead – they are booked with the office, and allocated to particular drivers on whom, for one reason or another, the company's management wants to bestow favour. In my case I was still at the stage where judicious favours were seen as investments in order to persuade me that this was really my dream career.

But in those early weeks I had no idea how rarely such work as this came through the datahead. I decided to radio the office and ask firstly if it was genuine and secondly how much I should charge for such a job. 'It's for real, love; you have to work out the fare between you and the customer and come to an agreement.' So I set about working out what was reasonable to charge. I knew it was about 70 miles from Leeds to Scarborough, and charged at full rate this would mean a single fare of about £80, and if I waited to do the return journey something more than double that. But this was more than I would normally take in a day, so what was reasonable? I decided to ask initially for £75 and then to talk about coming back should the customer wish me to wait for him.

I started wondering what kind of customer might call for a cab to Scarborough, and visualised a suave millionaire and a young attractive companion dressed in designer clothes with accessories by Gucci. Then the thought crossed my mind – did I really want to spend that long in someone else's company when relative solitude was one of the principal attractions of the job? I was still pondering this question when an elderly man came shuffling out of the side door and down the garden path towards me. Shabbily dressed and unshaven I wondered whether he was rich, eccentric, insane or a combination of all three. Perhaps nearing the point of shuffling off this mortal coil had he decided to blow a large wad of cash on a nostalgic trip to a favourite old haunt? Perhaps a reclusive millionaire acting on a whim who just fancied being driven to the seaside. Perhaps he had someone to see about something urgent – a family crisis? I was never to find out, but I was already having qualms about him simply because everything about his demeanour exuded resentful grumpiness, and I was not at all sure I wanted his company for the rest of the day for anything under four figures.

Climbing into the front seat of the car with the elegance and gracefulness of an arthritic hippo – and something of the odour of one too – he simply uttered one word – "Scarborough" and put his seat belt on. I decided that the matter of the fare could not be ignored at this stage of the venture so asked if he had any idea of what it was likely to cost at £1.20 per mile, and did he want me to wait to bring him back, in which case we needed to negotiate a rate for waiting and the return journey. The mention of the sum of £75 rendered him nearly apoplectic, as if he should be able to travel at least to Alpha Centauri for such a sum – this amid much wheezing, exuding of odours of dubious provenance and mildly abusive language.

By this point I had decided that even for three times the sum quoted I would far prefer a moderate day's takings to spending most of the day's shift in his company, so decided to further exacerbate his temper by outlining the additional costs of awaiting his pleasure in Scarborough and then driving him home.

Apart from the wheezing he suddenly became rather quiet and still, and I waited to see what kind of return of serve would come back over the net now the ball was firmly in his court. It must have been a full minute later that the exchange went from the odd to the surreal as brain and vocal chords cooperated to ask me to take him to the local pub less than a mile away instead. The sense of relief I felt was only marginally tempered by the thought of how much money I had potentially turned my back on, but the dominant thought was to wonder how anyone in their right mind could be sufficiently capricious to call a cab to take them 70 miles, walk out the front door anticipating a trip to the seaside and two minutes later decide on a pint at the local instead. Whether out of thankfulness at having saved so much money or because of a misplaced belief that I would be devastated at the misfortune of not enjoying his company whilst navigating the A64 to Scarborough I'm not sure, but telling me to keep the change he pressed a £5 note into my hand and exited with the same panache that had accompanied his embarkation some minutes previously.

I returned to the land of the mundane with more than a modest sigh of relief.

Whenever a job came through the datahead the first piece of information was always the name of the customer, where available. When one morning about half way through my first hour's work, while respectable folk are still abed and not even dreaming about breakfast, my datahead announced the arrival of a new job with the customer's name given as "Baked Beans", I had cause to wonder whether I was still in the land of Nod. The pick-up was from one of the many city centre hotels that had an account with the company, and sure enough on arrival a member of the kitchen staff emerged to greet me carrying what must be, I think, the largest tin of baked beans I have ever seen; it certainly would have contained enough to feed a posse for an entire week and guarantee some entertaining noises and smells around the camp fire for a similar period.

It turned out that the story was quite a simple one; another hotel on the other side of the city centre had discovered, on beginning to prepare for breakfast, that it had run out of beans and rung round other hotels in the hope of finding another establishment sufficiently altruistic to send over some of their surplus. In a spirit of generosity which I gather was the exception rather than the rule a chef had seen fit to take pity on the unfortunate hotel and extract them from their predicament – after all a full English breakfast without baked beans is much like a vindaloo without curry powder. I decided that such a receptacle was exempt from the law requiring passengers to wear seat belts, though from the way it was welcomed like a long-lost relative when I arrived at the second hotel I wondered whether I should have strapped it in just in case.

Jobs like these that involved inanimate objects rather than people were not infrequent, the most common sort arising from the contract my company had with the health service in West Yorkshire, and were generally satisfying in the sense that there was no one in the cab who you needed to make conversation with, be polite to or otherwise demonstrate any concern for. They tended to arrive particularly on night shifts or very early in the morning when no NHS transport was available, and this was the time of day when polite conversation was most difficult. So the absence of another homo sapien whilst transporting medical records, blood or other substances was often rather welcome, as was the sense that you were actually doing something useful for another human being whose recovery or even survival might be dependent on the material you were transporting.

To this day the job that causes me the most amusement in the realm of the vaguely odd or bizarre occurred one evening rush hour after a drop-off at the train station. I was asked to meet a customer who had driven to Leeds from the Home Counties, probably assuming that the city was little more than a village with a dirt track, mud huts, and tribal warriors dressed only in loin cloths. In any case she had been unable to locate her destination – even with the aid of the huge expensive GPS system adorning the windscreen and blocking around 50% of her field of vision. This kind of difficulty is not by any means as strange as it sounds, and once I realised where the customer was trying to go I understood the problem only too well – it was on the other side of the notorious inner city loop system from where she was stranded. Finally running low on fuel but with a bladder full to bursting point she had hit on the novel (and in my opinion ingenious) solution of calling a cab that would lead her to the required destination.

I decided to be magnanimous and sympathetic, and to respond appropriately to her request to drive slowly enough so she didn't lose me. Her relief on finally arriving was expressed by means of a broad smile and a very generous tip.

Most cities have some kind of manufactured method of keeping traffic moving round their centre as well as possible given that the streets were laid out well over a century ago for horse-drawn carriages, and not too many even of these. Such systems all have their own mysteries and only make full sense to those who are initiated into the lodge of those who regularly use them and have mastered their idiosyncrasies. But of all such systems it is surely the one in Leeds that must take the gold medal in the three mile vehicular obstacle race.

Known as the loop system, it is a series of roads connected at all sorts of odd angles to one another creating the shape of some grotesque polygon which renders the term "loop" oxymoronic to say the least. In my first month of cab driving I had been called to a destination on the opposite side of the loop that was tricky to locate, and was on my third circumnavigation of the city centre when I saw the hotel but couldn't see a way to get to it from the loop road, which was replete with traffic moving at sufficient pace to trigger speed cameras had there been any present. Unable to stop I was compelled to complete a fourth loop before I located the alleyway, barely wide enough for a Reliant Robin, through which I had to pass in order to reach it. The customer had, of course, long since gone, probably bundled into the cab of one of the many firms that sat outside such establishments hoping that someone would emerge and simply get in thinking this was the one they had ordered.

Having mastered circling the loop system clockwise – the way it is designed – the real art of the cabbie was to work out a better way of getting, for instance, from 12 o'clock to 10 o'clock without going via numbers 1-9. This took quite a while longer, involved discovering some obscure thoroughfares and one or two routes that were really not meant for cars at all. When after about six months I had mastered the whole thing I really felt I had graduated as a Leeds cabbie.

# 30

## CITY CENTRE WEST – THE SHIPPING FORECAST AND SAILING BY

It was, perhaps, at the mid-point of the second year of my sentence in what had become, by now, a very agreeable pattern of life with which I was very much at ease, that I began seriously to look again at the idea of returning to the world I had left behind. This was no easy decision; whilst the long hours spent sitting in a private hire car left me with a sensation of almost permanent tiredness, and with some extra girth round my middle due to the virtual impossibility of building a regular exercise routine into my weekly timetable, it was also comfortably familiar by now. Compared to my former existence this work environment was virtually stress-free. I was earning a good wage, and always had the opportunity of earning a little more should it be needed. One week I put in an extra shift in order to send some money to my eldest son who was struggling to have enough to live on at university. I really enjoyed an environment where I was able to see my weekly wage accumulating in the very tangible form of cash being placed into my hand. Ministry I knew to be poorly paid, and involved hard and often unappreciated work. In the stress stakes it resembled a button on one of my shirts now that I had put on a stone or two – one more cream cake and the uneven struggle to hold back the tide of human flesh would be history. The drop-out rate of ministers in my denomination had long since reached alarming levels, and various attempts to stem the tide seemed to have been largely futile; my own story, I discovered, was not particularly unusual.

So why go back to it all? Well there was the official reason which contained a grain of truth, and the real reason which held enough for several loaves of bread. To the ecclesiastical establishment and the few remaining pious friends I had failed to offend with the coarse language and humour that had made its way into my social intercourse I gave the impression that ministry was a divine calling, and ultimately if that is what you are created by the Almighty to do there is no real peace or satisfaction in anything else.

This was by no means untrue. Clergy of all shades and persuasions tend to be a slightly odd bunch in much the same manner as Morris Dancers, Bog Snorkellers and Train Spotters, and whether this is the way we are put together in the womb or the result of the sausage-machine training process of a theological college is really irrelevant – that's the way it is. But if I am honest most of this is bovine excrement. Concurrent with the repair to my self-esteem was the rediscovery of something I had feared was lost forever, my competitive instinct and refusal to concede defeat. Put simply I hated losing at anything, a questionable quality that had landed me in trouble in sports fixtures but helped to ensure far more wins than losses. My last job as a minister had been a failure, but the two preceding it had generally been regarded as successes, and such ignominy was no note on which to end a career. I had to give it one more go in order to prove – to myself in particular – that I was still hot stuff in the pulpit and vestry. So I entered the ecclesiastical marriage bureau for what I hoped would be the final time.

The various church bodies have different ways of sorting out which clergy go where; those with a hierarchical structure may have bishops who despatch their vicars and curates to livings sometimes with relatively little consultation. Others may have so few clergy anyway that a desperate congregation will grasp at any straw so long as it's wearing a clerical collar, for fear of being left on the shelf; but Baptist ministers are slightly different.

The way the process works in my church set-up is akin to some kind of ecclesiological dating agency. A group of senior ministers meet together once a month with a list of churches looking for ministers, and ministers looking for a fresh challenge – or, more frequently, looking to escape from the frying pan in the hope that the fire might not be quite so hot. Each church is matched up with a variety of potential suitors, whose details are then sent to those charged with the selection process for their particular establishment. Rather than "blue eyes, blonde hair, curvy, vivacious and looking for fun with a good sense of humour" (is anyone ever described in such missives as not having a GSOH?) ministers are described according to their churchmanship, their theological outlook and other such boring attributes.

Introductions made, everything is then left to be settled, if it seems appropriate, between church and minister. The leaders of the church always take the initiative to organise the first date, usually in the form of an introductory evening together with minimal physical contact and much discussion of generalities. A really good date may end with the equivalent of a peck on the cheek as a goodnight kiss. Some of these relationships result in second, third or even fourth dates, always with the whole church, and with increasing levels of intimacy, following which a decision is made whether or not to announce an engagement and set a date for the wedding.

Amazingly the process usually works pretty well.

My name had been sent to a dozen or more groups of church leaders who were considering my clerical curriculum vitae alongside that of several others. It was not many days before I began to receive enquiries about my availability and invitations to meet deacons, elders and other sundry lay representatives. I have always been flirtatious, eclectic and non-discriminatory at this stage of the procedure – even if a church profile gave me the heebie-jeebies; if nothing else it gave me an idea of what I didn't want just as (I imagine) a speed-dating evening facilitates a good choice by enabling you to eliminate some potential relationships with people you could imagine kissing about as easily as puckering up to the rear end of a rhinoceros.

So some minutes of calm during a night shift gave excellent opportunity to reflect on these various approaches, and on some of the more ephemeral questions that come into one's mind when contemplating a calling to represent the creator of the universe to a group of survivors of the multifarious assaults that currently fall upon the average nonconformist congregation. For me this opportunity occurred almost invariably in the period following midnight during my night shifts.

For some reason I was never able completely to fathom, most night shifts kept me busy until midnight, or a few minutes after, when most of the work that had flowed steadily from the suburbs and on the council estates dried up, and the only jobs immediately available were from the city centre. At this point most of the drivers who were working into the wee small hours would make their way to the nearest point of city night life at their disposal, and join the electronic queue for work.

The spot I almost invariably aimed for was the car park of a small commercial estate opposite one of the casinos from which work issued steadily through most of the night. I would almost always find myself at 12.15 or 12.20 in a queue behind at least a dozen drivers waiting for work from the same plot, which gave me the perfect opportunity for a power nap, nodding off whilst contemplating some of these deep questions.

Some people wake up grumpy on principal, others feel dreadful after just 15 or 20 minutes of sleep; I am fortunate enough to be able to drop off for a quarter of an hour and wake up feeling ready for almost anything and in good spirits, so the routine was to join the queue, put the seat back, lock the doors, and drift off while my number silently rose towards the top of the queue. Almost inevitably I was woken after about 15 minutes by the datahead summoning me back from the land of Nod. This was the time – and almost the only time unless there was a good football match on – that I switched on the radio, because either before, during or after my next job I would be comforted by the soothing tones of the Shipping Forecast preceded by the delightful, calming melody of Sailing By, just before Radio 4 handed over to the World Service.

What was it about Sailing By at 12.45 a.m. that made it so unmissable? Perhaps it was the juxtaposition of two contrasting maritime images. A melody redolent with suggestions of a tranquil sea with gentle ripples generated by the zephyr blowing offshore with just sufficient strength to fill the sails of the small dinghies ploughing their way across the bay catching the passing interest of families on a sun-drenched beach licking ice-creams. Then the Shipping Forecast with reports from coastal stations delivered with no background music and a voice straight from the waxworks museum warning of gales in Humber, Fastnet and the Irish Sea, not to mention the even graver horrors awaiting those who ventured into Hebrides, Bailey, South-east Iceland and North Utsire. There was something evocative about the images of a catamaran rocked by gentle waves off the coast of the English Riviera set alongside that of the grizzled skipper of a small fishing boat with more hair on his face than on top of it steering a steady course in a wheelhouse lashed by storms with the harbour lights of Stornoway just visible through the murky night; and in my image there was always a tin mug with piping hot tea that seemed to defy gravity while the storm tossed the vessel around like a toy, making the average white knuckle ride at the leading theme park seem like a children's roundabout at the local recreation ground.

All this seemed as a parable of life; which of the two images was the reality – the storm-tossed fishing boat off the north-west coast of Scotland or the sedate progress of the pleasure boat?

There is a whole world to ponder in that question and to the extent that my philosophical faculties were capable of such feats on the wrong side of midnight I did my best. I think I concluded that they were both genuine in their own way, but if you really wanted to appreciate what life in a boat was like you have to endure the rough stuff to appreciate the delights of the pleasure craft. In any case whatever I was doing, and whoever was in the cab at that time this was compulsory listening.

The other thing about the Shipping Forecast was that once it was complete, the National Anthem had been played and Radio 4 had begun transmitting the World Service, I knew I was into the home straight of my shift, and this was always a welcome moment, because by this stage I had been working for up to ten hours and I could just about begin hearing the call of my bed.

# 31

## CITY CENTRE EAST – CALL LANE AT 2 A.M.

No account of my time in the minicab world would be complete without some attempt to describe the scene in the centre of Leeds when the bars and clubs began to disgorge their customers before closing for the night, because this involved one of the most bizarre rituals of minicab driving that was as compulsive as it was frustrating. But first I need to explain a little about how the minicab world worked in practice rather than in theory in the early hours of the morning.

As I commented earlier the theory is that private hire cars (as opposed to Hackney Carriages) invariably have something like "Advance Bookings Only" written somewhere on the vehicle, or, even more ominously, "Journeys only insured when booked in advance," whereas proper taxis can pick up anyone who hails them in the street. Again in theory these rules are enforced by employees of the council, or occasionally the police, approaching vehicles and offering significant sums of money to private hire drivers to take them somewhere, or perhaps trying to hail them in the street. If the driver breaks the rules they will be informed of their misdemeanour and warned of impending prosecution and suspension of their licence.

That's the theory, but the practice is somewhat different. There were more private hire firms in and around Leeds than could be counted. I worked for the largest of these companies, which had the advantage of offering a steady flow of work around the clock; of course some hours were quieter than others, but then the number of drivers working fell off too, so for instance at 4 a.m. whilst there was only a trickle of work there were not many looking for it, and it was still possible to find enough to make it worth your while. There were a handful of companies who did their best to operate rigorously within the law, including a couple which, in numerical terms, could compete with my outfit. Once you went beyond that top half dozen firms, though, it was a very different story; most of the rest were small operations – some even being literally one man and a car – who had relatively little work that was pre-booked or came through a switchboard, particularly outside of normal waking hours. The drivers who worked for these companies were generally not subject to a company code of conduct as we were – the owner of the firm simply wanted to collect rent from his drivers, and for that consideration would allow them to sport the company logo on the side of the car and operate pretty much as they liked. In practical terms this meant that during a night shift they would have little or no work that came from their office, and made a living by plying for hire or piracy. Plying for hire means operating as a Hackney Carriage and picking up anyone flagging them down in the street, and piracy involves waiting in an area where one of the larger firms regularly has work and pretending to be the cab that the customer has ordered. They could get away with this for a number of reasons: Firstly, because most of the general public don't understand the distinction between Hackney Carriages and private hire cars they remain unaware – in spite of the warnings on the side of the car – that the driver is operating not only illegally but also without insurance for the journey involved. Secondly, in spite of occasional crackdowns and spot checks by the licensing authority and police, in reality the latter have no desire seriously to curtail the practice to a great degree. The principal objective of the police at two or three o'clock in the morning is to see everyone off the streets of the city centre and away from the area to their homes. A successful night is one in which no streets are spattered with bloodspots or vomit, no one is arrested and they don't suffer too much verbal or physical abuse; one can hardly blame them. So to start checking the credentials of all the private hire cars working is not only time-consuming, but counter-productive to their main objective.

Private hire drivers were thus able to operate outside the law with relative impunity. There were even car owners who had no connection with the taxi world whatever, who would put some kind of badge on their car – even a home-made "taxi" sign, and drive round the city centre late at night in the hope of finding someone sufficiently gullible – or inebriated – to climb in and pay a large sum of money for what was, in effect, a lift home.

Occasionally these ploys backfired; some of the student revellers got wise to the rules governing private hire drivers, and clambered aboard a car whose driver was plying for hire only to stiff him when they got out at the other end. I encountered a couple of drivers who were lamenting the appalling behaviour of the youngsters who had just got out and run off without paying into The Brewery flats, and appealed for my help. I suggested either calling the police or tracking down the 'phone number of the person who had booked the cab with their office; of course they could do neither because they were operating outside the law. Not only was I unsympathetic, I confess to a level of Schadenfreude, given how many of these drivers had stolen my fares when I had gone for a pick-up at a city centre venue.

So try if you will to imagine the hub of Leeds's night life and a thoroughfare named "Call Lane" at two o'clock in the morning. Wide enough to take three or four cars abreast, about 200 metres in length and, more significantly, a one-way street linked to the infamous inner city loop system. Both sides of the road were replete with drinking establishments, and many evenings saw all of them bursting at the seams; moreover they all seemed to close at about the same time.

The ritual would begin a few minutes before two o'clock with a job on my datahead calling for a pick-up in Call Lane. On one level my heart sank because I knew what I was in for but there was also something oddly endearing about the ritual played out in an entirely predictable fashion each night.

Arriving at the top of the street – if you could get into it at all – you were confronted by the spectacle of anything up to 100 private hire cars of all shapes and sizes representing more firms than you knew existed completely blocking the street in a scarcely believable display of taxi-driving anarchy. It was the automotive equivalent of lifting a manhole cover to investigate your blocked drain only to find a very large pile of amorphous excrement jamming the pipe. You were confronted with the sight of drivers of dozens and dozens of private hire cars who were operating illegally, looking just to pick up anyone willing to step into their vehicles or to steal the fare of another cabbie. They had, of course, arrived there a little earlier, and had no interest whatever in allowing the legitimately operating cars to pass through to pick up their fares until they had secured one of their own – or, more likely, someone else's. Those drivers who were operating within the law and those who had managed to persuade someone that they were actually the cab they had ordered (even though the legend adorning the car was different from the name of the company they had called) now found themselves stuck somewhere in the middle of the drainpipe and unable to move. The only means of clearing the drain was to apply pressure to those who were still causing the blockage by the enthusiastic and energetic use of the car's horn, which was perceived to act as a kind of plunger.

The Highway Code says of the car horn: -

Never use your horn aggressively. You MUST NOT use your horn
- While stationary on the road

- When driving in a built-up area between the hours of 11.30 p.m. and 7.00 a.m.
- Except when another road user poses a danger

Right – so that's simple enough then.

Clearly the authors of the national book on driving law and etiquette failed to include the exception to this rule which governs the drivers of private hire cars in the early hours of the morning in streets where bars, clubs and miscellaneous drinking establishments are emptying.

Whether out of frustration, anger or simply participation in some kind of nightly ritual I'm unsure, but nearly every driver in that melee must have been honking away almost repeatedly either to try to clear a route, attract the attention of customers (genuine or potential) or just as a means of gratuitous self-expression. It was as if an entire flock of geese had paused in the centre of the city en route to their migratory breeding-grounds, with each vehicle making a similar but slightly different sound. This built, at the height of the process, to a veritable cacophony of deafening noise. I never was sure whether there were people actually living in the immediate vicinity but if there were they would have needed to be either deaf or equipped with particularly effective earplugs to be getting any sleep. In any case it was quite a task to convince yourself that it was the middle of the night in a provincial English city rather than the evening rush hour in Beijing.

Funnily enough, and against the apparent odds, I usually though not always managed to track down my customers in Call Lane; they were probably the more savvy users of minicabs who knew the risks, financial and physical, of jumping in any car that presented itself, and used my firm regularly.

The other odd thing about this nightly ritual was that the impression you always had was that the prolific horn-sounding ritual actually worked, as if the sonic force of the noise was easing the poo through the drainpipe and out the other end. This was almost certainly only a perception; in truth as cars gradually filled up with customers and shoe-horned their way in a slalom-like fashion down the street the process would have happened anyway.

You might be forgiven for wondering where Her Majesty's constabulary were, and how they counteracted this flagrant defiance of the law. The simple truth was, of course, that they were sensible enough to be nowhere near Call Lane at 2 a.m. For one thing it would have taken half the West Yorkshire force to write out tickets to the renegade horn-blasters, and to check up on who was operating outside the law. But the main reason they made themselves scarce was because their objectives were achieved most easily by absence rather than presence. In order to make their collective life easier their interest was best served by getting the revellers safely out of the city centre as soon as possible; any kind of law enforcement would almost certainly have been counter-productive to this purpose, as well as clogging up the cells and generating mounds of tedious paperwork. I concluded that it would probably have taken a couple of murders with accompanying rivers of blood running off the kerb and down the gutter to arouse more than a passing interest from the Constabulary in the proceedings in Call Lane in the early hours. Amazingly enough as far as I know the anger of even the most irascible driver never quite plumbed those depths. I have to say that in this particular case I had great sympathy with the attitude of the police.

It seems an astonishing thing to admit, but I still somehow have a nostalgic longing for the Call Lane ritual.

# 32

## BRAMHOPE – BAD DRIVING

Some months into my foray into the world of taxi driving I had learned the painful way that I was not nearly as good a driver as I had thought, but I was hardly alone in assessing my ability behind the wheel at anything between "above average" and "exceptional". In the UK it is estimated that about 80% of drivers rate themselves at above average (the figure for the US is anything up to 93%!) This kind of statistic makes sense only in subjects like philosophy and theology where paradoxes and dichotomies defy semantic exactitude – and professional football where players apparently regularly give "110%". In the real and tangible world it is a statistical impossibility – only something just under 50% can be above average.

The answers to the question why this should be so are many and varied, and lie in the domain of the professional psychologist, but I reckon it is because at least in part we rate the faults of other drivers as being far more serious than our own. Take, for instance, the scenario where you are occupying the centre lane of a three lane motorway and, in a short while, but not quite yet, you will need to overtake something in the inside lane. You decide not to pull in but to save yourself the hassle of having to do the whole "mirror-signal-manoeuvre" thing and stay put because it's pretty quiet and, in any case, your speedometer is registering 72 mph and that's about the speed limit. Then some huge Tonka toy known fondly as a

4x4, driven in all probability by an overweight middle-aged bloke whose declining libido finds compensation in aggressive driving, appears from nowhere in your rear view mirror and if he's not doing a ton it isn't far off. He (I'm using the male personal pronoun because it usually, though not exclusively is a he) comes right up to your rear end before flashing his lights repeatedly and veering into the outside lane, tooting his horn and pointedly pulling in front of you long before a safe distance has been established. You are guilty, at the worst, of being a little dilatory in your lane discipline, whereas not only has he broken at least three laws in completing the manoeuvre (speeding, sounding horn, driving without due care and attention) he is also completely oblivious to these faults. His performance has, in his own eyes, been superb. Should he have a passenger he will sound off about "bloody tortoises who don't have a clue how to drive at speed on a motorway" without rating his own performance at anything less than exemplary. If there is no impressionable passenger he is likely soon to be busy on his 'phone – probably without the required hands-free kit – telling a friend about the appalling driving habits he is encountering today. If challenged he will assert his right to drive at that speed and in that fashion because both he and his vehicle are capable of far greater than average performance and the speed limit "in this day and age" of 70 mph is ridiculously low.

One day we will probably all get into cars that will, in effect, drive themselves, always obeying the rules of the road and travelling within the speed limit. At this point our friend will need to find another outlet to compensate for his inadequacies in other domains or else regularly take a cold shower.

The uncomfortable truth is that most of us do this at least to some degree – turning a blind eye to the driving beams in our own eye whilst being anxious to point out the tiniest speck in those we share the road with. So when asked whether we are above or below average as a driver we recall our latest experiences of those who are not driving as we consider they should and assess ourselves as being superior.

Having not had an accident for which I was culpable for many years I found that driving for a living cruelly exposed my weaknesses, and after two collisions for which I was in some measure responsible I came to the realisation that I had better revise my self-assessment and learn some lessons about defensive driving. I found the key was not to allow the red mist to rise when I was the victim of another driver's stupidity or aggression. I also managed to discipline myself to believe that I had not necessarily been singled out for special treatment and in the best traditions of English cricket umpiring give them the benefit of the doubt. Poor driving was generally attributed to incompetence rather than selfishness or a desire to offend. I am sure I have extended my life expectancy as a result.

There were, of course, exceptions to this demonstration of the spirit of generosity when overly aggressive drivers would try to force their way in front of you because, for some bizarre reason, cutting up a taxi or minicab was like collecting some kind of scalp. In places where there was heavy traffic, for instance when two lines of cars had to merge into one at road works, and someone decided that the normal rules of queuing and taking your turn didn't apply to them, I always tried to work out what kind of driver I was dealing with.

In this regard I think there are three fundamental types who propel their vehicle down the outside lane of a dual carriageway long after all other traffic has merged into a single file: –

1) Penis extension drivers – mostly though not exclusively men
2) Penelope Pitstop drivers, "silly me but aren't I cute" – mostly though not exclusively women
3) Oops, didn't see that coming drivers – more or less evenly spread across the gender divide

The first type hardly needs any further description: Often white van drivers or other miscellaneous tradesmen, not infrequently minicab drivers and almost universally men under the age of 40. You can see them in the door mirror – travelling at twice the speed limit down the outside lane, relishing the opportunity to demonstrate their machismo by forcing their way into any crevice in the single lane of traffic like a bull in a field full of cows on heat. If no crevice is available, they will thrust their penis extension towards any vehicle driven by someone who looks capable of being intimidated until a space appears. An advantage of spending so much time in the same make and model of car was that I knew where the boundaries of the vehicle were pretty much to the last millimetre, and so had a distinct advantage in any game of chicken with most drivers, who usually had to allow a little more space "just in case." One of the most satisfying parts of an average shift was to stop these characters forcing their way in front of me – and the joy was more than doubled if upon having to concede defeat they blasted their horn and / or made obscene gestures in my general direction. It created the sensation that we had just measured our willies and discovered that mine was somewhat longer than his, and there was nothing he could do about it.

The Penelope Pitstop drivers know exactly what they are doing but try to give the impression that they have driven down the outside of the traffic and suddenly discovered that they cannot proceed. They look imploringly at the driver they hope to charm with a "silly me" expression, flutter eyelids, smile and generally work hard at looking cute. "How can you not allow me in when I am so endearingly helpless?" The Sir Lancelot in the male psyche can find this "damsel in distress" act irresistible, and coming to the aid of the lady in question leaves a warm glow that is not even eradicated when the vehicle allowed in just manages to pass through the lights on amber while the gallant knight has to sit on his charger and wait for the next green.

Did I let these cute drivers in? It depended on how well my day was going, how sweet-looking they were, and whether they were the sort of driver I would much prefer to have in front of me where I could keep an eye on them rather than behind when anything could happen. But I confess to being susceptible to feminine charm and mild flirtation.

The third type – well, we've all been there. Driving in an area we don't know well and suddenly discovering we have put our vehicle in a position guaranteed to cause stress and / or embarrassment. You can always tell this type; unlike the penis extensions and sometimes the cuties they come to a grinding halt, indicate and look extremely uncomfortable. These I always let in. If in doubt having a look to see whether they were indicating was usually the giveaway; the aggressive types rarely bothered on the basis that if they indicate they are giving away their intentions, and that puts them at a disadvantage in the turf war over the space they are aiming for.

Some examples of bad driving were undoubtedly alcohol related. Most nights after about 1.30 a.m. the vast majority of vehicles on the road were taxis, private hire cars and emergency vehicles. I always enjoyed driving at this time of night because whilst there was still some aggressive driving – the police were particularly conspicuous for driving at twice the speed limit and passing through red lights whilst not answering an emergency call – generally the drivers knew what they were doing and their behaviour was predictable. Just occasionally I encountered a drunk driver weaving from one side of the road to the other, but more often I witnessed the aftermath of journeys cut short by those who had had just enough to drink to loosen their inhibitions and were convinced that they were perfectly fit to drive at whatever speed they chose.

Rarely a night shift passed without witnessing at least one scene of carnage where, in all probability, there had been serious injury, if not a fatality. Cars lying on their roofs, spread at grotesque angles somewhere off the road with doors, boot and bonnet open or wrapped around the proverbial lamp-post were common sights in the early hours. The most intriguing spectacle I recall was a car that was propped up vertically with its front bumper on the ground and rear end against the central support of a railway bridge carrying trains across a busy section of the ring road. It appeared to be unscathed by whatever turn of events had led to this scenario, and I spent the next half hour or more trying unsuccessfully to imagine a set of circumstances that would have caused it to come to rest in this position.

# 33

## East Park – Sundays

At some point in the middle of my minicab driving days I changed my mind about Sundays, less through any kind of force of reasonable argument and more by encountering the reality of what happens in an urban conurbation like West Yorkshire on what the Christian Church (mistakenly, really) calls the Sabbath. I remembered the campaign to Keep Sunday Special, of writing to my MP, praying earnestly that members of the House of Commons would see the importance of keeping a day a week free of commercial activity, all in the name of preserving something that was different about Sunday.

Of course the simple truth was that the churches up and down the land were frightened; dwindling, if not disintegrating attendances, could reach a state of meltdown if there were even more things to do on a Sunday than there had been previously. I recall the approbation I registered when the vicar of the parish church next to Villa Park (the nearest thing I have to a shrine outside of consecrated premises) decided to ring the church bells all the way through the football match that had been scheduled for a Sunday in protest at a yet further violation of the Sabbath.

Now I thought "What a prat!"

I suppose that going to church was what I had done on Sundays for virtually my whole life, and believed that this was the only authentic way to be a follower of Christ. Any initiative on the part of the authorities that paved the way for more opportunities for people to amuse themselves or work on Sundays was therefore yet further evidence of a government that was hell-bent on the destruction of the Church and, indeed, of organised religion. It would have been far less disingenuous to admit that, along with all other church leaders opposing this legislation, we were worried that those who had nothing better to do than attend "worship" on a Sunday might now have a more exciting alternative; that religious buildings might become something approaching derelict museums in the corporate life of the nation.

I realised within a couple of weeks of climbing into a minicab that Church was already such a cultural sideshow that it scarcely featured on the remotest fringes of the fairground. At an optimistic estimate 7-8% of the population attend church with some regularity, and this figure was somewhat lower in areas such as West Yorkshire. For most of the week – indeed for most of Sunday – the doors were shut and the buildings appeared lifeless. When most of the churches and chapels across the region did open their doors for a couple of hours on Sunday mornings (fewer and fewer held evening services) they exuded a general air that was about as welcoming as Stalag XIII on a rainy day. They were, put simply, an irrelevance to the cultural activity of the region even on the one day of the week they operated, and here they were asking for preferential treatment in order that people wouldn't go off and do other things they might actually enjoy.

The penny dropped at around 5.30 one Sunday morning about a year into my new career when I received a job to take someone from West Leeds to an industrialised area on the opposite side of the city. I thought how odd it was that anyone would be going to an area full of factories and waste land so early on Sunday, and was curious as to why. The customer was a pleasant, portly lady of maybe fifty years of age, whose appearance was quite similar to many of those who would later that morning be attending church.

Unable to restrain my curiosity I couldn't help but enquire about the purpose of her trip – perhaps there was a church of some sort there that held a very early mass. 'I'm going to the Car Boot of course, love' – delivered with the tone of one who could not understand why anyone would even vaguely consider an alternative pursuit.

'What – at this time of the morning?'

'I'm running a stall, love, and we have to be there by six to set up.'

Driving through the tunnel system that facilitated rapid transit from one side of the city centre to the other I felt a certain level of anxiety for the rather vulnerable looking lady in the rear of the car. As far as I was concerned I was dropping her off in the middle of an unpopulated urban desert fringed by some rather dodgy communities, and would she be safe?

The question was answered about half a mile from the point on the industrial estate for which I was heading when I almost collided with the tailback of vehicles waiting to enter the site; there were hundreds upon hundreds of pedestrians all heading the same way to a piece of waste land on which it would have been possible to fit several full-sized football pitches. The spectacle was jaw-dropping; that this many people would drag themselves out of bed at this hour on a Sunday to take part in such a weekly ritual when I was used to starting a service of worship at almost lunchtime and still having to wait for the latecomers to take their seats told me, once I had processed the information, all I needed to know about the place of the institutional Church in our society. And this was only the advance guard of the operation – once it opened properly and really got going there would be thousands of people converging on the area throughout the day, all excited about picking over other people's junk and maybe buying a couple of second-hand toys to take home.

For the first time since I had left my previous calling, and possibly the first time ever, I came face to face with the rather uncomfortable question as to whether the institution of Church has any useful place in our society, and was forced to attempt something like an honest evaluation of its significance. I reflected on how many people I had taken to or from church services since I began doing something that a decent percentage of the population would regard as useful on Sundays – driving a cab. The grand total was … one – though in fairness my tally would more than double in the next twelve months to reach a grand total of three. This calculation was simple enough, but on my way back from the place of pilgrimage, this veritable shrine of low-end consumerism, I calculated this in percentage terms of all work undertaken. Assuming I had by this stage worked about 50 Sunday day shifts, and assuming an average of 30 fares a day, I was looking at .067%.

Of course this hardly reflects churchgoing as a whole; most religious establishments of the Christian persuasion are in more well-to-do areas where car ownership is almost universal, and not even the most fastidious of the faithful would decline to drive on account of a mouthful of alcoholic communion wine. My brand of God-bothering only uses ghastly sweet non-alcoholic stuff, thanks to the ongoing influence of the Victorian Temperance movement, and possibly as a gesture of superior piety aimed in the general direction of the Established Church. This represented another absurd historical anachronism and more than a modicum of hypocrisy when nearly every church member I knew liked a glass of their favourite tipple with their Sunday lunch. Nevertheless I came to see for the first time with the sort of painful clarity that occurs when you are just waking up with a headache and someone pulls the blinds up on a bright summer morning just how much of a quaint leisure pursuit Sunday church attendance has become.

All week I would drive past the same church buildings and see them with doors locked shut. Even on Sundays the same doors were generally closed, except for an hour or two in the morning. During that brief window of opportunity the rare curious observer can usually see only a tiny bit of the interior, where typically there stands a slightly shabby looking elderly gentleman with a hand full of notice sheets waiting anxiously but with almost no expectation whatever to welcome the newcomer, and hoping against hope that this week will see the start of an upturn in attendances. He is a good man – he's probably been holding the fort for a decade or more; he does half the jobs in the chapel, from counting the meagre offering to replacing light bulbs, but those he welcomes week by week, year in year out are of a similar vintage to himself. He doesn't understand why people can't just give up an hour of their time to attend the Lord's House on the Sabbath. Were someone to try to explain why most of those driving past on their way to the car boot sale or other Sunday activities would fail to pluck up the courage to pass through the door and run the gauntlet of this one-man welcoming committee they would have their work cut out. They would have to explain that to enter through the hallowed portal would be the cultural equivalent of him entering the bookies and betting the contents of the offering plate on Accrington Stanley winning the F.A. Cup. This would almost certainly cause mortal offence and bewildered incomprehension in more or less equal measure.

Of course this is not the picture in all places of Sunday worship, but neither is it a caricature – this scenario is repeated in countless churches in countless towns, cities and villages all across the U.K. The mercy is that such chapels are closing through lack of anything resembling a viable congregation at a very rapid rate, and given another 20 years they will, in all probability, cease to be a feature of our cultural landscape. It has been predicted that the Christian Church will cease to exist in England by the middle of the century, and whilst this is probably not quite true it is certainly well on course to becoming so marginal that no one will any longer take notice of it, even if its buildings remain objects of historical interest.

The question of what the Church can do to change all this has been one that has occupied my mind, and occasionally my prayer life, for the last 40 years, ever since I was old enough to understand even something of the cultural anachronism that is so-called Christian Sunday worship. Of one thing I am convinced – that if there is to be anything like a recovery the various denominations must first come to terms with just what a total irrelevance to their society they have become. While the Church protests about legislation to give gay people equal rights, complains about the non-Christian nature of religious education in schools, not to mention assemblies that focus on morality and other world religions rather than on the Christian faith it will only be rearranging deckchairs on the Titanic. If at the same time it attempts to justify part of the Church of England hierarchy occupying unelected places in the House of Lords the true nature of the catastrophic decline will be masked behind a wall of self-righteous rhetoric as the more articulate apologists try to paper over the ever-widening cracks.

Perhaps the ultimate moment of truth came for me on the day of the Leeds marathon – like most marathons always run on a Sunday because that is the day most people are free, and the roads are at their quietest. The church I attended, for which I remain grateful as a therapeutic instrument in my healing process, was but a stone's throw (well perhaps a good three iron) from the route the runners would take, and was considered to be lively and active. The long road along which the runners would pass was buzzing with anticipation and teeming with life in anticipation of the display of vigour, athleticism and just plain doggedness that was about to pass their way. Water stations were staffed by enthusiastic volunteers, friends and families were excitedly awaiting their loved ones, flags were waving, and the atmosphere was of a carnival nature.

And there we were, 200 or so yards away, enacting what was for most of us a rather interesting version of a weekly ritual that would have been utterly, utterly meaningless to this fervent throng. I asked myself why we weren't in some way part of what was going on outside rather than being shut up in a second-rate mock-Gothic protuberance that might, with a certain generosity of spirit, have justified a place on the set of a 1930's Frankenstein film. If what we were indulging in was an encounter with the Might and Wisdom of Creation who delights in the attention of those he has fashioned in his image, why was the excitement and level of engagement at meeting him so feeble when compared to the thousands almost on our doorstep watching some people running past in fancy dress on a cool, damp Sunday morning?

Finding a way of addressing this conundrum was to be the lump of masonry from which the shape of the return to ministry I was contemplating was to be sculpted.

# 34

## Alwoodley – Encounters with the Gay Community

This is the point at which I should come out. Allow me to be honest about myself and confess that I am about as "straight" as I imagine it is possible to be. I find the male form, apart from a few notable exceptions where I find myself in envy of the physique of professional footballers and the like, to be unattractive in the extreme, and the thought of kissing another man is about as attractive as getting into a clinch with an amorous camel. It was, perhaps, because of this strong heterosexual orientation, and the traditional view of homosexual activity adopted by the Church, that I also have to come out as one of those who saw no real place for gay people in any Christian community. I confess this now with both embarrassment and shame, and with sincere apologies to those who may in any sense have suffered from the prejudices of people like myself. I owe the change in attitude to the experience of driving a cab around West Yorkshire, especially on night shifts.

I had no idea even of the existence of the "Gay Quarter" of the city until the first time I visited it late one evening at a time when I was still becoming acquainted with the different varieties of night-life on offer. The name on my screen read "Stephen" but I was honestly convinced that it must have been a mistake as what must surely have been a Stephanie emerged at a rate of knots wearing a long, flowing dress and high heels, to climb into the back seat offering the absolute minimum of exposure to any of the general public who may have been watching. Somewhat nonplussed I awaited instructions, which emerged from an unmistakably male set of vocal chords. This was a whole new world, and for almost the only time in my taxi-driving life I really didn't know what to say. What sort of banalities could I share with this character that wouldn't run the risk of sounding inane, embarrassing or offensive? Nothing came readily to mind, and this was clearly the common lot, as Stephen seemed either unable or unwilling to make any small talk. A mercifully short journey to what I would later recognise as the hub of the Leeds gay night-time scene ended with the opening of a beaded clutch-bag to pay the fare before Stephen disappeared into a doorway with marginally less haste than exhibited earlier.

Thankfully Stephen's apparent embarrassment was to prove to be unusual. Subsequent journeys to and from the same area taught me the obvious but, to be honest, completely unexpected truth that those in the homosexual community are just normal people like anyone else; it's only their sexuality that doesn't conform to the traditional expectations of society. The presence of a gay man in my cab was as unlikely to lead to a request for sexual favours as if the passenger was female, and I could freely chat to them about the same sorts of things I could chat to anyone else about. This sounds so ridiculously obvious now, but at the time the supposed "Christian" attitude I adopted to the gay community, born of the same sort of ignorant defensiveness that created my erstwhile prejudice against taxi drivers, seemed to make complete and irrefutable sense. It was, of course, justified by the rather selective texts from the Bible I used as a bulwark against the trebuchets of common sense.

Having said all of that it is somewhat interesting to note that on two of the three occasions on which I was propositioned for sexual favours, two were from homosexual men. The first of these was a polite enquiry as to my availability from a well-dressed individual returning from a day's work at a large office block. I was taken completely by surprise as I hadn't picked up a hint of any kind of attraction or of a non-heterosexual orientation. My polite refusal was met with an equally polite "No problem" and the encounter was at an end.

The second was more entertaining in that it involved a journey from the city centre with a rather hairy individual who was clearly somewhat the worse for wear after an evening in the pub. As is often the case with the loss of inhibition that accompanies inebriation this was increasingly manifested in emotional sentimentalism. I had learned long before that once people had this much alcohol in their bloodstream rational conversation was pretty-well impossible, so I had played all his comments and attempts to open a discussion on random subjects with the proverbial straight bat.

We reached his home in West Leeds whereupon he leaned across from the front seat, placing his face only inches from mine, and asked me meaningfully if I was married. I offered the firm response that this was so, and that my marriage had been the source of great happiness to me for something approaching thirty years. This was greeted with a sigh of disappointment and "What a shame", followed (after paying his fare) by another hopeful look before he resigned himself to a lonely night. I suspect that any disappointment was short-lived, since a drink-induced and very deep sleep could surely only have been averted by an intravenous supply of neat caffeine at this point. I smiled to myself, trying to work out how anything about my appearance or personality could be of remote interest to anyone of the same gender seeking a sexual encounter.

I heard stories of taxi drivers who were constantly offered sex as payment in kind for a taxi fare, but whatever it was I seemed to have that appealed to some of the male population of the region it was clearly lost on members of the fairer sex. There was some gentle light-hearted flirting, and I suppose there were a dozen or more occasions when women dropped hints that were I so inclined I could come in with them for a little late-night entertainment of an intimate nature. Only once was this made explicit, and I'm pretty sure that was the alcohol or other substance that was doing the talking. Fortunately – or, if I am to be slightly more honest unfortunately, none of those who dropped these hints were particularly attractive to me, so temptation was relatively easy to resist. Were one of the nubile and grossly underdressed students to offer me a drink in her room after a night out I might have been more hard pressed to resist, though as my wife says I would probably have experienced heart failure in the first few minutes of the encounter, so it is perhaps just as well that no such offer was ever received.

The most significant encounter with someone of a different sexual orientation is etched on my memory because it was this experience that forever changed the way I thought about the gay community as a Christian.

Gary was an executive with a multinational company who for whatever reason had been working late into the night and called a cab to take him from central Leeds to the other side of Bradford sometime after midnight. This was a terrific job to get for two reasons – firstly the length of journey meant a sizeable fare, and secondly he was sober – a rarity at this time of night, so there was a decent chance of a sensible conversation with an interesting individual. We soon started chatting about a range of subjects and, as was normal, he asked whether I had always been a cabbie as I didn't really sound like one. I revealed my former profession, he expressed polite interest, and the conversation moved on.

It was as we were approaching the centre of Bradford that he just dropped the question out. 'What does your church think about homosexuals?' This was fine – I had a ready-made answer that had been rehearsed in countless situations for decades, and had always served the purpose well. It went something like this; God designed people to be heterosexual and therefore homosexuality is not in line with what he requires. Some people, either through nature or nurture, find themselves attracted to people of the same gender. This is not sinful in itself, but if they have sexual relations with those they are attracted to that is wrong, and something the Church should not encourage. I was also anxious to put adultery and fornication in the same category, just to demonstrate that I was not really biased.

There was silence for a good 20 seconds before Gary responded.

'I'm a homosexual. Always have been. I've spent endless years asking God to make me straight, but it isn't happening, and I've given up trying. Does this mean God doesn't love me and won't want me?'

This was delivered without even a hint of accusation, self-pity or rebuke, just as an honest enquiry. I was struck dumb as the crass stupidity of the simplicity with which I had trotted out a particular line in rhetoric struck me between the eyeballs. What a pompous prat I must sound like.

More silence followed, eventually broken by me apologising for the prejudiced attitude that I now realised lay behind my answer to his quite reasonable question. What to say? I thought long and hard, then tried to undo some of the damage I had just inflicted on this affable human being whose company I had been enjoying for the last half hour or so.

'Look, I'm sorry, I've just realised how judgmental and illogical what I said must have sounded. Let me be honest; this is the first rational conversation I've ever had with a gay man on the subject, and my opinions are really born of the prejudice of ignorance. I'm really sorry, because in the last two minutes I've realised that the problem is not you but me. I can't truthfully believe that God doesn't have as important a place for you in his heart as for me, only you seem mercifully free from my kind of hang-ups and prejudices. I'm going to spend the rest of this week trying to work out what I really think.'

Gary was good-humoured and gracious; we had a long chat about the fortunes of the region's sports teams, and parted on very friendly terms, thanks only to his willingness not to rip me and my feeble reasoning to pieces.

This was a life-changing experience; I realised that so long as it is possible, from the exalted fortress of cosy evangelicalism, to lump together every person who is gay, lesbian or a transvestite, it is quite safe to make sweeping generalised statements that seem to make good biblical and theological sense. But then you meet someone like Gary, and realise that the gay community is full of such nice individuals, and arguments that work in relation to an amorphous mass of people simply don't hold water in relation to those you actually get to know.

In any case who was I to comment? Were my personal life to be subjected to the kind of scrutiny I was so willing to judge others by I would soon be classified as being far too hypocritical to begin pulling specks out of someone else's eye. I had for some absurd reason decided that same-sex genital activity was in the premier league of sin, whilst my little peccadilloes were of the stuff of a Sunday morning kick-about.

And then there was this quite ridiculous line taken by many church groups at the time – and even to the present day in some cases – that you can have homosexual orientation but if you gratify it that is the point where God becomes cross with you. Once you step back from that and offer it even a cursory analysis the total absurdity of the argument is shouting back in your face.

In this area I am still on a journey, trying to make sense of what the Bible says and what is actually happening all around me. I don't have all the answers by any means, but feel a lot more comfortable with the uncertainties than with the trite answers of my previous existence.

# 35

## MEANWOOD – THE FINAL DAYS

Only as the exit strategy from my strange and now not-so-new world was being implemented did I come to realise just how much the experience had changed me, and the realisation dawned that the way in which I understood the world would never be the same as it had been barely two years previously. Nothing of what I had experienced as a cabbie was particularly traumatic – it had been an oasis of calm in comparison to the final meetings at my previous incumbency, which had fluctuated somewhere between the vicious and the vitriolic most of the time.

The change resembled in many respects my discovery of the writings of George Orwell about a quarter of a century previously. The attraction of "1984" and "Animal Farm" had really been that they were such good yarns, and I was unaware of the subversion I was imbibing with each new page, breathing in a philosophical virus that would leave me with a complete inability ever to see the world in the same away again. It was as if explosive charges were smuggled in under my very nose, the detonation went unnoticed, but when I emerged all that was left of my former personal fiefdom was the rubble strewn around my ankles; whether or not I missed the old place was irrelevant – it was gone forever.

Fortunately (I think), unlike another of Orwell's heroes Dorothy, the child of the rectory in "A Clergyman's Daughter",

I had not lost my faith, but it was hardly the one I had cherished and nurtured before I started driving a minicab. The world I had come to inhabit had so altered my perspective that the only thing I was sure of in planning a return to clerical orders was that I could never ever do it in the way I had done it up to that point. I suppose on one level I had changed my religion rather than lost my faith. I wasn't wearing orange chiffon, chanting mantras or venerating species from the animal kingdom. It was still the Christian God I believed in, but not the same one I had grown up with. This old deity, whose strictures and virtues I had spent half a lifetime extolling, was distinctly unsympathetic to those who failed to reach the exacting standards I imagined he required of all those who worshipped him. Perhaps it was like the cathedral in Coventry that had been demolished by the Luftwaffe; the traditional, recognisable edifice that could be mistaken for nothing other than a cathedral of majestic proportions had been demolished, and in its place was something that looked quite different. I imagine when this happened there was a great deal of sadness among many who knew the old building on the grounds that this one doesn't really look anything like a cathedral. But if you can suspend your expectations of what a cathedral is supposed to look like and appreciate this architectural masterpiece for what it is you will see that it is every bit as much a place of worship as the old one, with a majesty and beauty that fits it for the modern age rather than the eighteenth century. My faith has changed for ever – it is less predictable, has a non-uniform shape and far fewer icons and other sacred objects, and even those that remain are much less venerated than they used to be. I dare to hope that it is softer, too – less judgmental and more conscious of its own weaknesses. I am very keen to keep the doors and windows open, and to add bits on or take bits off to make it more fit for the purpose for which it was designed. The only essential quality of this building is that God is in it, and maybe a God I have more uncertainties about than I did previously, but in whose presence I think I am increasingly comfortable.

This God I had come to believe in was the one whose compassion, common sense and generosity was embodied in the Jesus whose biography I now understood in terms of inclusivity; who went on an exhausting search for one stupid lost sheep which was in some economically insane way more important at that moment than the ninety nine who were being good little lambkins. The Jesus who only really seemed to get cross when confronted by rank hypocrisy – at which he got very cross indeed and was given to throwing furniture around. The Jesus who became the target of religious bigotry because he considered it more important – and more fruitful – to spend much of his time not with the outwardly pious but with the crooked, the corrupt and the sexually immoral on the grounds that they were the sick who knew they needed a doctor. The Jesus who willingly gave his own life with the promise that when he was lifted up on the cross he would draw everyone, not merely the religious elite, to himself.

On one level I was terrified of putting on a dog-collar (a metaphorical one in my case as I only possess one clerical shirt that has lasted for more than a quarter of a century, and which only makes appearances once or twice a year.) Somehow if I was to give this ministry thing one more go to see if I really had lost the plot or still had something to offer I had to ensure the best possibility of success, so I began to think of the kind of church I might work for and what characteristics it needed to exhibit. I listed the conditions necessary for the preservation of my sanity on a piece of paper during a quiet spell one evening when I knew that my profile had been sent to a wide range of churches for consideration. I drew up a specification and a list of resolutions that looked something like this: –

- I would never again play the game of church politics
- Whilst I would regard my relationship with God as a matter of the utmost importance I would never again take a church very seriously
- I would encourage people to ask honest questions about their faith in order to test its authenticity
- If this resulted in them discovering that the whole thing was a sham then so be it
- I would never again think that leading Sunday services is what church is all about
- I would treat religious bullshit in exactly the same as any other variety
- I would only work for a church that saw its primary role in relation to those outside its walls
- I would be true to myself and honest about my own struggles whilst avoiding self-indulgence and self-pity
- I would have nothing to do with superficial relationships characterised by conversations that never reached the crux of an issue
- I would respond to pious-sounding religious mumbo-jumbo by asking "what the fuck is that supposed to mean" (perhaps even including the expletive just to cause some gratuitous offence)
- I would never ever again leave myself in a position where I could face the prospect of being rendered unemployed and homeless at the whim of a capricious congregation

With these things in mind I set out to plan the kind of church I would be willing to work in – if any of them would have me now I had been in contact with the scrapings at the bottom of society's barrel. It wasn't long before I started receiving 'phone calls asking me to consider meeting the leaders of various churches, and the twin emotions of anxiety and excitement began to compete for space in my ample digestive tract.

Somehow I managed to find time to go and see the leaders of all the churches that made contact, believing that a personal encounter is the only way to gauge how things really stack up. I've found that there's no real substitute for hearing the unspoken communication – reading body language, observing eye contact and sensing other people's discomfort.

In this period I must have met seven or eight groups of church leaders, many of whom seemed to believe that in the great scheme of the ultimate redemption of humanity their little establishment was somewhere up there with the Vatican and Canterbury Cathedral. Others thought that their particular situation made them somehow quite unique in the annals of the history of Christendom, whereas they were, in reality, rather common mundane outfits with collective Walter Mitty delusions.

There was one group of leaders who I met and instantly felt kinship with, and became quite excited about working with. I went to meet them again to find they had added a new member to the team, whose whole demeanour made the hairs on the back of my neck stand on end. Put simply he appeared to be a clone of one of the worst abusers in my previous establishment, and I was thankful that I could recognise the type before the process went any further.

Others were groups of really nice people, but they had inhabited the cloisters of middle-class nonconformity for most of their lives and had somehow inured themselves to the harshness of real life. I tried to imagine them understanding the lives of the kind of people I had just spent a large part of two years with, and of them developing some kind of passion to make their church the kind of place where such folk would find a home; I tried in vain. The effort was futile, and I realised that whilst this had once been exactly the sort of refined, cosy environment I had allowed myself to become immersed in whilst becoming anaesthetised to the rest of the world it simply would not work any longer. I tried to explain once or twice, but the sympathetic nods and reassuring if non-committal "I see" or "I understand" was followed by an utterly unconvincing "but we can change." I passed over them in silence.

Eventually the profile I had been waiting for dropped noiselessly through the virtual letterbox of my email in-tray. A church that knew it was in trouble, knew the writing was on the wall in terms of any kind of future, and if they were to survive had to learn to be a Christian community in a completely different way to anything they had thought of before. No delusions of grandeur, just confused and saddened at the experience of having watched decades of constant numerical decline whilst being impotent to alter the relentless slide towards non-existence. I sat up, took notice, and set course for a series of meetings that would eventually see me installed in a situation where I had a licence to be as innovative and creative as I chose.

That was some eight years ago. For about half that time my wife and I kept our options open; I retained my private hire licence, my wife returned to West Yorkshire two days every week for work. We had enough put by for a deposit on a house, and if this ecclesiastical nirvana turned out to be another nightmare in disguise, or if we found that the wounds were simply too deep and the permanent injuries too pervasive for ministry to be a viable option, we had our escape route planned.

To my delight I found that the whole business came back as naturally as getting back on a bike, and the people who honoured me by asking me to be their minister really were what they claimed to be. Now approaching the final years of my working life I have a genuine contentment with my lot, mingled occasionally with a nostalgic yearning once again to drive the streets and byways of West Yorkshire in a battered old Skoda for a few pounds a trip. I have promised myself that retirement will present the opportunity to do some taxi driving in the leafy surrounds of north Northumberland where we have now bought our modest retirement home, and once again I will enjoy the thrill of wondering who is next going to step into the car and where the day will take me. But I will also be packing a flask of tea and some sandwiches.